cut here

The Complete Idiot's F

WordPerfect Shortcut Keys: The Top 40

Editing Shortcut Keys

Press	*To*
Ctrl+Z	Undo your last action
Ctrl+C	Copy the selected block
Ctrl+X	Cut the selected block
Ctrl+V	Paste the cut or copied block
Ctrl+Ins	Copy and paste the selected block
Ctrl+Del	Cut and paste the selected block
Alt+F4 or F12	Start block mode
F2	Search
Alt+F2	Search and replace
Ctrl+R	Repeat a key
Shift+F3	Display the Convert Case menu
Esc	Undelete

Navigation Shortcut Keys

Press	*To*
Ctrl+→	Next word
Ctrl+←	Previous word
Home, →	End of the line
Home, ←	Beginning of the line
Ctrl+↓	End of the paragraph
Ctrl+↑	Beginning of the paragraph
Home, ↓	Bottom of the screen
Home, ↑	Top of the screen
Page Dn	Beginning of next page
Page Up	Beginning of previous page
Home, Home, ↓	End of the document
Home, Home, ↑	Top of the document
End	End of the line
Ctrl+Home	Any page (Go to command)

General WordPerfect Shortcut Keys

Press	*To*
Shift+F10	Open a document
Ctrl+F12	Save a document
Shift+F7	Print a document
Shift+F3	Switch windows
Home, *n*	Switch to document *n*
Home, 0	See a list of open documents
F5	Start File Manager
Ctrl+F8	Select a font
F6	Bold characters
F8	Underline characters
Ctrl+I	Italicize characters
Ctrl+W	Use WordPerfect's symbols
Ctrl+F2	Start Speller
Home, F7	Exit WordPerfect

The WPMain Button Bar

Version 6's cool Button Bar (which you access by selecting **B**utton Bar from the **V**iew menu) puts a number of common tasks only a mouse click away. Here's a summary of the buttons from the WPMain Button Bar:

Button	***Command Equivalent***
File Mgr	**F**ile **F**ile Manager
Save As	**F**ile Save **A**s
Print	**F**ile **P**rint
Preview	**F**ile Print Pre**v**iew
Font	F**o**nt **F**ont
GrphMode	**V**iew **G**raphics Mode
TextMode	**V**iew **T**ext Mode
Envelope	**L**ayout **E**nvelope
Speller	**T**ools **W**riting Tools **S**peller
Grmatik	**T**ools **W**riting Tools **G**rammatik
QuikFndr	**F**ile **F**ile Manager **U**se QuickFinder
Tbl Edit	**L**ayout **T**ables **E**dit
Search	**E**dit Searc**h**
BBar Sel	**V**iew **B**utton Bar **S**etup **S**elect
BBar Opt	**V**iew **B**utton Bar **S**etup **O**ptions

alpha books

WordPerfect's Wondrous Windows

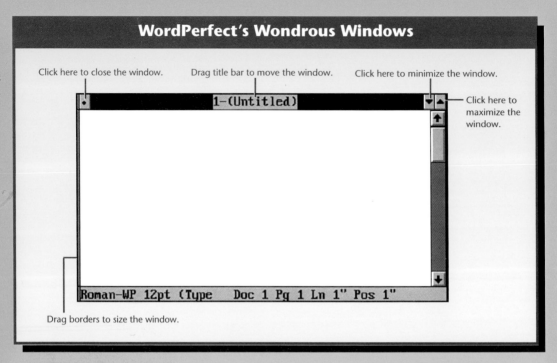

Click here to close the window.

Drag title bar to move the window.

Click here to minimize the window.

Click here to maximize the window.

1-(Untitled)

Roman-WP 12pt (Type   Doc 1 Pg 1 Ln 1" Pos 1"

Drag borders to size the window.

Dialog Box Buttons: The Big Two

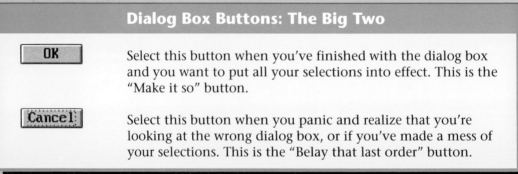

OK

Select this button when you've finished with the dialog box and you want to put all your selections into effect. This is the "Make it so" button.

Cancel

Select this button when you panic and realize that you're looking at the wrong dialog box, or if you've made a mess of your selections. This is the "Belay that last order" button.

The Ribbon: Formatting Made Easy

WordPerfect version 6 includes a fancy Ribbon tool that gives you easy access to some common formatting commands. To see it, select the **Ribbon** command from the **View** menu.

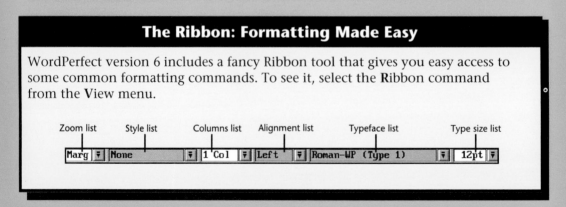

Zoom list   Style list   Columns list   Alignment list   Typeface list   Type size list

Marg ▼ None   ▼ 1 Col ▼ Left ▼ Roman-WP (Type 1)   ▼ 12pt ▼

The Complete
IDIOT'S
Guide to
WordPerfect™
2nd edition

by Paul McFedries

alpha
books

A Division of Macmillan Computer Publishing
201 W. 103rd Street, Indianapolis, Indiana 46290 USA

To Karen: For those times when you need to give WordPerfect technical support to total strangers in Thai restaurants.

©1994 Alpha Books

International Standard Book Number: 1-56761-499-X

Library of Congress Catalog Card Number: 94-71430

96 95 94   8 7 6 5 4 3 2 1

Interpretation of the printing code: the rightmost number of the first series of numbers is the year of the book's printing; the rightmost number of the second series of numbers is the number of the book's printing. For example, a printing code of 94-1 shows that the first printing of the book occurred in 1994.

Printed in the United States of America

Publisher
Marie Butler-Knight

Managing Editor
Elizabeth Keaffaber

Acquisitions Manager
Barry Pruett

Product Development Manager
Faithe Wempen

Development Editors
Seta Frantz
Heather Stith

Production Editors
Michelle Shaw
Phil Kitchel

Copy Editor
Audra Gable

Cover Designer
Scott Cook

Designer
Barbara Webster

Indexer
Bront Davis

Production Team
*Gary Adair, Dan Caparo, Brad Chinn, Kim Cofer, Lisa Daugherty,
David Dean, Jennifer Eberhardt, Beth Rago, Bobbi Satterfield,
Carol Stamile, Karen Walsh, Robert Wolf*

*Special thanks to C. Herbert Feltner for ensuring
the technical accuracy of this book.*

Contents at a Glance

Contents at a Glance

Contents at a Glance

Contents

8 Day-to-Day Drudgery II: Navigating Documents   75

9 Getting It Down on Paper: Printing Documents   83

Part II: Getting It Right: Editing Stuff   95

10 Deleting Text (and Undeleting It, Too)   97

11 Block Partying: Working with Blocks of Text   103

Introduction

If you've ever tried to have a conversation with a so-called computer "expert," you know they have this uncanny ability to make the rest of us feel like complete idiots within five seconds. They prattle on in their techno-jargon, throwing in the odd "of course" and "obviously" to make it clear that any fool with half a brain ought to know this stuff. Well, I say we thumb our collective noses at the world's computer geeks! Not only are we *not* idiots, but we're smart enough to know a thing or two ourselves:

- ☞ We're smart enough to know that "cool" isn't defined by how many back issues of *Popular Mechanics* we keep in the bathroom. We simply don't need a lot of technical details (and we don't wear pocket protectors, either).

- ☞ We're smart enough to know that it doesn't make sense to learn absolutely *everything* about WordPerfect. We just need to know enough to get our work done, thank you.

- ☞ We're smart enough to know that life's too short to read five kazillion pages of arcane (and mostly useless) information. We have lives to lead, after all.

A Book for Smart WordPerfect Idiots

If you're no fool but the computer gurus of the world make you feel like one, welcome to *The Complete Idiot's Guide to WordPerfect*. This is a book for those of us who aren't (and don't even want to be) computer wizards. This is a book for those of us who have a job to do—a job that includes working with WordPerfect—and we just want to get it done as quickly and painlessly as possible. This is *not* one of those absurdly serious, put-a-crease-in-your-brow-and-we'll-begin kinds of books. On the contrary, we'll even try to have—gasp!—a little fun as we go along.

You'll also be happy to know that this book doesn't assume you have any previous experience with WordPerfect. This means we'll begin each topic at the beginning and build your knowledge from there. But you won't find any long-winded discussions of boring technical details. With *The Complete Idiot's Guide to WordPerfect*, you get just the facts you *need* to know, not everything there *is* to know. All the information is presented in short, easy-to-digest chunks that you can easily skim through to find just the information you want.

How This Book is Set Up

I'm assuming you have a life away from your computer screen, so *The Complete Idiot's Guide to WordPerfect* is set up so you don't have to read it from cover to cover. If you want to know how to print, for example, just turn to the printing chapter. To make things easier to find, I've organized the book into five more or less sensible sections:

Part I—Day-to-Day Skills

WordPerfect follows the old 80-20 rule: you'll spend 80 percent of your time working with 20 percent of the program's features. The nine chapters in this section cover most of that 20 percent. You'll learn basic stuff such as starting WordPerfect (Chapter 3), using the keyboard and mouse (Chapter 4), saving your work (Chapter 7), and printing a document (Chapter 9).

Part II—Getting It Right: Editing Stuff

The benefits of a word processor over a typewriter are legion, but one of the biggest is being able to edit a document right on the screen. These three chapters show you how to delete—and undelete—text (Chapter 10), how to move chunks of text around (Chapter 11), and how to find stuff in your documents (Chapter 12).

Part III—Looking Good: Formatting Stuff

Because *looking* good is often as important as *being* good, WordPerfect gives you a fistful of ways to format your documents. The six chapters in Part III introduce you to these various options. You'll learn how to format individual characters (Chapter 13), lines and paragraphs (Chapter 14), and pages (Chapter 15). I'll also show you how to create envelopes and labels (Chapter 16), how to streamline your work with styles (Chapter 18), and more.

Part IV—Fiddling with Your Files

The documents you create in WordPerfect—whether they're letters, memos, or mystery novels—are stored inside your computer as *files*. This section shows you how to work with multiple files at once (Chapter 19), how to use File Manager, WordPerfect's answer to the DOS command line (Chapter 20), and how to find files quickly with QuickFinder (Chapter 21).

Part V—Wielding WordPerfect's Tools

The book ends with eight chapters that take you through some of WordPerfect's collection of tools and utilities. Chapters 22 and 23 check out the spell checker, thesaurus, and grammar-checker that are built right into WordPerfect. You'll also get to play with graphics (Chapter 24) and tables (Chapter 25), and I'll show you how to customize WordPerfect (Chapter 27). The final chapter takes you through the necessary drudgery of installing WordPerfect (just in case you can't talk some knowledgeable guru into doing it for you).

The Complete Idiot's Guide to WordPerfect also includes a glossary that'll help you make sense of all those bizarre computer terms, as well as a handy tear-out reference card that gives you easy access to important (or just plain handy) WordPerfect information.

What's New in the Second Edition

Sending a book out to market is a little like watching one of your kids leave home and head out into the world. Will they be all right? Will other people accept them? Will they be successful in their chosen field? Will they be displayed prominently at the front of the store? (Well, okay, we probably don't want our kids displayed prominently in the front of stores.) I'm happy to report that The Complete Idiot's Guide to WordPerfect's first venture into the cold, cruel world has been a resounding success. I've received a lot of comments from people saying they liked the book and really enjoyed the approach. Thanks!

The only complaints I heard were from people who wanted more! Well, you got it. This second edition beefs up the coverage of the same

WordPerfect features you use every day. The second edition also includes the following:

- ☞ A greater emphasis on those WordPerfect features that can make your writing life easier. For example, I've moved the coverage of the insanely convenient Button Bars and Ribbon to an earlier chapter (Chapter 5). This way, as you read the rest of the book, I can point out which buttons you can use to work with the other WordPerfect features.

- ☞ Increased coverage of WordPerfect's formatting features. This includes coverage of creating envelopes and labels, as well as how to use styles to make formatting a breeze.

- ☞ The "Wielding WordPerfect's Tools" section includes new chapters on using graphics and tables. These are features that can give even the most mundane document a truly professional touch (and, best of all, they're remarkably easy to use).

- ☞ There is, as I've already mentioned, a separate "WordPerfect Ideas" chapter that gives you all kinds of ways to put WordPerfect to work at home and at the office.

Features of This Book

The Complete Idiot's Guide to WordPerfect is designed so you can get the information you need fast and then get on with your life. If you ever need to type something (which does come up occasionally with word processors), it will appear like this: **type this**.

It seems WordPerfect has thousands of features, and most of them are accessible by pressing certain *key combinations* on your computer's keyboard. I explain more about this in Chapter 4, "Keyboard and Mouse Basics," but you should know that I'll be writing these key combinations by separating the two keys with a plus sign (+). For example, I might say something like "press **Ctrl+F12** to save a document." The "Ctrl+F12" part means you hold down the Ctrl key, tap the F12 key, and then release Ctrl. (Don't worry: you are in no way required to memorize these keyboard contortions to become a competent WordPerfect user.)

Also, look for the following icons that will help you learn just what you need to know:

These boxes contain notes and technical information about WordPerfect facts that are (hopefully!) interesting and useful.

This icon defines geeky computer terms in plain English.

WordPerfect made a lot of changes in the leap from version 5.1 to 6. Where there are differences, this icon points out the appropriate 5.1 instructions.

There are always dangerous ways to do things on a computer—and this icon will tell you how to avoid them.

If you rearrange the letters in "complete idiot," you end up with "de cool tip time," and that's just what this icon means. It presents you with handy tips that show you easier ways to get things done in WordPerfect.

Acknowledgments (The Kudos and Huzzahs Dept.)

Ah, so many people to thank, so little time. From the first edition, let's start with Acquisitions Editor Steve Poland: thanks for thinking of me. Development Editor Faithe Wempen: it was great being a team again; thanks for another job well done. Managing Editor Liz Keaffaber: thanks for keeping me in line (take a vacation!). Production Editor Annalise DiPaolo: always a pleasure (good luck in the future). Copy Editor Barry Childs-Helton and Tech Editor Kelly Oliver: thanks for making me look good.

The second edition was graced by the presence of Development Editors Seta Frantz and Heather Stith, Copy Editor Audra Gable, and Production Editor Michelle Shaw. Thanks to all for another great job!

Part I
Day-to-Day Skills

Let's face it, WordPerfect is one intimidating program: all those installation disks, the overstuffed manual bursting at the seams. The good news is that most of that stuff doesn't apply to the likes of you and me. All we really need are a few basic features that'll let us get our work done with a minimum of fuss and bother. In a sense, that's what this whole book is about, but the chapters here in Part I set the stage for everything else. You'll be learning the basics, such as how to start WordPerfect, how to use your keyboard and mouse, and how to use things like the pull-down menus and dialog boxes to make your life easier. Believe me, if you can get through this part (and if you can dress yourself, you can handle any of this), the rest will be a day at the beach.

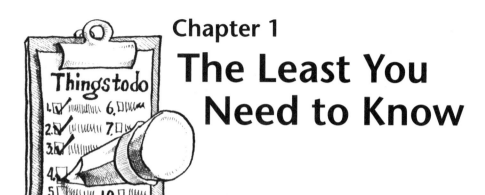

Chapter 1
The Least You Need to Know

I know, I know. You can't wait to get started. What is it? A looming deadline? Unfettered curiosity? A type-A personality? Well, not to worry. This chapter gets you up to speed quickly by presenting a "just-the-facts" description of the 10 most important WordPerfect tasks. Of course, each of these items is discussed in more detail elsewhere in the book, so if you'd like to know more, I'll also point out the relevant chapters as we go along. If you're one of those people who likes to read ahead to the good parts, this chapter's for you.

1. Starting WordPerfect

To start WordPerfect, you need to be at the DOS prompt. (The DOS prompt looks like C:\> or maybe just C>.) If your computer starts off in some kind of menu system, you need to exit the menu to get to DOS. Once you're in DOS, make sure you're logged onto the drive on which you installed WordPerfect. To do this, just type the drive letter followed by a colon (:), then press Enter. For example, to change to drive C, type **C:** and press **Enter**. Now peck out **WP** on your keyboard and press the **Enter** key. You'll know all is well if you see the WordPerfect logo on your screen (as shown on following page). See Chapter 3, "Diving In: Your First WordPerfect Session," for more information.

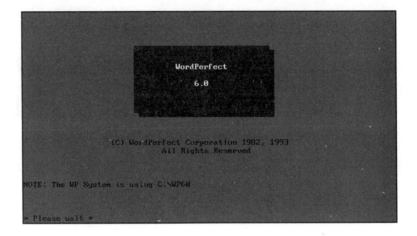

You'll see this screen while WordPerfect cranks itself up to speed.

Whenever I ask you to type something, I'll show the appropriate text in capital letters. This is only to make the text easier to read; it doesn't mean you have to use capitals. Unless it's absolutely required (and I'll let you know if it is), you can enter most text in uppercase, lowercase, or any combination of the two that strikes your fancy.

2. Entering Text

Once WordPerfect is loaded, you can start typing right away. There are no complicated commands to run, and no messy formulas to remember. You don't even have to press Enter at the end of every line, the way you do with a typewriter (where the same key is called "Return"). WordPerfect wraps your prose onto the next line, free of charge. The only time you need to press **Enter** is when you want to start a new paragraph. If you make a mistake, just press the **Backspace** key to wipe it out.

Chapter 3, "Diving In: Your First WordPerfect Session," gives you a few more tips about entering text. For the lowdown on editing your documents, skim through Part II, "Getting It Right: Editing Stuff."

3. Using Pull-Down Menus

Pull-down menus are hidden menus that list the various commands that are available for each WordPerfect task. To pull down a menu with the keyboard, find the letter in the menu name that is underlined or appears in a different color. Then just hold down the **Alt** key and press the letter.

Or, with a mouse, move the mouse pointer into the *menu bar* area (the horizontal strip along the top of the screen) and click on the name of the menu you want to pull down. ("Click" means to press and release the left mouse button.)

Once you have your menu displayed, you can select a command. With your keyboard, you use the up and down arrow keys to highlight the command you want and then press **Enter**. With a mouse, you simply click on a command.

In version 5.1, press **Alt+=** to display the menu bar, find the letter in the menu name that appears in a different color, and then press the corresponding key to pull down the menu.

To learn more about pull-down menus, see Chapter 5, "WordPerfect the Easy Way: Menus, Button Bars, and More."

4. Opening a Document

When you start WordPerfect, you get a blank screen that's ready for your typing. If you'd prefer to work with an existing document, you need to open it. To do so, you pull down the File menu and select the **Open** command (or you can simply press **Shift+F10**) to display the Open Document dialog box (shown below). Now type the full name of the file into the

To open a file with version 5.1, press **Shift+F10**, type in the name of the file at the bottom of the screen, and then press **Enter**.

Filename box. If the file is in a different drive or directory, be sure to include the drive letter and/or the directory name. When you're ready, select the **OK** button or press **Enter**.

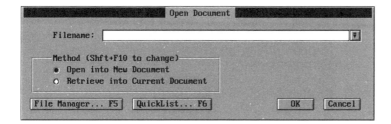

Use the Open Document dialog box to specify which file you want to open.

For more information on the Open command, see Chapter 7, "Day-to-Day Drudgery I: Opening, Saving, and Closing." To learn more about dialog boxes, see Chapter 6, "Talking to WordPerfect's Dialog Boxes."

5. Saving a File

To save a new file in WordPerfect 5.1, press **F10**, type in the name at the bottom of the screen, and then press **Enter**.

One of the most gut-wrenching experiences in computerdom is to work on a document for hours and then lose everything because of a system crash or power failure. You can minimize this damage by saving your work regularly; just pull down WordPerfect's File menu and select the Save command, or press **Ctrl+F12**. If you're saving a new file, the Save Document dialog box will appear. Use the Filename box to give the file a name. When you're ready, select **OK**.

See Chapter 7, "Day-to-Day Drudgery I: Opening, Saving, and Closing," for more details about saving your work.

6. Marking a Block of Text

Much of what you do in WordPerfect—whether it's cutting, copying, formatting, or printing—involves highlighting a block of text beforehand to let WordPerfect know what text you want to act on. Here's how you do it:

- ☛ With the keyboard, position the cursor to the left of the first character in the block, and then select the Block command from the Edit menu (or press **Alt+F4**). Now use the arrow keys (or Page Up and Page Down if you have a lot of ground to cover) to highlight the block.

- ☛ With a mouse, point at the first character in the block, and then drag the mouse to move the pointer over the block.

You'll find lots more block info in Chapter 11, "Block Partying: Working with Blocks of Text." To learn how to drag a mouse, see Chapter 4, "Keyboard and Mouse Basics."

7. Formatting Characters

To make your documents stand out from the crowd, use WordPerfect's *character formatting* commands. With these commands you can do simple formatting like adding bold and italics, but you can also get into fancy stuff like different fonts, outlining, and shadowing. Just pull down the Font menu and select the appropriate command, or press **Ctrl+F8** and choose options from the Font dialog box that appears (see below).

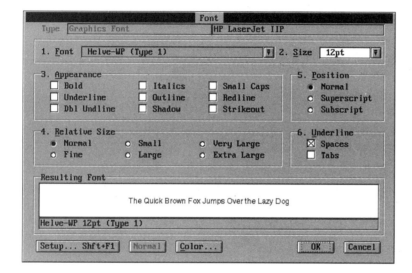

The Font dialog box is an easy way to format several character attributes at once.

The full scoop on all this can be found in Chapter 13, "Making Your Characters Look Good."

8. Undoing a Mistake

The WordPerfect programmers thoughtfully included an Undo command you can use to reverse your most recent action. This is great if you've just made a formatting gaffe, or if you "cut" when you should have "copied." To use the Undo feature, just pull down the Edit menu and select the Undo command (you can also simply press **Ctrl+Z**).

But wait, there's more. WordPerfect also has an Undelete feature that can get you out of trouble if you've just deleted your entire day's work. To

Version 5.1 doesn't have an **Undo** command, but you can Undelete text by pressing **F1**.

use it, first select Undelete from the Edit menu (or press **Esc**). Your most recent deletion will appear highlighted in the text, and the Undelete dialog box will appear with two options: Restore and Previous Deletion. Select **Restore** to restore the highlighted text. Select **Previous Deletion** to take a look at text deleted previously (WordPerfect stores the last three deletions). When you have the text you want, select **Restore**.

You'll learn about Undo in Chapter 11, "Block Partying: Working with Blocks of Text," and Undelete in Chapter 10, "Deleting Text (and Undeleting It, Too)."

9. Printing a File

Once you've finished working with a document, you'll want to print a copy to show off to your friends and colleagues. To do this, pull down the File menu and select the Print/Fax command. The Print/Fax dialog box that appears (see below) enables you to specify how much of the document to print, the number of copies, and various other settings. When you're ready to print, select the Print button.

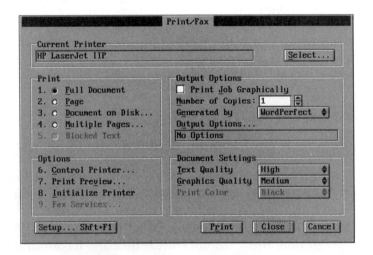

Use the Print/Fax dialog box to set your print options.

For more printing particulars, take a look at Chapter 9, "Getting It Down on Paper: Printing Documents."

10. Quitting WordPerfect

When you've finished with WordPerfect, you can quit the program by pulling down the File menu and selecting the Exit WP command (or press **Home** and then **F7**). This displays the Exit WordPerfect dialog box, with a list of your open files. If necessary, select the documents you want to save, and then select the **Save and Exit** button. If you aren't saving any documents, select the **Exit** button.

To quit version 5.1, press **F7** and respond to the prompts at the bottom of the screen.

See Chapter 3, "Diving In: Your First WordPerfect Session," for some additional information on quitting WordPerfect.

(zen text)

Chapter 2
Word Processing: A Primer

In This Chapter

☛ What is word processing?

☛ Is word processing a good thing?

☛ How does WordPerfect fit in?

☛ What's new with version 6?

☛ Occasional outbursts as the author gets a thing or two off his chest

Word processing. Personally, I've never liked the term. It sounds so cold and so, well, computer-like. I mean, processing words? What the heck does that mean? The bank processes checks, the IRS processes tax returns. Who processes words? We write them, play with them, misuse them, misspell them, forget them; but process them? No.

But the computer geeks of the world decided long ago that's what it should be called, so it looks like we're stuck with it. Despite these misgivings, this chapter takes a look at this whole word processing thing. What is it? What can you do with it? Why should you care?

What Is Word Processing?

Well, in the most basic, watch-their-eyes-glaze-over terms, *word processing* is using a computer to write, edit, format, and print documents. Yeah, I know, it doesn't sound very glamorous, but it's not really supposed to be. I mean, think about it. Most of the writing we do is grunt work anyway: memos, letters, essays, diatribes, and tirades of one sort or another. All we really need is to get the words down, dot the i's and cross the t's, make it presentable, and then get some hard copy that we can ship out. Everything else—whether it's putting together a newsletter or writing a doctoral thesis—is just an extension of this basic stuff.

Your Computer Is Not a Typewriter

All word processors have some kind of work area that you use for writing. Generally speaking, you just start pecking away on the computer's keyboard, and the characters appear like magic on the screen.

Works just like a typewriter, right? Wrong. Oh sure, the keyboard looks somewhat familiar: the letters and numbers are arranged more or less the same, the Spacebar is where it should be, and your old friends the Shift and Tab keys are there. Things may look the same but, baby, this ain't no Selectric.

The biggest difference, of course, is that the word processor has the muscle of a full-fledged computer behind it. Computers may be a lot dumber than we are (and don't let anyone tell you otherwise), but even the cheapest PC clone is way smarter than the most high-falutin' typewriter. For example, on a typewriter, a bell sounds to warn you when you near the end of a line. That's not bad, but the dumb beast still expects you to finish the line yourself and then press the Return key (or—gasp—crank the carriage return bar) to start a new line. A word processor, on the other hand, handles this chore for you: when you near the end of a line, you can blissfully continue typing, and the program will start a new line automatically (that's called *word wrap*). It'll even carry over any word you happen to be in the middle of.

Editing: Getting It Right

Word processors really begin to earn their stripes when it comes time to make changes in a document. With a typewriter, you can fix small mistakes, but you still have to fumble around with correction ribbons or (yuck) that ugly White-Out stuff. If you leave out a sentence or paragraph accidentally, forget about it. You've got to type the whole thing over.

Word processors, though, live to fix mistakes. Type the wrong character? Just press a button to delete it. Forget a paragraph? Simply insert it where it needs to go. Want to move a section of text from the beginning of the document to the end? No problem: just "cut" it out and "paste" it in the appropriate place. Want to replace every instance of "affect" with "effect"? (I can never remember which is which.) Most word processors have a "search and replace" command that'll do just that.

And this is just the tip of the iceberg. A full-featured program, such as WordPerfect, has all kinds of strange and wonderful ways to get the job done right (including, thank goodness, a spell checker!).

Formatting: Looking Good on Paper

Writing and editing are important of course, but the area where word processors really shine is *formatting*. It's not enough, in these image-conscious times, merely to hand someone a piece of paper with a bunch of words on it. Documents today need impact to get their message across. The formatting options in most word processors can help.

You can use **bold** to make things stand out, or *italics* for emphasis. You can center text or set tabs with just a few keystrokes. Some of the better programs also allow you to organize your words into columns or wrap them around a picture. In the really high-end word processors (such as WordPerfect), you can even add professional features such as footnotes and tables of contents without breaking a sweat. If you can picture it in your head, you can probably do it with today's word processors.

Printing: Getting Hard Copy

Once you've finished changing a document, you'll need to print it out for others to see. This sounds like there wouldn't be much to it; just run some sort of "Print" command and the thing prints. But you can also choose to print only certain parts of a document (a single page or even a single paragraph, for example), or you can print multiple copies, or, if you have more than one printer, you can choose which one you want to use. Some programs, like WordPerfect, even let you see a page-by-page preview of what the document will look like.

Is Word Processing a Good Thing?

This may sound like a silly question to ask after extolling the numerous virtues of word processing programs. And it may be moot in any case, because word processing is by far the most popular category of computer software. Some people do have concerns, however, about what word processing is doing to our minds—so we may as well tackle those before going any further.

Problem #1: Word Processors Encourage Sloppy Writing

This is the most common problem put forth by so-called "writing experts." You usually hear three kinds of complaints:

☛ If a section of text doesn't work for some reason, people using word processors don't rewrite the whole thing from scratch. Instead, trying to get their point across, they tend to insert more words and sentences. The usual result is bloated, overexplained thoughts that ramble incoherently.

In computer slang, constantly rewriting a section of text is known as **churning**.

☛ Most word-processor screens show only about a half a page at a time, so people tend to see the trees (words, sentences, and paragraphs) instead of the forest (the entire document). As a result, word processed documents tend to lack organization, and they often end up with separate pieces of the overall argument scattered willy-nilly.

☛ The advent of the electronic thesaurus has made it easier to utilize cumbrous, orchidaceous words that serve only to obfuscate intendment and subjugate perspicuity.

My answer to these charges is that word processors don't write sloppily, *people* do. Forthwith, here are some suggestions you can use to avoid sloppiness in your own prose:

☛ Wherever possible, read your text out loud. If it doesn't flow off your tongue, it won't flow through someone's brain.

☛ If a sentence or paragraph doesn't feel right, try rewriting it from scratch instead of patching it up. If you can't bring yourself to delete it, at least move it off the screen where you can't see it (and so won't be influenced by it).

☛ A good word processor (such as WordPerfect) has outlining features that can help you organize large documents. This is a bit of an advanced topic, but it's worthwhile to learn before starting on that new novel.

☛ The best writing is clear and straightforward, without a lot of pretentious words that confuse more than they impress.

Problem #2: Word Processors Waste Time

You could see this one coming. Today's top-of-the-line word processors have so many bells and whistles that you can end up spending all your time fussing about with obscure fonts and complicated desktop publishing features. People often compound the problem by printing the document every time they make the slightest change. This just wastes paper and consumes valuable natural resources.

Again, these are behavioral problems, not word processor problems. On the one hand, it really is best to keep your work simple and to avoid cluttering documents with fancy elements. This will help make your text readable and your meaning clear. On the other hand, the best way to get familiar with any kind of software is to experiment with different features and try out whatever looks interesting. You won't wreck anything, and most programs will warn you if you're about to do anything disastrous. And besides, you've gotta have *some* fun.

SPEAK LIKE A GEEK

Programs that come fully loaded with complicated options are called **fritter-ware** because you end up frittering away your time playing around with the fun stuff instead of getting work done.

Problem #3: Word Processors Create Illiterates

The same people who complained that calculators would turn our kids into math dropouts are now crying that computer spell checkers and grammar checkers will turn us all into illiterate slobs who wouldn't know a participle if it was dangled in front of us.

This one's easy to answer, folks: nuts to them, I say! If we can get our machines to handle the rote work of spelling and grammar, I'm all for it. After all, meaning is what's most important. Why not take the time that would normally be spent with our noses in dusty dictionaries and use it to craft our concepts and polish our prose?

How Does WordPerfect Fit Into All This?

If word processing dominates the software industry, WordPerfect dominates the word processing industry, with something like 60% of the market. So what's the big deal? Well, it's hard to say, actually. Prior to version 6, the program was quirky—to say the least—and somewhat intimidating for beginners. (WordPerfect 6 changes all that, as you'll see shortly.)

All that aside, however, there's no doubt that WordPerfect has something for everyone. If all you need is basic editing features for things like letters and memos, WordPerfect will handle these chores with a few simple commands. If you need to put together large, complex documents, WordPerfect has features such as outlining, indexing, and footnotes that'll handle the biggest job without complaint. If your interests lie more toward desktop publishing (creating newsletters, brochures, and the like), WordPerfect can do page layout, columns of text, and graphics with the best of them. In other words, WordPerfect works the way you do, not the other way around.

Version 6 is a vastly changed product from its predecessors. It brings to the table a number of new features that put the program in line with some industry standards (such as pressing the **F1** key to get help) and make the program both easier to use and more powerful. Here's a quick summary of some of the new features:

- ☞ A "graphics mode" that lets you see on screen what your document will look like when it's printed.

- ☞ The capability to open up to nine, count 'em, nine documents at once. This makes it easy to compare two or more documents, and to move text from one document to another.

- ☞ An industry-standard interface that uses pull-down menus and dialog boxes (I'll explain what these things mean as we go along) to make your life easier.

☛ A new Ribbon and Button Bar; these give you easy access to the commands and features you use most often.

☛ A built-in grammar checker.

☛ QuickFinder, a new utility that lets you find your documents quickly.

☛ Improved printing functions, such as Print Preview (which you use to view your document page-by-page before printing it out) and envelope printing.

This book covers most of these new version 6 features, but don't feel left out if you have an older incarnation of the program. Any major differences in version 5.1 are spelled out in separate sidebars for handy reference. (If you have 5.0, you can still get by with no problems, because it's not all that different from 5.1.)

The Least You Need to Know

This chapter took you on a quick tour of the shiny, happy world of word processing. Here's a recap of some of the sights we saw along the way:

☛ Word processing is a dumb name for using a computer to write, edit, format, and print documents.

☛ Your keyboard may look like a typewriter but, thanks to the computer in the box behind it, it's a lot smarter and a lot easier to use than a typewriter. Most editing and formatting commands are just a few keystrokes or mouse clicks away.

☛ Word processing is a good thing if you approach it the right way. Keep things simple, use the program's features to make your life easier, and don't be afraid to experiment.

☛ WordPerfect is the most popular word processor by far, because it works the way you do. Version 6 has all kinds of cool new features that'll keep you entertained for hours.

**You could fit a lot of haiku
on this page.**

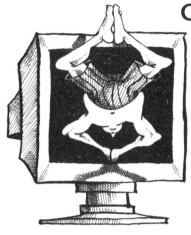

Chapter 3

Diving In: Your First WordPerfect Session

In This Chapter

- A heartwarming story about skiing
- Starting WordPerfect
- Taking a tour around the screen
- Entering text
- Exiting WordPerfect

The first time I ever went skiing, my friends (who, of course, were all experts and had little patience for a rank beginner) took me for a couple of token runs down the bunny hill and then whisked me to the top of some huge mountain. (With friends like these…!)

In our travels down the mountain, we'd often come upon the steep, mogul-filled hills that my friends loved. However, they scared the heck out of me, so I'd just tuck in behind everyone else and hope for the best. Happily, I always seemed to struggle down somehow, but I'd see groups of skiers standing at the top, fidgeting nervously, afraid to go down, but not able to turn back. In honor of these nervous-nellies, I developed my skiing motto: "Better a leg broken by boldness than a spirit broken by fear."

I tell you this story now, as we stand at the edge of WordPerfect Hill, to inspire you to, as the ads say, "just do it." Follow my lead and you're sure to come through unscathed.

Preflight Checklist

Before starting WordPerfect, you should make sure you've got everything you need. Here's a quick checklist:

❑ Is your computer on?

This is, of course, important. Make sure not only that your computer is up and running, but that anything else you'll need (such as your monitor or printer) is also powered up and ready to go.

❑ Is WordPerfect installed?

If the program hasn't yet been installed, you have two choices:

☞ Find the nearest computer nerd and ask him or her to install the program for you. This is the easiest method (for you, anyway), and you'll find most computer gurus can be bribed with the appropriate junk food or a well-aimed compliment (such as calling them a "guru" instead of a "nerd").

☞ If you can't find a guru or you'd like to give it a go yourself, you'll find WordPerfect's installation program to be friendlier than most. Chapter 29, "Installing WordPerfect," takes you through the required steps.

SPEAK LIKE A GEEK

Because of the obvious geeky associations, the term **nerd** is now considered bad form. The politically correct phrase of choice is **technically advantaged**. (By the way, just to prove that I'm no slave to the PC set, what do you call a nerd who graduates from college? Boss.)

❑ Are you at the DOS prompt?

Before you can start WordPerfect, you need to be at the DOS prompt. (Ewww, DOS! Don't worry, we'll only be making a brief stop in bad old DOS-land before moving on.) The DOS prompt looks like C> or C:\> or some variation on this theme. If you don't see anything that looks like this, you're probably in some other program. Here are some possibilities:

- The MS-DOS Shell program. If you see **MS-DOS Shell** at the top of your screen, hold down your keyboard's **Alt** key and press **F4** to return to DOS.

- Some kind of menu system. Your computer may be set up with a menu system that gives you a list of programs to run. If you're lucky, you may see a "WordPerfect" option. If so, great! Just select the option to start WordPerfect, and then skip to the section titled "Checking Out the WordPerfect Screen," later in this chapter. Otherwise, look for an option called "Exit to DOS," or "Quit," or something similar. You can also try pressing the **Esc** key.

❑ Is the ambiance just right?

Make sure your surroundings are comfortable and your favorite computer accessories are nearby (a good strong cup of coffee, relaxing background music, a copy of *Feel the Fear and Do It Anyway*, etc.).

The Three-Step Program for Starting WordPerfect

Without further ado, here are the steps you need to follow to get WordPerfect up and running:

1. If necessary, change to the drive on which you installed WordPerfect by typing the drive letter, followed by a colon (:), and pressing the **Enter** key. For example, to change to drive C, type **C:** and press **Enter**.

2. Type **WP** and press **Enter**. Yup, that's all there is to it: just peck out two lousy little letters, and you're on your way. No complicated commands to remember or snaggled syntax to scratch your head over. Ah, if only everything in life were so simple.

3. If you're starting WordPerfect for the first time, a box will appear on the

In DOS, however, things can *always* go wrong. After entering the **WP** command, you may see the following ominous message on your screen:

Bad command or file name

Yikes! Remain calm and take a deep breath. All you need to do is change to the directory where WordPerfect is installed. If you're using version 6, type **CD\WP60** and press **Enter**; for version 5.1, type **CD\WP51** and press **Enter**. Then try starting the program again.

screen to ask you for your registration number. Dig out your WordPerfect Certificate of License, type in the registration number listed on the certificate, and then press the **Enter** key to move on. (If you've lost your Certificate of License already, don't worry about it; just press **Enter** to continue without entering the number.)

Checking Out the WordPerfect Screen

WordPerfect will take a few seconds to crank itself up to speed. When it finally does, you'll see the screen shown here.

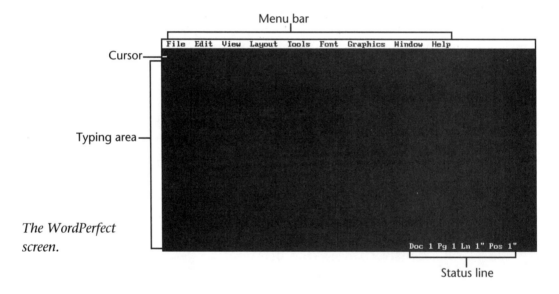

Menu bar

Cursor

Typing area

The WordPerfect screen.

Status line

There's not a lot to see, is there? It's almost disappointing, in a way. I mean, after loading all those disks this is all we get? Welcome to the WordPerfect philosophy: "Hide as much stuff as possible, to maximize the amount of text that can be displayed on the screen." This is a good idea for experienced word jockeys, but it can intimidate the heck out of beginners who haven't the faintest idea where to find what they need. This, then, will be our mission in this book: to seek out new WordPerfect life and new WordPerfect civilizations; to boldly go where you've never gone before. (Cue music.)

Explaining the Few Things You Can See

The WordPerfect screen may be stark, but it's not empty. Here's a quick rundown of what's there:

☞ **The typing area**   This is the blank expanse that covers everything but the top and bottom lines of the screen. This is where it all happens; everything you type will appear in this area. Think of it as the electronic equivalent of a blank sheet of paper.

☞ **The cursor**   This small, blinking line has a single purpose in life: it tells you where the next character you type will appear. Go ahead and press a letter on your keyboard. See how it shows up on the screen right above where the cursor was? The cursor itself leaps ahead to tell you where your next character will appear. (Press **Backspace** to get rid of the character you just typed.)

☞ **The menu bar**   This is the top line of the screen. Although you'd never know to look at it, this innocuous-looking line is actually your gateway to every single WordPerfect feature. This prodigious feat is accomplished by the miracle of *pull-down menus*. You'll learn all about these magical beasts in Chapter 5, "WordPerfect the Easy Way: Menus, Button Bars, and More."

If you're using version 5.1, you may not see the menu bar. To display it, just hold down the **Alt** key on your keyboard, press the equals sign (=), and then release **Alt**.

☞ **The status line**   This is the bottom line of the screen (my screen only shows info on the right side, but yours may also display some stuff on the left). Although it looks pretty incomprehensible, the information is actually quite useful (although you probably won't appreciate it until you've used the program a bit). Here's a summary of what's there:

Info	*What It Means*
Doc 1	With WordPerfect 6, you can open as many as nine documents at once. (With version 5.1, you can open two at once.) This info helps keep things straight by telling you which one you're currently working on (Doc 1, Doc 2, Doc 3, and so on).

Pg 1   This is the page number you're on (Pg 1, Pg 2, and so
           on).

Ln 1"   This tells you which line the cursor is on. The posi-
           tion is measured in inches—that's what the double-
           quote symbol (") means—from the top of the page. It
           starts at 1" because you have a one-inch margin at the
           top of the page.

Pos 1"   This tells you which column the cursor is in. The
           position is measured in inches from the left edge of
           the page. Again, it starts at 1" because there's a one-
           inch margin on the left side of the page.

Margins are the (usually) empty areas that surround your text on the page. WordPerfect's standard margins are one inch high on the top and bottom edges of the page, and one inch wide on the left and right edges. See Chapter 15, "Making Your Pages Look Good," to learn how to change margin sizes.

Now What?

Okay, you've got this big-bucks word processor loaded, the cursor is blinking away insistently, the large, blank typing area seems to cry out to be filled with happy little characters. What else do you need to know before getting started? Well, in a word, nothing! That's right, just start pecking away on your keyboard, and your brilliance will be displayed for all to see. This is the beauty of WordPerfect (if beauty is the right term): the program gets out of your way so you can get down to the business of writing.

Here are a few things to watch for when typing:

☞ If you're used to typing with a typewriter, you may be tempted to press the Enter key when you approach the end of a line. Fortu-nately, you don't have to bother, because WordPerfect handles that chore for you. When you've filled up a line, WordPerfect moves the text onto the next line automatically. Even if you're smack in the middle of a word, the program will automatically truck the entire word onto the next line, no questions asked. The only time you need to press **Enter** is when you want to start a new paragraph.

☞ If you make a mistake, just press the **Backspace** key to wipe it out. (If you don't see any key with the word "Backspace" on it, look for a left-pointing arrow (←) on the right end of the keyboard row that has all the numbers.)

☛ As you type, some of the information on the status line will change. For example, as you move across the screen, the column position (Pos) will increase, and as you move to a new line, the row position (Ln) will increase.

☛ If you're entering a lot of text, you may be startled to see a line suddenly appear across the screen. No, there's nothing wrong with your screen. It just means you've moved to a second page; to show you where one page ends and the next begins, WordPerfect displays a line. As proof that you're on a new page, check out the status line: WordPerfect bumps the page number (Pg) up to 2, and resets the line position to 1" (since you're now at the top of a new page).

The feature that starts a new line automatically is called **word wrap**.

A page-divider line is called a **page break**.

Checking Out Graphics Mode

One of the truly impressive new features you get with WordPerfect 6 is the ability to work with the program in *graphics mode* (as opposed to the normal *text mode*). Using graphics mode has three major advantages:

☛ When you format your documents (such as making characters bold or italic, or using different fonts), you can see the changes right on the screen, instead of having to wait for a printout. The following picture shows you an example of what I mean.

☛ With WordPerfect's graphics mode, what you see on your screen is what you get when it's printed. This not only saves time when you're formatting and laying out your documents, but it also saves trees because you don't have to print out every little change to see if it looks right.

The feature that enables you to see on your computer screen what you end up getting from your printer is called *WYSIWYG* (What-You-See-Is-What-You-Get). It's pronounced—for what it's worth—*wizzy wig*. I swear I'm not making this up. (After you've used WordPerfect for a while, you'll probably come up with your own versions of the WYSIWYG acronym: When Your Screen Indicates Where You Goofed; When You See It, Won't You Gag?; Why Your Screen Inadvertently Will Yield Garbage. Hey, who said computers were no fun?)

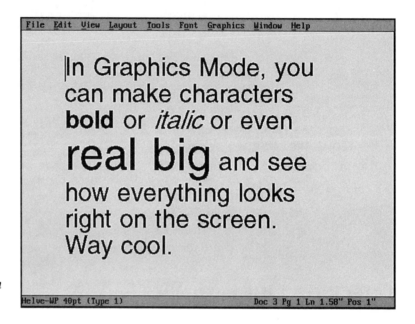

| File Edit View Layout Tools Font Graphics Window Help |

In Graphics Mode, you can make characters **bold** or *italic* or even **real big** and see how everything looks right on the screen. Way cool.

Helve-WP 40pt (Type 1)   Doc 3 Pg 1 Ln 1.58" Pos 1"

An example WordPerfect screen in graphics mode.

☞ WordPerfect becomes a *graphical user interface* (or GUI—which is pronounced *gooey* for short). This fancy phrase just means that the various WordPerfect elements—the pull-down menus and dialog boxes that you'll be learning about in the next few chapters—appear in spiffy 3-D formats. This is not only pretty, but it actually makes the program easier to use.

Are there any disadvantages to graphics mode? Well, only one: the program runs a little slower in graphics mode. But, to my mind, the speed penalty is easily outweighed by the added conveniences.

I'll be using graphics mode for all the screen pictures you'll see in the rest of the book. To make it easier to follow along, you might want to switch to graphics mode yourself. It's easy: just hold down the **Alt** key on your keyboard, and tap the letter **V**. This displays one of WordPerfect's pull-down menus. Release **Alt** and press the letter **G**. Your screen will go black for a second or two, and when it returns, you'll be in graphics mode.

When you switch to graphics mode, you won't notice many different elements right off the bat. The menu bar and status line appear in a different color, and the cursor becomes a vertical bar, but that's about it for now. The other differences will appear as we go along.

Getting Help

If you run into a problem with WordPerfect, or if you simply find yourself in a strange part of town, you want to get help fast before panic sets in. Thoughtfully, the WordPerfect programmers have provided you with a handy, on-line Help system. You start this system in one of two ways:

☞ Press **F1** to get help that is *context-sensitive*. This means the help screen that appears is related to whatever task you're in the middle of.

In version 5.1, press **F3** to get context-sensitive help.

☞ Select a command from the **Help** menu. (You can display the **Help** menu by holding down **Alt**, pressing **H**, and then releasing **Alt**. See Chapter 5, "WordPerfect the Easy Way: Menus, Button Bars, and More," for details.)

I won't go into the details of the Help system here. However, if you think you'll be using it regularly, read ahead to Chapter 6, "Talking to WordPerfect's Dialog Boxes," to learn how to navigate the Help system's dialog boxes. (By the way, to close a Help dialog box, just press **Esc**.)

Exiting WordPerfect

I know, I know, you're just starting to have fun, and here I am telling you how to exit the program. Well, you've gotta do it sometime, so you may as well know the drill.

The following steps tell you how to exit WordPerfect without saving your work. If you have a document that you want to save for posterity, skip ahead to Chapter 7, "Day-to-Day Drudgery I: Opening, Saving, and Closing," to learn the gory details.

You can combine steps 1 and 2 by pressing your keyboard's **Home** key, then pressing the **F7** key.

1. Begin by pressing **Alt+F** (press and hold down the **Alt** key and press **F**). You'll suddenly see a big list of stuff appear on your screen. This is another example of the pull-down menus I mentioned earlier.

2. Ignore everything you see except the line at the bottom of the list that says **Exit WP**. There are a number of ways to select this command, but for now, the easiest is simply to press **X**. You'll see a box on your screen titled **Exit WordPerfect**.

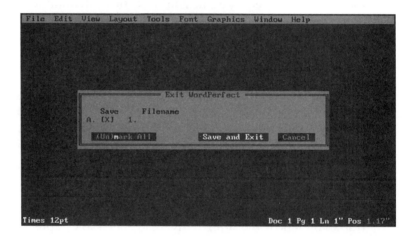

3. You have three choices at this point:

☞ If you see a little rectangle inside the Exit WordPerfect box that simply says **Exit**, just press **Enter**.

☞ If you see a rectangle that says **Save and Exit**, press **M** (this tells the program that you don't want to save your work). Then press **Enter**.

☞ If you change your mind and decide you don't want to exit after all, just press the **Esc** key.

To quit version 5.1, first press **F7**. You'll see the following prompt in the status line:

Save document? No (Yes)

Press **N** to select No. Now you'll see another prompt:

Exit WP? No (Yes)

Press **Y** to select Yes and exit WordPerfect.

The Least You Need to Know

In this chapter, you made the big leap and learned how to start WordPerfect. The rest of the chapter wasn't terribly strenuous (I hope), but here's a quick summary anyway:

- ☞ To start WordPerfect, make sure you're in DOS, and then type **WP** and press **Enter**.

- ☞ The WordPerfect screen is mostly empty (this is the typing area), but it does include three other elements: the cursor, the menu bar, and the status line.

- ☞ To enter text, just start typing. Remember that you don't have to press Enter at the end of each line.

- ☞ WordPerfect 6 features an impressive new graphics mode. To switch to it, hold down **Alt**, press **V**, and then press **G**.

- ☞ To exit WordPerfect, hold down **Alt**, press **F**, and then press **X**. In the **Exit WordPerfect** box that appears, press **Enter** (if you see just the Exit button) or press **M** and **Enter** (if you see the Save and Exit button).

**You say, How much more blank could
a page be? and the answer is, None.
None more blank.**

Chapter 4
Keyboard and Mouse Basics

In This Chapter

☛ A tour around the keyboard

☛ WordPerfect keyboarding basics

☛ The mouse made easy

"Garbage in, garbage out." That's an old expression computer geeks like to use to explain why things go haywire in software programs. Feed computers junk, and you get junk back: the dumb beasts just aren't smart enough to know the difference. In other words, input is everything.

When it comes to using WordPerfect, you have two ways to input data (that is, to put stuff into your computer): the keyboard and the mouse. You don't have to become a keyboard connoisseur or a mouse maven to use WordPerfect, but to avoid the "garbage in" thing, it helps to digest a few basics. This chapter tells you all you need to know.

The Keyboard: A Guided Tour

Keyboards come in all shapes and sizes; like the proverbial snowflake, it seems no two are alike. However, they all share a few common features, and most are laid out more or less the way you see here.

A typical PC keyboard. Just to be a pain, your computer manufacturer may have put the keys in slightly different positions.

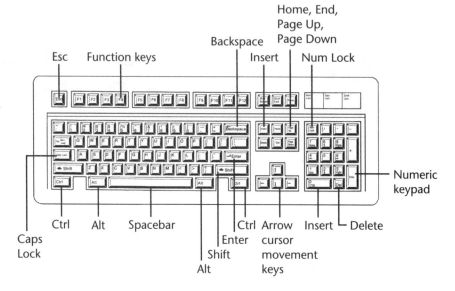

TECHNO NERD TEACHES...

The keyboard shown is called an Enhanced Keyboard. Most older computers come with lesser keyboards that have only 10 function keys and on which the arrow movement keys are mixed in with the numeric keypad keys. These aren't devastating problems, but they can be inconvenient because WordPerfect does use function keys F11 and F12, and separate cursor keys are much easier to use. If you're thinking of buying a new keyboard, though, be careful. Some older machines can't handle the Enhanced Keyboard.

Letters, Numbers, and Other Strangers

The bulk of the keyboard is taken up by the basic letters, numbers, punctuation marks, and other special characters that you'll be using most often (and some, like ~ and ^, that you may never use). Computer geeks refer to this area as the *alphanumeric keypad*.

Typing teachers always suggest limbering up your fingers before getting down to heavy typing. One of the best ways to do this is to type out *pangrams*—sentences that use all 26 letters of the alphabet. The standard pangram that everybody (sort of) knows is *The quick brown fox jumps over the lazy dog.* This is fine, but it's a bit dull. Try some of these on for size:

Pack my box with five dozen liquor jugs.

The five boxing wizards jump quickly.

Sexy zebras just prowl and vie for quick, hot matings.

Judges vomit; few quiz pharynx block.

Shift and Caps Lock

Just like on a typewriter, you use the Shift key to get capital letters. For keys with two symbols (except the ones on the numeric keypad; I'll talk about those later), hold down **Shift** to get the upper symbol. If you want to type nothing but capital letters for a stretch, it's better to press the **Caps Lock** key (which is similar to a typewriter's Shift Lock key). Note, however, that the Caps Lock key only works for letters; to get the other symbols (such as $ and +), you still need to use **Shift**. When you want to switch back to normal letters, just press **Caps Lock** again.

When Caps Lock is on, the Caps Lock indicator on your keyboard lights up, and in WordPerfect's status line, **Pos** changes to **POS**.

Ctrl, Alt, and Those Bizarre WordPerfect Key Combinations

If you press **Ctrl** (it's pronounced "control") or **Alt**, nothing much happens; but that's okay because nothing much is supposed to happen. You don't use these keys by themselves, but as part of *key combinations* (the Shift key often gets into the act as well).

Try an example so you can see what I mean. Hold down the **Ctrl** key with one hand, use the other to tap **W** on your keyboard, and then release **Ctrl**. Like magic, a box entitled WordPerfect Characters appears on your screen. The point of this exercise isn't to do anything with this box (which you can get rid of by pressing the **Esc** key twice, or turn to Chapter 13, "Making Your Characters Look Good," to figure out what it does), but to show you that you can get WordPerfect's attention simply by entering certain combinations of keys. Using the **Ctrl** and **W** combo is like saying "Yo! I wanna see the WordPerfect Characters box on the screen!"

WordPerfect has all kinds of these strange-but-useful key combinations, so we need some kind of shorthand for verbose instructions such as "Hold down the **Ctrl** key, tap **W**, and then release **Ctrl**." From now on, instead of this mouthful, I'll just say "Press **Ctrl+W**" (or whatever).

Just to make things confusing, WordPerfect has a second kind of key combination where you press and release one key (say, Home) and then press and release another (say, 1). For these, I'll say something like "Press **Home, 1**."

The Esc Key

If you find yourself in some strange WordPerfect neighborhood, and you're not sure what to do next, you can usually get back to Kansas—not by clicking your ruby slippers, but by pressing the **Esc** key until things look more familiar. If you're in the typing area, however, Esc activates WordPerfect's Undelete feature (see Chapter 10 to get the scoop on Undelete).

The Cursor Control Keys

One of the principle differences between a word processor and a typewriter is that the word processor lets you leap around to any place in the document to fix blunders or just to check things out. You do this with the *cursor control* keys, which you'll find either on a separate keypad or mixed in among the numeric keypad keys. You'll be learning all kinds of fun navigation stuff in Chapter 8, "Day-to-Day Drudgery II: Navigating Documents," but for now, here's a quick summary of some basic cursor control techniques:

Press	To move the cursor
←	Left one character
→	Right one character
↑	Up one line
↓	Down one line
Page Up	To the top of the previous page
Page Down	To the top of the next page

The Numeric Keypad

On each type of keyboard, the numeric keypad serves two functions. When the Num Lock key is on, you can use the numeric keypad to enter numbers. If Num Lock is off, the keypad cursor keys are enabled, and you can use them to navigate a document. Some keyboards (called *extended keyboards*) have a separate cursor keypad so you can keep Num Lock on all the time.

If you press a key in the numeric keypad and, instead of a getting a number, you go racing off to another part of the document, you probably have Num Lock turned off. Just tap the **Num Lock** key to enable the numbers.

You usually have two ways to tell when Num Lock is on. On your keyboard, look for a light under the Num Lock indicator. In WordPerfect itself, watch Pos in the status line. If Num Lock is on, Pos will either be highlighted (if you have version 6.0 and you're in text mode), or it'll be blinking (in version 5.1).

The Function Keys

The *function keys* are located either to the left of the alphanumeric keypad or across the top of the keyboard. There are usually 12 function keys (although some older keyboards have only 10), and they're labeled F1, F2, and so on. In WordPerfect, you use these keys either by themselves or as part of the key combinations we looked at earlier. For example, the Home, F7 key combination is a quick way to exit WordPerfect (press just **F7** in version 5.1).

A Note About Notebook Keyboards

If you're ever forced to type for an extended period on a notebook or laptop keyboard, you have my deepest sympathies. These suckers are not only cramped, they have all the feel of a piece of cement. To make things even worse, there's usually no separate numeric keypad, so the cursor control keys are scattered willy-nilly. On some notebooks, the cursor keys are hidden among the letters, and you have to hold down a special key (usually labeled "Fn") to get at them. Yuck!

So what's my point? Well, just that you need to be a little more careful when using a notebook keyboard. Fingers that would normally fly (relatively speaking) on a regular keyboard will be bumping into each other in the cramped confines of the notebook layout. One solution that many notebooks offer is the option to hook up a separate numeric keypad—or even a full-fledged keyboard. You should check into this; it's definitely worth it.

WordPerfect Keyboarding for Non-Typists

As I've said, getting the most out of WordPerfect doesn't mean you have to become some kind of touch-typing, thousand-words-per-minute keyboard demon. Heck, I've been using computer keyboards for years, and I wouldn't know what touch-typing was if it bit me in the face. In this section, we'll just go through a few things that should make your life at the keyboard easier.

The Enter Key Redux

When you use a typewriter, a little bell goes off as you near the end of each line. This sound warns you to finish off the current word (or to add only a couple of small ones) and then press Return to start a new line. WordPerfect frees you from this old-fashioned drudgery because it starts new lines for you automatically. If you're smack in the middle of a word, this feature will even transport the entire word to the next line. So even though you ex-typewriter types may be sorely tempted to do so, *don't* press Enter as you near the end of a line. Just keep typing—WordPerfect will handle all the hard stuff. (You'll probably find you miss the little bell, though. Oh, well.)

You *can* press **Enter** when you need to start a new paragraph. WordPerfect creates a new blank line, and moves the cursor to the beginning of it. You can also use Enter to insert blank lines in your text. Just position the cursor at the beginning of a line and press **Enter**. The new line appears above the current line.

The feature that starts a new line automatically is called **word wrap**.

Quick Fixes: Using Backspace and Delete

You'll be learning all kinds of fancy techniques for editing your documents in Part II. For now, though, you can use the Backspace and Delete keys to get rid of small typos. Just use the arrow keys to position the cursor appropriately, and then use these keys to make corrections:

Backspace   Use this key to delete the character immediately to the left of the cursor. (If your keyboard doesn't sport a key that says "Backspace" on it, look for a left-pointing arrow: ←.)

Delete   Use this key to delete the character immediately to the right of the cursor (if you're in graphics mode) or immediately above the cursor (if you're in text mode).

Switching to Typeover Mode

If you position the cursor in the middle of some text, anything you type is inserted between the existing characters. If you're redoing a few words, you could delete them first and then retype, but it's often easier to just type over them. To do this, you need to put WordPerfect in *typeover mode* by pressing the **Insert** key. (I know, I know, that doesn't make sense, but bear with me.) You'll see the word **Typeover** appear in the bottom left corner of the screen, and when you type now, the new characters replace the existing ones. To resume normal operations, just press **Insert** again.

The problem with typeover mode is that, one of these days, you'll forget to turn it off, and you'll end up wiping out all kinds of important prose. When this happens, press **Ctrl+Z** to undo the typeover, and then press **Insert** to return to Insert mode.

Key Combination Contortions

WordPerfect has a key combination for just about anything you'd ever want to do with the program, and I'll be letting you in on many of them as we go through this book.

Most people find it faster to use one hand for these key combinations, but I'll warn you now to expect some real contortions. This is especially true for key combos that use either Ctrl or Alt and the function keys. Some of these nasty devils can be quite a stretch for all but the biggest hands. (Although things are made easier by some thoughtful computer companies that put Ctrl and Alt keys on both sides of the Spacebar.) My advice? Don't strain yourself unnecessarily; use two hands if you have to.

Mouse Machinations

Learning how to use a mouse is by no means an essential WordPerfect survival skill. You'll find, however, that it makes many everyday tasks just plain faster and easier. The good news is that using a mouse takes no extraordinary physical skills. If you can use a fork without poking yourself in the eye, you'll have no trouble wielding a mouse.

The arrow (or block) that moves on your screen when you move the mouse is called the **mouse pointer**.

The Basic Mouse Technique

A mouse is a marvelous little mechanical miracle that can seem incomprehensible to the uninitiated. The basic idea, though, is simple: you move the mouse on its pad or on your desk, and a small arrow moves correspondingly on the screen. (If you're using version 5.1, or if you're in version 6's text mode, you'll see a small block instead of an arrow.) By positioning the arrow on strategic screen areas, you can select text, operate the pull-down menus and Button Bars, and choose all kinds of WordPerfect options. Not bad for a rodent!

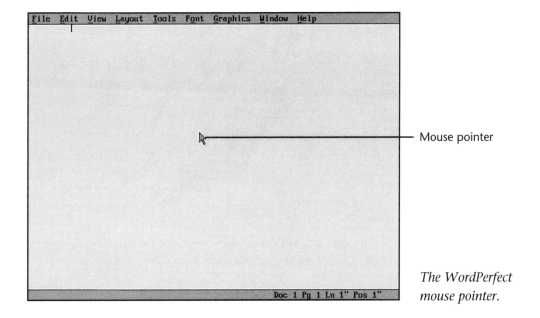

The WordPerfect mouse pointer.

Using a mouse is straightforward, but it does take some getting used to. Here's the basic technique:

1. Turn the mouse so that its cable extends away from you.

2. Place your hand over the mouse in such a way that:

   ☛ the part of the mouse nearest you nestles snugly in the palm of your hand.

   ☛ your index and middle fingers rest lightly on the two mouse buttons (if your mouse has three buttons, rest your fingers on the two outside buttons; leave the middle one alone for now).

   ☛ your thumb and ring finger hold the mouse gently on either side.

If you don't see the mouse pointer on your screen, but you know you have a mouse installed, just wiggle the mouse a bit and the pointer should appear. WordPerfect always hides the pointer whenever you type something.

The proper way to hold a mouse.

3. Move the mouse around on its pad or on your desk. Notice how the mouse pointer on the screen moves in the same direction as the mouse itself.

A person who spend lots of time in front of his screen is called a **mouse potato** (the computer equivalent of a couch potato).

The Hard Part: Controlling the Darn Thing!

Moving the mouse pointer is simple enough, but controlling the pesky little thing is another matter. Most new mouse users complain that the pointer seems to move erratically, or that they move to one part of the screen and run out of room to maneuver. To help out, here are a few tips that will get you well on your way to becoming a mouse expert:

☞ Don't grab the mouse as if you were going to throw it across the room (although you may, on occasion, be tempted to do so). A light touch is all you need.

☞ The distance the mouse pointer travels on the screen depends on how quickly you move the mouse. If you move the mouse very slowly for about an inch, the pointer moves about the same distance (a little more, actually). However, if you move the mouse very fast for about an inch, the pointer races across the screen.

☞ If you find yourself at the edge of the mouse pad but the pointer isn't where you want it to be, simply pick up the mouse and move it back to the middle of the pad. This doesn't affect the position of the pointer, but it does allow you to continue on your way.

Here's a list of the kinds of actions you can perform with a mouse:

Point To move the mouse pointer so it rests on a specific screen location.

Click To press and release the left mouse button.

Double-click As you might expect, double-clicking means to quickly press and release the left mouse button twice in succession.

Drag (This has nothing to do with dressing funny.) To press and hold down the left mouse button, and then move the mouse.

The Least You Need to Know

This chapter gave you the lowdown on using the keyboard and mouse in WordPerfect. Here are a few highlights:

☞ Most of your typing time will be spent pecking out letters, numbers, and punctuation in the alphanumeric keypad.

☞ You use the **Ctrl** and **Alt** keys (and sometimes **Shift**) in combination with other keys to access WordPerfect's commands. In this book, key combinations separated by a plus sign (such as Ctrl+W) mean you hold down the first key, press the second key, and then release the first key. Key combinations separated by a comma (such as Home, F7) mean you press the first key and then press the second key.

☞ The cursor control keys help you move around in a document. They appear in a separate keypad or mixed in with the numeric keypad (in which case, you have to turn Num Lock off to get at them).

☞ Use the numeric keypad to enter numbers into your documents quickly. Make sure Num Lock is turned on before using these keys.

continues

continued

☛ The function keys are the 12 (or sometimes 10) keys labeled F1, F2, and so on. In WordPerfect, you use these either by themselves or in combination with other keys to run certain commands.

☛ A mouse can make WordPerfect easier to use, but it does take some getting used to.

Chapter 5

WordPerfect the Easy Way: Menus, Button Bars, and More

In This Chapter

- What are pull-down menus?
- How to use pull-down menus with the keyboard and mouse
- Checking out the oh-so-handy Button Bars
- Easy formatting with the Ribbon thing
- Rambling ruminations on desks, drawers, and the Dead Sea Scrolls

As I've said before, the WordPerfect philosophy is to get out of your way by presenting you with a clean and uncluttered screen. However, you (or your company) didn't shell out the big bucks just so you could type all day. To get the most out of your WordPerfect investment, you need to use the program's other features.

How do you access those features? Well, if you read the last chapter, you know that one way is through the use of key combinations. But key combinations, while often quicker, have two major drawbacks:

☞ You either have to memorize them (shudder) or you have to interpret WordPerfect's arcane templates (a task akin to deciphering the Dead Sea Scrolls).

☞ They can be physically brutal unless you have basketball-player-sized hands.

Fortunately, there are easier alternatives: *pull-down menus*, *Button Bars*, and the *Ribbon*. The pull-down menus group commands in logical chunks, they're a snap to use, and you still maintain access to every WordPerfect feature. The Button Bars and Ribbon are even handier because they enable mouse users to access common WordPerfect tasks with a click or two of a button. Sound good? Then read on, and I'll show you how they work.

What the Heck Are Pull-Down Menus?

Take a good look at the desk you're sitting at. (If you're not sitting at a desk, picturing one in your head will do.) You've probably got an area where you do your work, surrounded by various tools (pens, pencils, and so on) and things that keep you informed (such as a clock and calendar). Probably you also see a few drawers, from which you get your work and in which you store your desk tools.

The WordPerfect screen is a lot like a desk. You do your work in the typing area, of course, and you have the status line to keep you informed. You also have pull-down menus that work, in fact, just like desk drawers. When you need to get more work (for example, to open a document) or access a WordPerfect command, you simply open the appropriate menu and select the menu option that runs the command.

Why You Pull "Down" Instead of "Up" or "Out"

Why are they called "pull-down" menus? Well, because they're hidden inside the menu bar at the top of the screen. Selecting any one of the nine menu bar options (File, Edit, View, and so on) displays a menu of choices, such as the File menu shown here.

*WordPerfect's File
pull-down menu.*

The effect, you'll note, is as though you pulled the menu down from the menu bar. (Hey, sometimes this stuff actually makes sense!)

How to Use Pull-Down Menus with the Keyboard

The secret to using pull-down menus from the keyboard is to look for the underlined letter in each menu bar option. (If you're not in graphics mode, look for the different colored letter in each option.) For example, look at the "F" in File, the "E" in Edit, and so on. These underlined letters are the menus' *hot keys*.

The choices you see in a pull-down menu are called **commands**. You use these commands to tell Word-Perfect what you want it to do next.

How do they work? Simple: you just hold down **Alt**, press the hot key on your keyboard, and then release **Alt**. For example, to pull down the File menu, use the **Alt+F** key combination.

Once you have a menu displayed, you need to select one of the commands. This is simple enough. You just use the up and down arrow keys to highlight the command you want, and then press **Enter**. Depending on which command you select, one of three things will happen:

If you have version 5.1, and you don't see the menu bar on your screen, just click the right mouse button to display it.

To pull down a menu in version 5.1, first display the menu bar by pressing **Alt+=**. You'll see the File option highlighted. Either press the menu's hot key or use the left and right arrow keys to highlight the option you want, and then press **Enter**.

☞ WordPerfect will carry out the command.

☞ Another menu will appear. In this case, use the arrow keys to select the command you want from the new menu, and then press **Enter**.

☞ A dialog box will appear, asking you for more information. See Chapter 6, "Talking to WordPerfect's Dialog Boxes," for details on using dialog boxes.

How to Use Pull-Down Menus with a Mouse

If you have a mouse, using pull-down menus is a breeze. All you do is move the mouse pointer into the menu bar area and click on the name of the menu you want to pull down. For example, clicking on File in the menu bar pulls down the File menu.

Once you have your menu displayed, you then simply click on the command you want to execute. As I explained in the keyboard section, one of three things will happen, depending on the option you select:

☞ WordPerfect will carry out the command.

☞ Another menu will appear. In this case, just click on the command you want to execute from the new menu.

☞ WordPerfect will display a dialog box in order to get further info from you.

While you're getting the hang of all this, occasionally you may find that you pull down a menu and discover you don't want to select any of its commands. No problem; you can remove the menu by simply pressing **Esc** twice (yes, it has to be twice). If you find that you've pulled down the wrong menu, use the left or right arrow keys to cycle through the other menus.

More Fun Pull-Down Menu Stuff

If you've been pulling down some menus, you may have noticed a few strange things. For example, did you notice that some commands have a triangle on the right-hand side of the menu? Or that some are followed by three ominous-looking dots? Or that others also list a key (or key combination)? These are just a few of the normal features found in all pull-down menus, and you can take advantage of them to make your life easier. The rest of this section summarizes these features. I'll be using the Edit menu (shown below) as an example, so you might want to pull it down now to follow along.

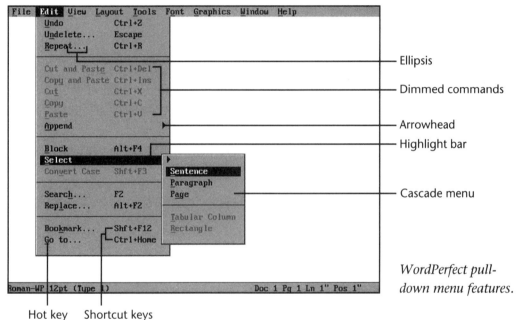

WordPerfect pull-down menu features.

The highlight bar   As you move through a menu with your keyboard, a black bar appears across the menu. This is called the *highlight bar* and it indicates the current command. As I've said, one way you can choose a command is by pressing **Enter** when that command is highlighted.

More hot keys   Every command in a version 6 pull-down menu has one underlined character (or a character that appears in a different color, if you're in text mode). This is the command's *hot key*; when the menu is displayed, you can select that command by simply pressing the underlined letter on your keyboard. For example, in the Edit menu, you could select the Go to command by simply pressing **G**.

Shortcut keys   Some menu commands also show a key or key combination on the right-hand side of the menu. These are called *shortcut keys*; using shortcut keys, you can bypass the menus altogether and activate a command quickly from your keyboard. For example, you can select the Edit menu's Replace command by simply pressing **Alt+F2**. (If you try out this command, press **Esc** twice to remove the box that appears. To learn about the Replace feature, see Chapter 12, "Search and Ye Shall Replace.") Once you've worked with WordPerfect for a while, you may find it faster to use these shortcut keys for some of the commands you use most often.

Arrowheads   With some commands, you'll see an arrowhead ▶ on the right side of the menu. This tells you that yet another menu will appear when you select this command. For example, choose the Select command from the Edit menu to see a menu of selection commands. (Press **Esc** to remove the new menu.)

When a command displays another menu, the new menu is called a **cascade** menu.

The ellipsis   An *ellipsis* (...) after a command name indicates that a dialog box will appear when you select the command. WordPerfect uses dialog boxes to ask you for more information or to confirm a command you requested. For example, if you select the Edit menu's Search command, a dialog box appears to ask you what you want to search for. (Press **Esc** twice to remove this dialog box.) See Chapter 6, "Talking to WordPerfect's Dialog Boxes," for more dialog box details.

The dimmed commands   You'll sometimes see menu commands that appear in a lighter color than the others. These are called *dimmed commands*, and the dimming indicates that you can't select them (for now, anyway). Generally speaking, if you see a dimmed command, it means that you must do something else with the program before the command will become active.

For example, the Edit menu's Copy command (among others) is usually dimmed. As you'll see in Chapter 11, "Block Partying: Working with Blocks of Text," you use the Copy command to copy chunks of text from one part of a document to another. Before you can use Copy, however, you first need to tell WordPerfect which text you want to copy (this is explained in Chapter 11). Until you do that, WordPerfect dims the Copy command so you can't use it.

Check marks   Some commands operate like light switches: they toggle certain features of an application on and off. When the feature is on, a small check mark appears to the left of the command to let you know. (If you're operating in text mode, WordPerfect uses an asterisk (*) instead of a check mark.) Selecting the command (or, sometimes, a different command) turns off the feature and removes the check mark. If you select the command again, the feature is turned back on, and the check mark reappears.

Let's work through an example so you can see what I mean:

1. Pull down the View menu and take a look at the Pull-Down Menus command; it should have a check mark beside it. This means that WordPerfect's menu bar is active.

2. Now select the Pull-Down Menus command. This deactivates the command, which means that WordPerfect removes the menu bar from the screen.

3. The fact that you can't see the menu bar doesn't mean you can't access the menus. To prove it for yourself, press **Alt+=** or click the right mouse button. WordPerfect redisplays the menu bar. (This is only temporary, however; if you press **Esc**, the menu bar disappears again.)

4. To bring back the menu bar full-time, first display the menu bar and select the View menu. Notice how the Pull-Down Menus command no longer has a check mark beside it? Now select the Pull-Down Menus command. WordPerfect reactivates the menu bar.

The Button Bars: Easy Command Access

If you thought the pull-down menus were handy, wait until you get a load of version 6's new *Button Bars*. To check them out, pull down the View menu and take a look at the Button Bar command; if it doesn't have a check mark beside it, go ahead and select it. (If it does have a check mark, press **Esc** twice to return to the document.) This displays the Button bar, as shown on the following page. As you can see, the Button Bar is a collection of buttons with cute little pictures and hard-to-read text.

Although you get a Button Bar in text mode, it's pretty pathetic. To get the neat pictures, make sure you're in graphics mode.

WordPerfect 6's
Button Bar.

└─ Scroll buttons   Button Bar

Using the Button Bar

Each of the buttons you see represents a common WordPerfect task. All you have to do is click on a button, and WordPerfect executes the task. For example, clicking on the Print button displays the Print/Fax dialog box. To see more buttons, click on the downward-pointing arrow on the left side of the Button Bar; to get back, click on the upward-pointing arrow (these arrows are called the *scroll buttons*).

As a public service throughout this book, I'll let you know whenever a WordPerfect feature is accessible from a Button Bar button by adding a picture of the icon like this:

   Click on this button to display the Print/Fax dialog box.

Sorry keyboard users, the Button Bar is only accessible with a mouse.

Displaying a Different Button Bar

WordPerfect actually comes with no less than seven different Button Bars (you can only display one at a time, however). Why so many? Well, the other Button Bars are designed for specific tasks. For example, if you'll be doing a lot of character formatting, you'll probably want to display the Fonts Button Bar because it's chock full of buttons that perform various character formatting chores. (Check out Chapter 13 "Making Your Characters Look Good," to sink your teeth into this character-formatting stuff.)

To display a different Button Bar, pull down the View menu, choose the Button Bar Setup command, and then choose the Select command from the cascade menu. WordPerfect displays the Select Button Bar dialog box, shown on the following page. The Button Bars box contains a list of the available Button Bars (FONTS, LAYOUT, and so on). Double-click on the name of the Button Bar you want displayed. WordPerfect returns you to the document and replaces the current Button Bar with the one you selected.

 You can also display the Select Button Bar dialog box by clicking this button in the WPMAIN Button Bar.

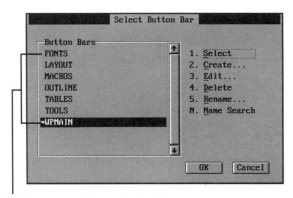

Use the Select Button Bar dialog box to display a different Button Bar.

Double-click on one of these Button Bar names.

The Ribbon: Easy Formatting Access

Just when you thought things couldn't get any easier, WordPerfect 6 also includes yet another new screen element: the Ribbon. The Ribbon is a collection of lists that give you easy mouse access to some of WordPerfect's formatting features. To display the Ribbon, pull down the **View** menu and activate the **R**ibbon command. The Ribbon appears just below the menu bar, as shown here. (For clarity, the screen below only shows the Ribbon. However, WordPerfect is perfectly happy to let you display a Button Bar at the same time.)

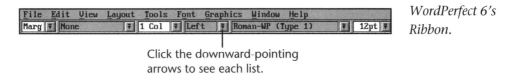

WordPerfect 6's Ribbon.

Click the downward-pointing arrows to see each list.

Each Ribbon object has a list of formatting choices. You display the lists by clicking on the downward-pointing arrows. (You can hide a list by pressing **Esc**.) As with the Button Bars, I'll show you how to use each Ribbon list in the appropriate sections of this book.

The Least You Need to Know

This chapter explained WordPerfect's pull-down menus and showed you how to use them with both a mouse and keyboard. You also learned about the Button Bars and the Ribbon. Here's a summary of what you now know:

☞ Pull-down menus are a lot like desk drawers because they "store" tools (commands) that you use with WordPerfect.

☞ To pull down a menu with the keyboard, look for the menu's hot key, press and hold **Alt**, and then press the hot key on your keyboard.

☞ To pull down a menu with the mouse, simply click on the menu name in the menu bar.

☞ Once a pull-down menu is displayed, you can select a command by using your keyboard's up and down arrow keys to highlight the command and pressing **Enter**. If you have a mouse, just click on the command you want.

☞ To display the Button bar, pull down the **View** menu and activate the **Button Bar** command.

☞ To display the Ribbon, pull down the **View** menu and activate the **Ribbon** command.

Chapter 6
Talking to WordPerfect's Dialog Boxes

In This Chapter

- ☛ What is a dialog box?
- ☛ Getting around in dialog boxes
- ☛ Learning about dialog box buttons, boxes, and lists
- ☛ Odd dialog box details for curious computer consumers

As you work with WordPerfect, little boxes will appear incessantly on your screen to prompt you for more information (and generally just confuse the heck out of things). These are called *dialog boxes*, and they're WordPerfect's way of saying "Talk to me!" This chapter looks at these chatty little beasts, and offers some helpful tips for surviving their relentless onslaught.

A Note to Users of Version 5.1

If you're using WordPerfect 5.1, the good news is that you don't have to learn about dialog boxes—because there aren't any! (They were introduced in version 6.) The bad news is that you have something even worse: menus. Menus are sort of like dialog boxes (they're boxes that ask you for more information), but they're pretty stark and unappealing (and they lack the gnarly 3-D effects you get in version 6's graphics mode). However, you need to know how to use them to get through the program, so here's a quick course:

Menu choices will appear in one of two forms. The first is a simple list of options, like this:

Print

1 - Full Document

2 - Page

3 - Document on Disk

4 - Control Printer

5 - Multiple Pages

To select the option you want, just press the number (or, in some cases, the letter) listed to the left of the option. In this example, you'd press 1 to select the Full Document option. If you use a mouse, you can just click on the option you'd like.

The second kind of menu displays a bunch of information and then lists your options at the bottom of the menu, like this:

1 Move; 2 Copy; 3 Delete; 4 Append

Again, to select one of these choices, just press the appropriate number or click on the option with your mouse.

In simpler situations, WordPerfect doesn't display a menu at all. Instead, you'll see a prompt on the status line that will either look something like this

Exit WP? No (Yes)

or like this

Document to be saved:

In the first case, you answer the question by pressing **Y** (for Yes) or **N** (for No), or by clicking on the appropriate answer. In the second case, WordPerfect wants you to type something (such as the name of a document). Type your response and then press **Enter**.

Where Do They Come From?

Dialog boxes may sometimes seem to appear out of nowhere, but they generally show up after you select certain options from WordPerfect's pull-down menus or press certain key combinations. Whether or not a dialog box appears depends on whether or not the program needs more information from you. For example, if you select the File menu's Open command, WordPerfect displays the Open Document dialog box (shown below) to ask you the name of the document you want to open.

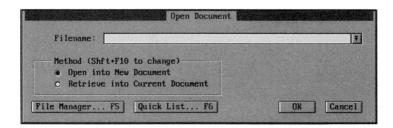

If you select the Open command, WordPerfect asks you for the name of the file you want to open.

You can always tell when a command will generate a dialog box by looking for three dots (...) after the command name. These three dots (they're known as an *ellipsis*) tell you that some kind of dialog box will appear if you select the option. This gives you time to prepare yourself mentally for the ordeal to come.

Dialog Box Basics

Before we can talk any more about dialog boxes, we need to get a specimen on the screen. If you pull down the File menu and select the Print/Fax command, you'll see the Print/Fax dialog box shown here. This one should serve us nicely (don't worry, you won't actually have to print anything).

Check box Dialog box title Text box Spinner

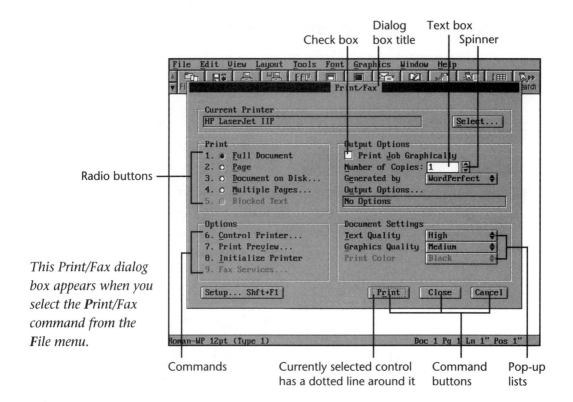

Radio buttons —

This Print/Fax dialog box appears when you select the Print/Fax command from the File menu.

Commands   Currently selected control   Command   Pop-up
             has a dotted line around it   buttons   lists

Before getting started, here are a few points about dialog boxes to keep in mind:

☞ Dialog boxes always have a title at the top of the box. This lets you know if you selected the right command.

☞ Dialog boxes like to monopolize your attention. When one is on the screen, you can't do other things such as enter text in the typing area or select a pull-down menu. Deal with the dialog box first, and then you can do other things.

☞ The various objects you see inside a dialog box are called *controls* because you use them to control the way the dialog box works.

Navigating Controls

Before you learn how these controls operate, you need to be able to move among them. (This section applies only to keyboard users. Mouse users select a control merely by clicking on it.)

The first thing you need to figure out is which control is currently selected. (This can be easy or hard depending on how many controls the dialog box has.) You need to look for the control that has its name surrounded by a dotted outline (or, in text mode, look for the control that is highlighted). Think of this as a "You are here" sign on a map. When you first display the Print/Fax dialog box, for example, the Print button at the bottom of the box has the dotted outline, so it's currently selected.

Once you know where you are, you can move around by pressing **Tab** (to move, more or less, left to right and top to bottom through the controls) or **Shift+Tab** (to move right to left or bottom to top). Go ahead and try some experiments in the Print/Fax dialog box. Each time you press Tab (or Shift+Tab), make sure you can find the selected control before moving on.

If you see a number or letter beside a control, you can select it simply by pressing the letter or number on your keyboard. For example, in the Print/Fax dialog box you'd select the **Page** control by pressing **2**.

Most WordPerfect dialog boxes organize related controls into groups and surround them with a box. The Print/Fax dialog box, for example, has five such groups (Current Printer, Print, Output Options, Options, and Document Settings). When you're inside one of these groups, you can usually select another control in the group simply by pressing the underlined letter in the control. For example, if you're in the Output Options group, you could select the Number of Copies control by pressing **N**.

Working with Radio Buttons

Radio buttons are WordPerfect's equivalent of the old multiple-choice questions you had to struggle with in school. You're given two or more choices, and you're only allowed to pick one. In the Print/Fax dialog box, the Print group contains five radio buttons.

TECHNO NERD TEACHES...

Why are they called *radio buttons*? Well, they're named for those old car radios where you had to push a button to select a station; this would release the currently selected station, so you could only have one station selected at a time. The radio buttons in a dialog box work just the same way.

As you can see, a radio button consists of a small circle with a label beside it that tells you the name of the control. Remember that the purpose of a dialog box is to get more information from you. By selecting the Print/Fax command from the File menu earlier, you told WordPerfect that you wanted to print something. These radio buttons are WordPerfect's way of asking "What, exactly, do you want to print?" Your mission (should you choose to accept it) would be to activate one of these buttons and then move on. (Don't worry too much about what the various options mean. I'll explain all in Chapter 9, "Getting It Down on Paper: Printing Documents.")

How do you activate a radio button? From the keyboard, you need to press **Tab** until the radio button you want is selected (its name is surrounded by a dotted outline) and then press either the **Spacebar** or **Enter**. Notice how a black dot appears inside the circle when you activate one of the buttons. If you have a mouse, simply click on the option you want (you can either click on the button itself or on its name).

If your mouse or keyboard skills aren't quite up to snuff yet, you may select the wrong radio button. No problem-o. Just select the correct one, and WordPerfect will deactivate the incorrect one automatically.

Working with Check Boxes

The real world is constantly presenting us with a series of either/or choices. You're either watching Oprah or you're not; you're either eating Heavenly Hash or you're not. That kind of thing. Word-Perfect handles these sorts of yes-or-no, on-or-off decisions with a control called a *check box*. The check box presents you with an option that you can either activate (check) or not.

In the Print/Fax dialog box, for example, the Print Job Graphically control is a check box. This control is on when an "X" appears in the square, and it's off when the square is empty. (Call me crazy, but wouldn't it make more sense if an activated check box actually had a check mark in it instead of an X? Just thought I'd ask.)

To activate a check box from the keyboard, press **Tab** until the check box you want is selected, and then press the **Spacebar**. To deactivate the check box, press the **Spacebar** again.

To activate a check box with a mouse, click on the box or on its name. To deactivate the box (remove the "X"), just click on the box again.

Working with Text Boxes

A *text box* is a screen area you use to type in text information such as a description or a file name. When you select a text box, you'll either see a blinking horizontal cursor inside the box (if it's empty) or highlighted text (if it's not). The Print/Fax dialog box has a single text box: the Number of Copies control.

When the text in a text box is highlighted, it means that it will be replaced by whatever you type. To avoid replacing the entire text, just press the left or right arrow key to remove the highlight, and then position the cursor appropriately.

To use a text box from your keyboard, press **Tab** either until you see the cursor in the box or until you see the text in the box highlighted, and then begin typing. To use a text box with a mouse, click anywhere inside the box and then type in your text. (As with regular text, you can fix mistakes in a text box by pressing the **Backspace** and **Delete** keys.)

Working with Spinners

Spinners are controls that let you scroll up or down through a series of numbers. Spinners have two parts:

☞ On the left you'll see a text box you can use to just type in the number you want.

☛ On the right you'll see two buttons with upward- and downward-pointing arrows. Click on the upward-pointing arrow to increase the number shown in the text box. Click on the downward-pointing arrow to decrease the number.

In the Print/Fax dialog box, the Number of Copies control has a spinner attached to it.

Working with Pop-Up Lists

Pop-up lists are controls that let you select from a list of choices. The button face always shows the current selection. In the Print/Fax dialog box, each of the controls in the Document Settings group is a pop-up list.

To work with a pop-up list from the keyboard, use **Tab** to select the button name and then press **Enter** to display the list of available choices (the current selection has an asterisk (*) beside it). Use the up and down arrow keys to highlight the choice you want, and then press **Enter**.

With a mouse, place the pointer over the appropriate pop-up list and press and hold down the left mouse button. In the list that appears, keep the mouse button pressed and move the mouse up and down until the selection you want is highlighted. Then release the button.

Dialog Box Commands

Many dialog boxes also include simple commands that work much like the commands in a pull-down menu. In the Print/Fax dialog box, for example, each of the items in the Options group (Control Printer, Print Preview, Initialize Printer, and Fax Services) is a command.

To select a command with your keyboard, press **Tab** until the command is selected, and then press **Enter**. With a mouse, just click on the command.

Working with Command Buttons

The Print/Fax dialog box also includes a number of controls called *command buttons* (for example, there are four along the bottom: Setup, Print, Close, and Cancel). When you select a command button, you're telling WordPerfect to execute the command written on the face of the button.

To select a command button from the keyboard, press **Tab** until the command button you want is selected, and then press **Enter**. To select a command button with a mouse, you just click on the button.

WordPerfect uses command buttons for all kinds of things, but two are particularly common: OK and Cancel. You use the OK button (the Print/Fax dialog box doesn't have one) when you're finished with the dialog box and you want to put all your selections into effect. Think of this as the "Make it so" button. Use the Cancel button when you panic and realize that you're looking at the wrong dialog box or when you've made a mess of your selections. Think of this as the "Belay that last order" button.

Working with Drop-Down Lists

At this point, the Print/Fax dialog box has outlived its usefulness. Select the **Cancel** button to remove it from the screen, and then select the Font command from the Font pull-down menu. This displays (surprise, surprise) the Font dialog box, which I'll use to explain what drop-down lists are.

A *drop-down list* is like a combination of a text box and a pull-down menu. You can type in the option you want or you can select it from a list that drops down (hence the name) when you select it. Drop-down list boxes usually contain lists of related items such as font names or document files. (The controls on WordPerfect's Ribbon are all drop-down lists. See Chapter 5, "WordPerfect the Easy Way: Menus, Buttons Bars, and More," to read more about the Ribbon.) The Font dialog box has two drop-down list boxes: Font and Size. Here's what your screen should look like when the Font list is dropped down.

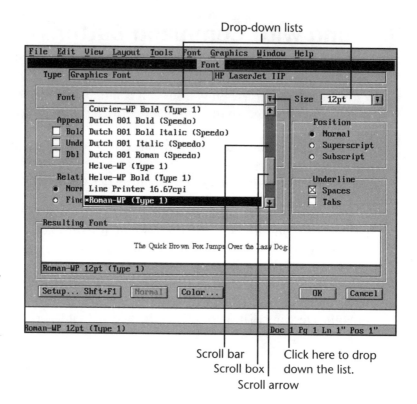

The Font dialog box, with the Font drop-down list dropped down.

Drop-down lists

Scroll bar
Scroll box
Scroll arrow

Click here to drop down the list.

To use your keyboard to select an item from a drop-down list, follow these steps:

1. Press **Tab** until either the name of the drop-down list is selected or until the current value in the list's text box is highlighted.

2. If the list's name is selected, press **Enter** to open the list. If the list's current value is highlighted, you open the list by pressing the down arrow key instead. (I'm sure it's little inconsistencies like these that have made most WordPerfect users old before their time.)

3. Type in your selection or use the up and down arrow keys to highlight the item you want.

4. Press **Enter**.

To use a mouse to select an item from a drop-down list, follow these steps:

1. Click on the downward-pointing arrow on the right side of the control. This opens the list to display its options.

2. Double-click on the item you want. If you don't see the item, use the scroll bar to view more of the list. (If you're not sure how a scroll bar works, read on.)

A Brief Scroll Bar Primer

You'll be learning more about scroll bars in Chapter 8, "Day-to-Day Drudgery II: Navigating Documents," but I'll give you a brief introduction here so you'll be able to use the drop-down lists.

Some lists contain too many items to fit inside the box that drops down. In this case, a scroll bar appears on the right hand side of the box to make it easier to navigate the list. The box inside the scroll bar (it's called, appropriately enough, the *scroll box*) tells you where you are in the list. For example, if the scroll box is halfway between the top and the bottom of the scroll bar, you're approximately halfway down the list.

Here's a neat-o tip that can save you oodles of time. Once the drop-down list is open, press the first letter of the item you want. Word-Perfect leaps down the list and highlights the first item in the list that begins with the letter you pressed. If you keep typing, Word-Perfect tries to find any item that matches the letters you've entered.

To navigate a list with the scroll bar, use the following mouse techniques:

☞ To scroll through the list one item at a time, click on either the upward-pointing arrow at the top of the scroll bar (to move up) or the downward-pointing arrow at the bottom of the scroll bar (to move down).

☞ To jump quickly through the list, click inside the scroll bar between the scroll box and the top (to move up) or between the scroll box and the bottom (to move down).

☞ To move to a specific part of the list, drag the scroll box up or down.

The Least You Need to Know

This chapter showed you the ins and outs of using dialog boxes to communicate with WordPerfect. We covered a lot of ground and you learned all kinds of new things. If it's not all clear in your head right now, don't worry about it because, believe me, you'll be getting plenty of practice. In the meantime, here's some important stuff to remember:

☞ WordPerfect uses dialog boxes to ask you for more information or to confirm that the command you've selected is what you really want to do.

☞ Keyboard jockeys use the **Tab** key (or **Shift+Tab**) to move through the dialog box controls.

☞ Some controls display a number or letter to the left. You can select these controls simply by pressing the number or letter on your keyboard.

☞ Many controls have underlined letters. When you're in a group, you can select these controls by pressing the letter on your keyboard.

Chapter 7

Day-to-Day Drudgery I: Saving, Opening, and Closing

In This Chapter

- ☛ Saving a document
- ☛ Saving a document under a different name
- ☛ Opening and retrieving a document
- ☛ Closing a document
- ☛ Cat waxing and other handy skills

WordPerfect, especially version 6, is jam-packed with powerful features that let you do everything but wax the cat. But even with all that power at your fingertips, you still need to take care of mundane drudgery such as opening, saving, and closing documents (the subjects of this chapter) and navigating your way through large files (which I'll save for Chapter 8).

Save Your Work, Save Your Life

Most people learn about saving documents the hard way. For me, it was a power failure that wiped out an entire day's writing. Believe me, that kind of thing can make you old before your time.

Why is saving necessary? Well, when you open a document, Word-Perfect copies it from its safe haven on your hard disk to the volatile confines of your computer's memory. When you shut off your computer (or if a power failure forces it off), everything in memory is wiped out. If you haven't saved your document to your hard disk, you'll lose all the changes you made.

Saving a New Document

When you first start WordPerfect, the program displays a blank typing area that you can use to begin a fresh document. If you've used this blank file, you can save your work by pulling down the File menu and selecting the Save command, or by pressing F10. WordPerfect needs to know the name you want to use for the new file, so it displays the Save Document dialog box shown below.

You can also access the Save Document dialog box by clicking on this button in the WPMAIN Button Bar.

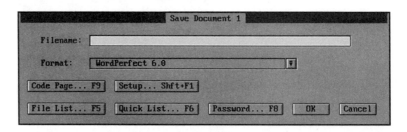

When you save a new document, WordPerfect displays the Save Document dialog box so you can name the file.

In the Filename text box, enter the name you want to use. File names usually contain a period flanked by a *primary name* on the left and an *extension* on the right. Extensions are optional, but most people use them because they're handy for identifying what type of file you're dealing with. For your WordPerfect documents, for example, use something like .WP or .DOC.

When naming your documents, make sure you observe the Sacred Filename Commandments handed down by the great DOS Gods:

I Thou shalt not use more than eight characters for the file's primary name.

II Thou shalt not use more than three characters for the file's extension.

III Thou shalt separate the primary name and the extension with a period.

IV Thou shalt not use a space or any of these other forbidden characters:

+ = \ | [ ] ; : , . < > ? /

V Thou shalt not take the name of an existing file.

When you finish typing in the file name, select the **OK** button. If all is well, WordPerfect saves the file and returns you to the document. However, if you enter an illegal name, WordPerfect will do one of the following:

When you save a new file in 5.1, you see this prompt:

Document to be saved:

Just type in a name (abiding by the Sacred Filename Commandments, of course), and press **Enter**.

☛ If your primary name is too long, WordPerfect lops it off at eight characters; if your extension is too long, WordPerfect spits out the extraneous letters and just uses the first three characters.

☛ If you enter an illegal character in the name, WordPerfect displays an **Invalid filename** error message. Select **OK** to close the error message box. Then return to the Save Document dialog box, expunge the offending character, and then try again.

☛ If you give the document the name of a file that already exists, WordPerfect displays a dialog box warning you that you are about to replace an existing file and asks you whether that's really what you want to do. Replacing the file will mean it's gone for good—and no amount of hocus-pocus will get it back. If you're absolutely, positively sure you won't ever need the other file, select **Yes**; otherwise, select **No** to return to the Save Document dialog box, and then enter a different file name.

To make saving even easier, use this handy shortcut key combination: **Ctrl+F12**.

Version 5.1 isn't quite so simple. After selecting the Save command, you see the following prompt:

Document to be saved:

The name of the file will appear as well. Press Enter, and WordPerfect (as though it didn't believe you), prompts you with this:

Replace filename? No (Yes)

Press **Y** to select Yes.

Saving an Existing Document

Once you've saved a new document, you're not out of the woods yet. If you make changes to the file, you need to save them as well. Happily, WordPerfect makes further saves so easy I can explain the whole process in a single sentence: To save the document you're working on, pull down the File menu and select the Save command. That's it! WordPerfect automatically updates the old copy of the file on your hard disk with the current version of the document.

How Often Should You Save?

Saving your work is vital, but few people do it often enough. How often is "often enough"? Take this quiz to see if you know:

You should save your work if:

(a) You pause while you think of what to say next (a common occurrence for many of us).

(b) You've just entered a long passage.

(c) You've just formatted a large section of text.

(d) You've just rearranged a bunch of stuff.

(e) You've just retrieved another document into the current one.

(f) About 10 minutes or so have passed since your last save.

(g) There's a thunderstorm raging outside your office.

(h) All of the above.

The answer, of course, is (h) All of the above. Saving is so easy that you really should do it as often as you can. Use (a) through (g) as a guideline for deciding when it's time to save. (You may be wondering why the heck you need to save your work during thunderstorms. Superstition? No. The problem is that lightning strikes can cause power surges in electrical outlets. Don't worry, you're in no danger of being jolted through your keyboard; but these surges do have a nasty habit of wreaking untold havoc on your sensitive data.)

Saving a Document When You Exit WordPerfect

You'll recall that to exit WordPerfect you select the Exit WP command from the File menu. If you attempt to exit WordPerfect without saving the current file, the Exit WordPerfect dialog box (shown below) appears.

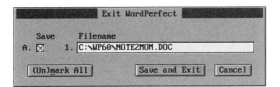

When you exit WordPerfect, the program gives you an opportunity to save your work.

Here are your options:

☞ If you have saved the document before, its name will appear in the Filename text box. Select the **Save and Exit** button to save the document and exit WordPerfect.

☞ If the document is new, enter a file name in the Filename text box, and then select the **Save and Exit** button.

☞ If you don't want to save your changes, turn off the Save check box and select the **Exit** button.

Saving While Exiting in Version 5.1

You exit version 5.1 by selecting Exit from the File menu. WordPerfect then asks if you want to save the current document. If you don't want to save it, press **N**; otherwise, press **Y**. If you're saving a new document, you'll be prompted for a file name. Enter the name and press **Enter**. Another prompt will appear (this is the last one, I promise), asking you if you want to exit WordPerfect. Select **Yes**.

Saving a Document Under a New Name

The File menu also includes a Save As command. This command is a lot like Save, except that you can save the file under a new name or to a new location. This is useful for creating a new file that is very similar (but not identical) to an existing file. Instead of creating the new file from scratch, just open the existing file, make the changes, and then use the Save As command to save your changes to the new file. The old file remains as it was.

Version 5.1 has no Save **As** command. To save the current document under a different name, select **S**ave from the **F**ile menu. When WordPerfect prompts you for the name of the document to be saved, delete the displayed name (using the Backspace key), enter the new name, and then press **Enter**.

Text that you reuse over and over is called **boilerplate**. It's the word processing equivalent of the old maxim, "Don't reinvent the wheel."

When you select Save As from the File menu (you can also simply press **F10**), our old friend the Save Document dialog box appears with the name of the current file in the Filename text box. Enter the new file name and then select the **OK** button. WordPerfect closes the old file, copies the text to the new file, and then opens the new file.

You can also save a document under a different name by clicking on this button in the WPMAIN Button Bar.

Getting Documents: Opening Versus Retrieving

In most of your WordPerfect sessions, you'll work with an existing document you saved sometime in the past. WordPerfect gives you two ways to do this: you can open a document or you can retrieve one.

When you *open* a document, WordPerfect sets up a fresh typing area, displays the document, and positions the cursor at the beginning of the file. When you *retrieve* a document, WordPerfect makes a copy of the entire file and then inserts it into the current document at the cursor position. This is a handy way of reusing material in another document.

How to Open a Document

To open a document, pull down the File menu and select the **Open** command (or you can press **Shift+F10**). You'll see the Open Document dialog box shown below.

*Selecting the **Open** command from the File menu displays the Open Document dialog box.*

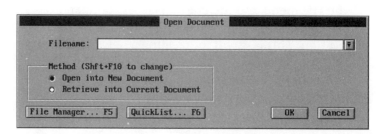

If you know the name of the document, enter it in the **Filename** text box and select **OK**. If you worked with the document recently, display the Filename drop-down list (either click on the downward-pointing arrow or move the cursor into the Filename box and press the down arrow key) to see the names of the last four files you opened. If the file you want is in the list, great! Just select it and WordPerfect opens it for you. For reference, WordPerfect displays the name of the opened file in the status line.

TECHNO NERD TEACHES...

Did you know you can tell WordPerfect to display a document automatically when you start the program? Sure! When you start WordPerfect at the DOS prompt, simply add a space after the **WP** and type the name of the document. For example, to open a document called STARTME.DOC, enter the following:

WP STARTME.DOC

Press **Enter** and, a few seconds later, WordPerfect loads and displays the file.

If you're not sure about the name, you can tell WordPerfect to display a list of files by following these steps:

1. In the Open Document dialog box, select the **File Manager** button or press **F5**. You'll see another dialog box called Specify File Manager List.

2. WordPerfect is asking you to specify which directory you want displayed. If you have no idea what a directory is, just select **OK**. (I'll give you the lowdown on weird DOS things like directories in Chapter 20, "Using WordPerfect's File Manager"). If you're familiar with directories, make whatever changes are necessary in the Directory text box, and then select **OK**. The File Manager appears on-screen, as shown on the following page.

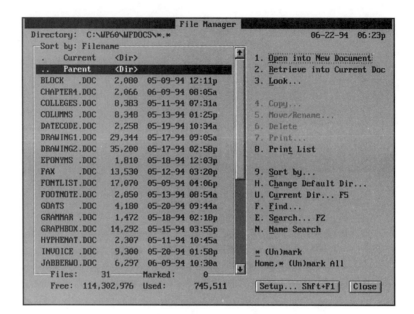

Use the File Manager to select the file you want to open.

3. Yikes! Pretty scary-looking, huh? Luckily, you can safely ignore most of the gobbledygook you see. Just use the up and down arrow keys to highlight the file you want to open, and then press **Enter**, or click on the Open into New Document command.

How to Retrieve a File

When you want to retrieve a file, first position the cursor at the point where you want the new text to appear. Then select the **Retrieve** command from the File menu to display the Retrieve Document dialog box (see below). Enter the name of the document in the Filename text box, or use the File Manager as described in the previous section.

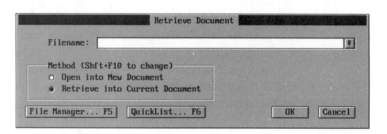

Selecting the Retrieve command from the File menu displays the Retrieve Document dialog box.

How to Open and Retrieve a File in WordPerfect 5.1

To open a file in version 5.1, first close the current file (as described later in this chapter). Then select **Retrieve** from the File menu, and you'll see the **Document to be retrieved:** prompt in the status line. Enter the name of the document and press **Enter**.

Once you have either the Open Document or Retrieve Document dialog box open, you can toggle between them by pressing **Shift+F10**.

To retrieve a file in version 5.1, first position the cursor appropriately and then select **Retrieve** from the File menu. When prompted for a document, enter the name and press **Enter**.

A Fresh Beginning: Starting a New Document

As I mentioned earlier, WordPerfect displays a new document when you first start the program. However, you can start a fresh file anytime you want. All you do is pull down the File menu and select the New command. (To start a new document in 5.1, just close the current document, as described in the next section.)

Closing a Document

When you're done with a document, you should close it to make room for other files. To do so, simply pull down the File menu and select the Close command.

In 5.1, you close a document by selecting **Exit** from the **File** menu. When you are prompted to save the document, select **Yes**, and then press **Enter** when WordPerfect displays the file name. (Unless, of course, you want to save the file under a different name. To do that, change the displayed name and press **Enter**.) WordPerfect asks if you want to replace the file. Select **Yes**. WordPerfect, ever relentless with the questions, now asks if you want to exit the program. Select **No**.

The Least You Need to Know

Now that was a chapter! WordPerfect sure seems to like complicating simple tasks such as saving and opening documents. Here's a summary of what you need to know:

- ☞ You should save your documents as often as you can to avoid losing any work. All you have to do is select the **Save** command from the **File** menu, or press **Ctrl+F12**.

- ☞ When you save a new document, WordPerfect asks you to enter a name for the file. Be sure to follow DOS's arcane file-naming rules or you'll get an error message.

- ☞ If you want to save a document under a different name, use the **File** menu's Save **As** command or press **F10**.

- ☞ To open a document, select **O**pen from the **File** menu (or press **Shift+F10**) and enter the name of the file in the Open Document dialog box.

- ☞ To retrieve a file, select **R**etrieve from the **File** menu and enter the name of the file in the Retrieve Document dialog box.

- ☞ To close a document, use the **File** menu's **C**lose command.

Chapter 8

Day-to-Day Drudgery II: Navigating Documents

In This Chapter

- ☛ Navigating a document with the keyboard
- ☛ Using WordPerfect's Go to command
- ☛ Navigating a document with a mouse
- ☛ Using scroll bars
- ☛ Tales of a thousand-and-one key combos

A lot of what you create in WordPerfect will be short letters and memos that fit right on-screen. But you'll also create longer documents, and what you see in the typing area will only be a small chunk of the entire file. To see the rest of the document, you'll need to learn a few navigational skills. Now, I'm not talking about navigating the Baja 500 or anything—just a few simple skills to help you get around. With this chapter riding shotgun, you'll get through just fine.

To get the most out of this chapter, you should follow along and try each of the techniques as I present them. For best results, open (or create) a document that's larger than the screen.

Navigating with the Keyboard

WordPerfect has a fistful of ways to navigate your documents from the keyboard. In this section, you'll work your way up from short hops between characters and words to great leaps between screens and pages.

Navigating Characters and Words

The simplest move you can make in a document is to use the left and right arrow keys to move left or right one character at a time. If you have a bit of ground to cover, try holding down the key. After a slight delay, the cursor will start racing through each line. (Notice that when it hits the end of one line, it starts over at the beginning of the next.)

When you hold down an arrow key, the speed at which the cursor moves is governed by two factors: the *delay* after the first movement, and the *repeat rate* (the rate at which the keyboard repeats the key). For the fastest possible keyboard response (i.e., the shortest delay and the quickest repeat rate), exit WordPerfect and type the following at the DOS prompt:

MODE CON DELAY=1 RATE=32

Press **Enter** to put these settings into effect. Now restart WordPerfect, and your arrow keys will whizz the cursor around the screen. If you want to play around with different settings, you can enter any value from 1 to 4 for the delay (the lower the value the smaller the delay), and any value from 1 to 32 for the repeat rate (the greater the value the faster the rate).

If you need to jump over a couple of words, hold down the **Ctrl** key and then use the left or right arrow keys to move one word at a time. If you're in the middle of a long word such as "hippopotomonstrosesquipedalian" (which is a very, very long word that means "pertaining to very, very long words"), use **Ctrl+left arrow** to move quickly to the beginning of the word.

Navigating Lines and Paragraphs

If you need to move up or down one line at a time, use the up or down arrow key. If you're at the bottom of the screen and you press the down arrow, the text will move up so you can see the next line. (The line that used to be at the top of the screen heads off into oblivion; but don't worry, WordPerfect keeps track of everything.) A similar thing happens if you're at the top of the screen (unless you're at the top of the document): if you press the up arrow, the text moves down to make room for the next line. Moving text up or down like this is called *scrolling* through the document.

To move to the beginning of the current line, press **Home** and then the left arrow key. To move to the end of the current line, press **Home** and then the right arrow (or you can just press the **End** key).

If you need to jump around a paragraph at a time, use **Ctrl+up arrow** (to move up one paragraph) or **Ctrl+down arrow** (to move down one paragraph).

Navigating Screens, Pages, and Documents

For really big documents, you need to know how to cover a lot of ground in a hurry. WordPerfect, of course, is up to the task.

To move to the top of the screen, press the minus key (–) on your keyboard's numeric keypad. (You can also press **Home**, **up arrow**.) To move to the bottom of the screen, press the numeric keypad's plus key (+), which is also equivalent to **Home**, **down arrow**. Keep pressing these keys to navigate the document one screenful at a time.

For multi-page documents, press **Page Up** to move to the beginning of the previous page or **Page Down** to move to the beginning of the next page.

Once you start hopping madly through a file, get your bearings by keeping your eyes on the status line's data. The Pg setting will tell you which page you're on, and the Ln setting tells you where you are in the current page.

If pressing plus or minus on your numeric keypad only produces plus or minus signs in your text, turn **Num Lock** off, or try holding down the **Shift** key when you press the plus or minus key on the keypad.

For truly large leaps, press **Home**, **Home**, **up arrow** (yes, you press Home twice) to move to the beginning of the document, or press **Home**, **Home**, **down arrow** to move to the end of the document.

Navigating with the Go to Command

No document jockey's arsenal of navigation tricks would be complete without WordPerfect's Go to command. If you select Go to from the Edit menu (or press **Ctrl+Home**), you'll see the Go to dialog box shown here.

Use the Go to command to jump strategically through a document.

Go to enables you to jump to specific parts of a document at warp speed. Here's a summary of what you can do once the Go to dialog box is displayed:

With all these key combinations, you occasionally may find that you jump somewhere you didn't intend to. If this happens, press **Ctrl+Home** to start the **Go to** command, and then press **Ctrl+Home** again. This takes you back to your original position.

- ☛ Press the up arrow to go to the top of the current page.

- ☛ Press the down arrow to go to the bottom of the current page.

- ☛ Type a number and press **Enter** to move to the top of that page number.

- ☛ Type a character to move to the next occurrence of that character. (This only works if the character isn't too far away; specifically, you have to be within 2,000 characters of the character you want to go to.) Also, make sure you enter the correct case for the character (for example, entering **a** only finds "a"; it won't find "A").

Navigating with the Repeat Command

Instead of wearing out your fingers on the keyboard, use the Repeat command to do the work. Just press **Ctrl+R** (or select Repeat from the Edit menu) to display the Repeat dialog box (shown below), and then press whatever key you want repeated. If you press, say, the down arrow, WordPerfect moves down eight lines.

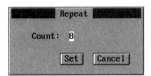

In version 5.1, press **Esc** to activate the **Repeat** command.

Why eight? Well, that's the number that appears by default in the Repeat dialog box. If you'd like to use a different number, press **Ctrl+R**, type in the number, and then press the key you want repeated.

Use the Repeat dialog box to repeat a keystroke and save wear and tear on your fingertips.

Navigating with the Mouse

Keyboard users, of course, can't have *all* the fun. If you like using a mouse, you can navigate a document with it just as well. Here are the basic techniques:

- ☞ To move the cursor to any spot on the screen, just click on the spot.

- ☞ To scroll the text down, position the pointer at the bottom of the typing area, hold down the right mouse button, and then drag the pointer down into the status line.

- ☞ Scrolling text up is similar: position the pointer at the top of the typing area, hold down the right mouse button, and then drag the pointer up towards the menu bar.

These techniques are fine, but to really get around with a mouse, you have to learn about scroll bars.

Scroll Whats?

Scroll bars are a lot like elevators. They sort of look like elevator shafts, and like your favorite Otis device, they serve a dual purpose: they can tell you where you are, and they can take you somewhere else.

Sorry, version 5.1 has no scroll bars.

Before you can use 'em, though, you need to display 'em. Just pull down the View menu, select the Vertical Scroll Bar command, and you'll see a scroll bar on the right side of the screen, as shown here.

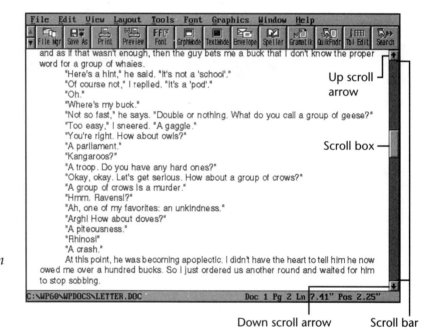

A WordPerfect screen with a vertical scroll bar.

Here are a couple of things to note about scroll bars before we move on:

- ☞ The size of the scroll box depends on how big your document is: the bigger the document, the smaller the scroll box.

- ☞ The View menu also has a Horizontal Scroll Bar command. You can use this scroll bar to scroll left and right in documents that are too wide to fit on the screen.

Where Am I? The Scroll Bar Knows

Thanks to my innately lousy sense of direction (I've been known to get lost getting out of bed in the morning), I always seem to lose my way in any document longer than a couple of pages. Fortunately, I have scroll bars to bail me out. The idea is simple: the position of the scroll box tells me my relative position in the document. So, for example, if the scroll box is about halfway down, I know I'm somewhere near the middle of the file. In this sense, the scroll box is a little like the floor indicators on an elevator.

Can I Get There from Here? Navigating with Scroll Bars

The real scroll bar fun begins when you use them to move around in your documents. There are three basic techniques:

☞ To scroll vertically through a document one line at a time, click on the scroll bar's up and down scroll arrows.

☞ To leap through the document one screen at a time, click inside the scroll bar between the scroll box and the scroll arrows. For example, to move down one screenful, click inside the scroll bar between the scroll box and the down scroll arrow.

☞ To move to a specific part of a document, drag the vertical scroll box up or down to the appropriate position. For example, to move to the beginning of a document, drag the scroll box to the top of the scroll bar.

The Least You Need to Know

This chapter concluded our look at document drudgery by examining a few easy navigation techniques. Here's the lowdown:

☞ Use the left and right arrow keys to move left and right one character at a time.

☞ Use **Ctrl+left arrow** or **Ctrl+right arrow** to jump left or right one word at a time.

☞ The up and down arrow keys move you up or down one line at a time.

☞ **Ctrl+up arrow** moves you up one paragraph, and **Ctrl+down arrow** moves you down one paragraph.

☞ Press minus (–) or plus (+) on the numeric keypad to move to the top or bottom of the screen.

continues

continued

☞ **Page Up** moves you to the beginning of the previous page, while **Page Down** moves you to the top of the next page.

☞ The **Go** to command (**Ctrl+Home**) gives you more control over your document-leaping.

☞ When navigating with a mouse, just click to move to a spot you can see, or use the scroll bars to navigate the entire document.

☞ To display the vertical scroll bar, pull down the **V**iew menu and activate the Vertical Scroll bar command.

Chapter 9

Getting It Down on Paper: Printing Documents

In This Chapter

- The basic printing steps
- Printing a selection of pages
- Printing an unopened document right from your hard disk
- Using WordPerfect's handy Print Preview feature
- Selecting a different printer
- Magic, mirrors, movie trailers, and other miscellaneous mumbo-jumbo

Okay, you've managed to peck out a few words on the keyboard, and maybe you've even gotten used to the idea of not pressing Enter at the end of each line. But before we move on to the editing and formatting stuff, perhaps you'd like to print out your creation for all to see. This is one of my favorite parts because, no matter how much I work with computers, I don't feel right until I see those pages come slithering out of my printer. To that end, this chapter takes you painlessly through the basics of printing with WordPerfect.

In this section, I'm assuming you've already set up a printer within WordPerfect (normally you do this during installation). If, when you access the Print/Fax dialog box as described below, the Current Printer area says **NO PRINTER SELECTED**, you don't have a printer set up. To remedy this, see "Adding a Printer to Word-Perfect," later in this chapter.

Basic Printing

Without further ado, let's get right to the basic steps that let you print a document in WordPerfect:

1. Make sure your printer is ready to go:

    ☞ Is it plugged in to both the wall and your computer?

    ☞ Is it turned on?

    ☞ Is it *on-line*? (Most printers have an "On-Line" light that tells you. If the light isn't on, press the **On-Line** button.)

    ☞ Is there enough paper for your document?

2. Once your printer is warm and happy, open a document and then decide how much of it you want to print. (Refer to the section titled "Printing an Unopened Document," to learn how to print documents without opening them.)

    ☞ If you want to print the whole thing, skip to Step 3.

    ☞ If you want to print only a single page, place the cursor anywhere on that page.

    ☞ If you want to print a block, select the block. (You select a block by pressing **Alt+F4** or **F12**, and then using the arrow keys to highlight what you need. If you have a mouse, just drag it over the appropriate text. See Chapter 11, "Block Partying: Working with Text Blocks," for details.)

3. Pull down the File menu and select the **Print/Fax** command, or press **Shift+F7**. You'll see the Print/Fax dialog box, shown below.

     You can also display the Print/Fax dialog box by clicking on this tool in the WPMAIN Button Bar.

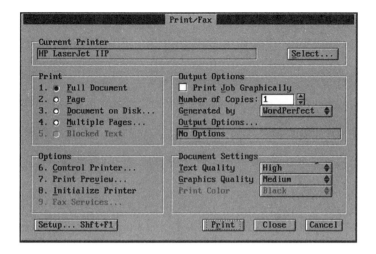

WordPerfect's Print/ Fax dialog box contains all the options you need to print your documents.

4. Use the Print group's radio buttons to tell WordPerfect what to print:

Full Document	This option prints everything.
Page	This option prints only the current page.
Document on Disk	This option magically prints a document without having to open it. See "Printing an Unopened Document," later in the chapter.
Multiple Pages	This option prints only the page numbers you specify. See "Printing Multiple Pages" to learn more.
Blocked Text	This option prints only the currently selected block.

5. If you need more than one copy, enter the number you want in the Number of Copies spinner.

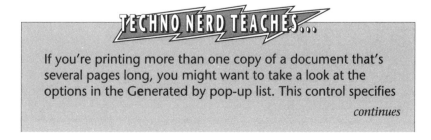

TECHNO NERD TEACHES...

If you're printing more than one copy of a document that's several pages long, you might want to take a look at the options in the Generated by pop-up list. This control specifies

continues

> *continued*
>
> whether you want WordPerfect or the printer to generate the
> multiple copies. For example, suppose you want three copies
> of a two-page document. If WordPerfect generates the
> copies, things take a little longer, but the copies get *collated*,
> which means the entire document gets printed one copy at a
> time. If the printer does it, the job will print faster, but you'll
> get three copies of page 1, and then three copies of page 2.

6. Use the Text Quality pop-up list to indicate how nice you want
   your text to look. If you're printing a final draft, select **High** for
   the best looking output. If you're just printing out a copy to see
   how things look, you can save some ink (or toner, if you have a
   laser printer) by selecting **Medium** or even **Draft** quality.

7. When you've finished picking your options, select the **Print**
   button to set everything in motion.

Printing Multiple Pages

If you only need to print a few pages from a document, select **Print/Fax**
from the File menu, and then select the **Multiple Pages** radio button in the
Print/Fax dialog box. In the Print Multiple Pages dialog box that appears
(see below), use the **Page/Label Range** text box to specify the pages you
want printed. The following table shows you how to enter the page numbers to let WordPerfect know which pages to print (the letters *a*, *b*, and *c*
represent page numbers you can enter):

Use	To print
a	Page *a*. For example, enter **3** to print only page 3.
a, b, c	Pages *a*, *b*, and *c*. For example, enter **1, 3, 5** to print pages 1, 3, and 5.
a–b	Pages *a* to *b*. For example, enter **2–5** to print pages 2, 3, 4, and 5.
a–	From page *a* to the end of the document. In a 10-page document, for example, enter **5–** to print page numbers 5 through 10.

Use	To print
–a	From the beginning of the document to page *a*. For example, entering **–6** prints page numbers 1 through 6.
a, b, c–d	Pages *a* and *b*, and pages *c* through *d*. For example, enter **1, 3, 6–10** to print pages 1, 3, and 6 through 10.

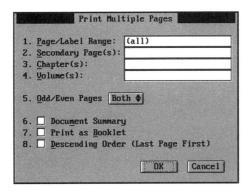

Use the Print Multiple Pages dialog box to specify the page numbers you want to print.

The Print Multiple Pages dialog box gives you several other options, as well:

☛ If you've been using secondary page, chapter, or volume numbers, use the **Secondary Page(s)**, **Chapter(s)** or **Volume(s)** text boxes to specify which ones you want to print. (See Chapter 15, "Making Your Pages Look Good," to get the poop on adding page, chapter, and volume numbers to your documents.)

☛ If you need to print only odd or even pages, select either **Odd** or **Even** from the **Odd/Even Pages** pop-up list.

☛ If you want the last page in the range printed first (which is handy if your printer spits out the pages face up), activate the **Descending Order (Last Page First)** check box. You can use the **Descending Order** check box even if you're printing the entire document. Just make sure the **Page/Label Range** says (**all**).

Make sure you type the page numbers in ascending numerical order. WordPerfect will choke if you enter something like 8–3 or 6,1.

When you finish selecting all the options you want in the Print Multiple Pages dialog box, click the OK button to return to the Print/Fax dialog box.

Printing an Unopened Document

One of WordPerfect's handy timesaving features is its capability to print an unopened document. This feature saves you from having to go through the whole hassle of opening the file, printing it, and then closing it again.

To try this voodoo out, select **Print/Fax** from the **File** menu, and then select the **Document on Disk** radio button. You'll see the Document on Disk dialog box as shown below. In the Document Name text box, enter the name of the file you want to print. (If you're not sure of the name, select the File List button or press **F5**, press **Enter** when the Select List dialog box appears, and then use the File List dialog box to select the document.)

Use the Document on Disk dialog box to specify the document you want to print.

When you're ready, select **OK**. WordPerfect displays the Print Multiple Pages dialog box, so you can specify a print range, if you like. Enter your options and select **OK**. Once you're back in the Print/Fax dialog box, select the Print button.

Using Print Preview

One of my favorite things about going to the movies is watching the trailers for upcoming films. Maybe that's why I like WordPerfect's Print Preview feature. It's like a trailer for the document you're about to print (without all the hype). You see exactly what your printout will look like, headers, footers, page numbers, and all. True, you can see all that stuff with version 6's graphics and page modes. But Print Preview shows you the big picture: you see a full page on your screen, so you can see how the whole thing fits together.

You can crank up Print Preview using any of these three methods:

☞ Select Print Preview from the **F**ile menu.

☞ If you're already in the Print/Fax dialog box, select the Print Preview command.

☞ 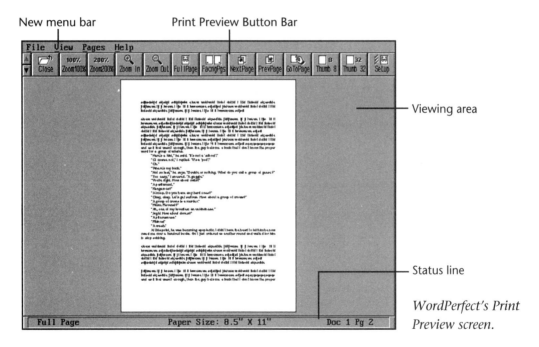 Click on the Print Preview button in the WPMAIN Button Bar.

Whichever method you use, the Print Preview screen appears, as shown in the following figure.

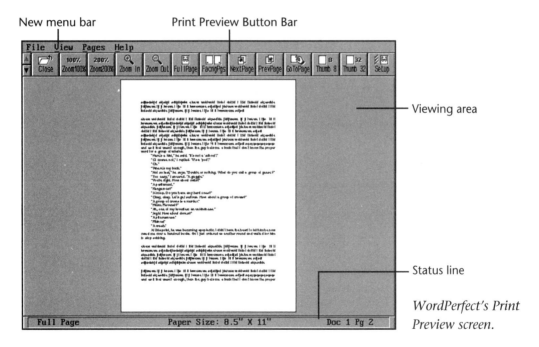

WordPerfect's Print Preview screen.

This screen is a little different from the one you're used to, so let's check out its various parts:

Menu bar   Print Preview has a scaled-down menu bar, but you use it just like the regular one.

Button Bar   The Print Preview screen has its own Button Bar that gives you push-button mouse access to each of the Print Preview features.

Viewing area   This is where WordPerfect displays your document. You can "zoom" in and out to see more detail or less detail.

Status line   Print Preview's status line shows slightly different info from what you see on the normal one. You see the current View (Full Page, 100%, etc.), the paper size, and the usual Doc and Pg values.

The next couple of sections show you how to use different Print Preview views and how to navigate your document. When you're finished with Print Preview, pull down the File menu and select Close, or press **F7**.

 You can also close Print Preview by clicking on this button in the Print Preview Button Bar.

Selecting Different Views

Print Preview normally displays your documents one page at a time in *Full Page view*, which scales down each page so that you can see the whole thing on your screen. This is great for checking out the overall layout of each page, but if you need to see more detail or more pages at once, you need to select the appropriate command from the View menu (or click on the corresponding button in the Print Preview Button Bar). Here's a summary:

Select	Or Click On	To
100% View	100% Zoom100%	See each page at the actual printed size
200% View	200% Zoom200%	See each page at twice the actual printed size
Zoom In	Zoom In	Increase the size of the page by 25%
Zoom Out	Zoom Out	Decrease the size of the page by 25%
Full Page	FullPage	View the current page

Select	Or Click On	To
Facing Pages	FacingPgs	View two consecutive pages at once
Thumbnails	Thumb 8	Display several pages at once. A cascade menu appears from which you can select the number of pages you want to view

Navigating Your Document

To see other pages in your document, use the commands in the **Pages** menu. Here's a summary:

Select	Or Click On	To
Go To Page	GoToPage	Display the Go To Page dialog box. Enter the page number you want to see, and then select OK
Previous Page	PrevPage	Go to the previous page
Next Page	NextPage	Go to the next page

Cancelling a Print Job

If you send a job to the printer and then decide you don't want to print it after all, you may be able to cancel the job in midstream. Here are the steps you need to follow:

1. Select Print/Fax from the File menu to display the Print/Fax dialog box, and then select the Control Printer command. The Control Printer dialog box appears, as shown on the next page.

2. Use the up or down arrow keys to highlight the job you want to cancel, and then select the Cancel Job command. If you want to cancel multiple jobs, highlight each one and press the **Spacebar**. A dialog box appears, asking if you want to cancel all the marked print jobs.

Current print jobs —

*WordPerfect's Control
Printer dialog box
keeps you apprised of
your print jobs, and
lets you cancel them
at any time.*

```
╔══════════════════ Control Printer ══════════════════╗
┌─Current Job─────────────────────────────────────────┐
│ Job Number: │2          │    Page Number:  │3      │ │
│ Status:     │Printing   │    Current Copy: │1 of 1 │ │
│ Message:    │None                                   │ │
│ Paper:      │Letter (Portrait) 8.5" x 11"           │ │
│ Location:   │Continuous feed                        │ │
│ Action:     │None                                   │ │
│                                                      │ │
│ Percentage Processed: │22 │                          │ │
└──────────────────────────────────────────────────────┘
┌─Job─Document───────────Destination──────┐ ▲  1. Cancel Job
│ 2   C:\...\LETTER.DOC    LPT 1          │    2. Rush Job
│ 3   C:\...\FAX.DOC       LPT 1          │    3. * (Un)mark
│ 4   C:\...\INVOICE.DOC   LPT 1          │    4. (Un)mark All
│                                          │ ▼
└──────────────────────────────────────────┘
┌Text──────Graphics─────Copies─Priority─┐  ┌─Stop─┐  ┌──Go──┐
│High       Medium        1     Normal   │  └──────┘  └──────┘
└────────────────────────────────────────┘  ┌Network... F8┐ ┌Close┐
```

3. Select **Yes** to cancel the jobs and return to the Control Printer dialog box.

4. Select **Close** to return to the document.

TECHNO NERD TEACHES...

The Control Printer dialog box has all kinds of other neat stuff. For example, you can watch the boxes in the Current Job group to see how a print job is progressing. And if something goes wrong with the job, you'll see a message in the Action box, and WordPerfect will tell you what you need to do. If you want to pause a job (say, to add more paper to the printer), select the Stop button; to resume printing, select the Go button. You can also send a print job that you need right away to the head of line. Just highlight the job, and then select the Rush Job command. When WordPerfect asks you to confirm that you want to rush the job, select Yes. (Note, however, that if a job is already printing, WordPerfect will restart the printout from the beginning once the rush job is done.)

Selecting a Different Printer

If you're lucky enough to have more than one printer, you can switch between them in WordPerfect fairly easily.

You may have noticed when printing that the Print/Fax dialog box shows you the name of the currently selected printer in the Current Printer box. To change this printer, choose the Select button beside it. This displays the Select Printer dialog box. Use the up and down arrow keys to highlight the printer you want (or just click on it with your mouse), and then choose the Select command. WordPerfect returns you to the Print/Fax dialog box and displays the name of the selected printer in the Current Printer box.

Adding a Printer to WordPerfect

If you get a new printer for Christmas (hey, why not?), or if you didn't set up your printer when you installed WordPerfect, you need to add the printer so WordPerfect knows what to do with your printouts. Follow these steps to add a printer:

1. In the Print/Fax dialog box, choose the Select button to display the Select Printer dialog box.

2. Choose the Add Printer command. WordPerfect displays the Add Printer dialog box, shown below.

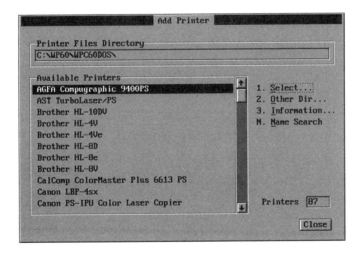

Use the Add Printer dialog box to select the printer you want to add to WordPerfect.

3. In the Available Printers list, highlight your printer, and then choose the Select command. The Printer Filename dialog box appears.

4. Select **OK**. WordPerfect displays the Information dialog box.

5. Select **Close**. Yet another dialog box appears (I told you these things were relentless). You can ignore everything and just select **OK** to return to the Select Printer dialog box.

6. Select **Close** to return to the Print/Fax dialog box.

The Least You Need to Know

This chapter showed you how to get hard copies of your WordPerfect documents. Since you'll likely be doing a lot of printing with WordPerfect, a quick review of the basics wouldn't hurt:

- ☞ Before printing, make sure your printer is ready for action. Check to see that it's plugged in, the cables are secure, it's turned on (and on-line), and that it has enough paper to handle the job.

- ☞ To print, pull down the **F**ile menu and select the **P**rint/Fax command (or just press **Shift+F7**). Enter your options in the Print/Fax dialog box, and then select the **P**rint button.

- ☞ You don't need to print the entire document each time. If you like, you can print just a block, the current page, or a range of pages. For the latter, select the **M**ultiple Pages option in the Print/Fax dialog box and enter the pages you want to print in the Multiple Pages dialog box that appears.

- ☞ To print an unopened document, select the **D**ocument on Disk option from the Print/Fax dialog box. Enter the name of the file you want printed and then select **OK**. Enter the pages to print, select **OK**, and select Print.

- ☞ Print Preview lets you see exactly how your document will look when it's printed. Just select the Print Preview command from the **F**ile menu or, if you're in the Print/Fax dialog box, select the Print Preview option.

- ☞ To select a different printer, choose the **S**elect button in the Print/Fax dialog box, highlight the printer you want, and then choose the **S**elect option.

Part II
Getting It Right: Editing Stuff

If, as they say, the essence of good writing is rewriting, then word processors ought to make us all better writers because rewriting—or editing—is what they do best. WordPerfect, in particular, has an impressive array of editing tools. The chapters in this section give you the basics of editing your prose in WordPerfect. You'll learn everything from simple deleting (and, thankfully, undeleting) to shuffling great hunks of text to new locations. I don't know if it'll make you a better writer, but it'll sure make you a heck of a rewriter.

Chapter 10

Deleting Text (and Undeleting It, Too)

In This Chapter

- Deleting one character at a time
- Deleting one word at a time
- Deleting entire pages
- Using the Repeat and Undelete features
- A small slice of the author's life

I moved recently, and it only took me five minutes of packing to realize something: I never throw anything away. I found old gum wrappers; ticket stubs from every baseball, football, hockey, and basketball game I'd ever attended; an ancient (and British!?) version of Monopoly. And books! Don't get me started with books!

I have the same trouble throwing things away when I'm writing. As my editor will tell you, I have a hard time deleting *anything*. I think I just get too attached. However, WordPerfect doesn't; in fact, it gives you all kinds of ways to nix troublesome text. This chapter will show you how.

Before going on any kind of deletion rampage, you should know that there's a section at the end of this chapter called "To Err Is Human, to Undelete Divine." If you wipe out anything you shouldn't have, skip ahead to that section to see how to make everything okay again.

Deleting Characters

WordPerfect makes it easy to expunge individual characters. You have two options:

☞ Press the **Delete** key to delete the character to the right of the cursor (or, if you're in text mode, the character above the cursor).

☞ Press **Backspace** to delete the character to the left of the cursor. (If your keyboard doesn't have a **Backspace** key anywhere in sight, look for the key with the left-pointing arrow ←, instead.)

In **Typeover mode**, your typing replaces existing characters. With **Insert mode**, your typing is inserted between existing characters.

If you want to delete several characters in a row, hold down **Delete** or **Backspace** until all the riffraff is eliminated. (Be careful, though: the cursor really picks up speed if you hold it down for more than a second or two.) You can also switch to Typeover mode, and simply overwrite the text you want deleted. Just press **Insert**, and you'll see the word **Typeover** in the status line. To return to Insert mode, press **Insert** again.

Deleting Words

To handle any stray words that creep into your documents, WordPerfect enables you to delete entire words with a single stroke. Just position the cursor anywhere inside the word you want to blow away, and press **Ctrl+Backspace**. If you place the cursor between two words and press **Ctrl+Backspace**, WordPerfect deletes the word to the left of the cursor.

For really fine-tuned deleting, you can even delete portions of a word. Here's how:

☞ To delete from the cursor to the end of a word, press **Home**, **Delete**.

☞ To delete from the cursor to the beginning of a word, press **Home**, **Backspace**.

Deleting Lines

WordPerfect lets you delete a portion of a line, or even (with just a little extra work) an entire line. For starters, if you just need to delete text from the cursor to the end of the line, press **Ctrl+End**.

Deleting an entire line takes an extra step: first place the cursor at the beginning of the line (by pressing **Home**, **left arrow** or by clicking to the left of the line), and then press **Ctrl+End**. (To learn how to delete entire sentences and paragraphs, see Chapter 11, "Block Partying: Working with Blocks of Text.")

Deleting Pages

If you've really made a mess of things, you may need to obliterate great big chunks of text. One handy way to do this is to delete everything from the cursor to the end of the page. You do this by pressing **Ctrl+Page Down**. Just to be safe, you should scroll down to the bottom of the page before using Ctrl+Page Down to make sure you're not going to wipe out anything important.

Since this is such a destructive command, WordPerfect asks if you're sure you want to go through with it, as shown here. Just select **Yes** to continue (or, of course, **No** to cancel).

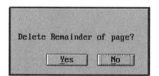

When you press Ctrl+Page Down to delete from the cursor to the end of the page, WordPerfect—ever cautious—asks you to confirm.

Repeat Deleting

The **Repeat** command gives you a handy way to speed up your deletion chores. Just select **Repeat** from the Edit menu (or press **Ctrl+R**), and then press the appropriate deletion key or key combination. The default repeat value is 8

In version 5.1, press **Esc** to select the Repeat command.

(which means that if you press Delete, for example, WordPerfect will delete eight characters), but you can use whatever value you need. Just type the number you want in the Repeat dialog box. Unfortunately, **Repeat** doesn't work with the Backspace key.

Press **F1** to crank up the Undelete command in version 5.1. You'll see the following prompt at the bottom of the screen:

Undelete: 1 Restore; 2 Previous Deletion: 0

Press **R** (or **1**) to restore a deletion. Press **P** (or **2**) to see the other deletions.

To Err Is Human, to Undelete Divine

Let's face facts: everybody deletes stuff accidentally, and one day you'll do it, too. It's one of those reality things (like nose hair and paying taxes) that we just can't avoid. The good people at Word-Perfect know this, and the gurus in their programming department came up with a way to ease the pain: the Undelete command. This command, as its name implies, miraculously reverses any of your three most recent deletions (which, believe me, has saved my bacon on more than one occasion).

Here are the steps to follow to undelete something:

1. Get whatever cursing, fuming, and gesticulating you normally do when you've just deleted your last three hours' work out of the way first. You need a clear head for what's to come.

2. Select U**n**delete from the Edit menu or press **Esc**. As you can see in the figure that follows, WordPerfect displays the Undelete dialog box, adds the last deletion back into the text, and highlights it so you can see it clearly.

WordPerfect adds your last deletion back into the text.

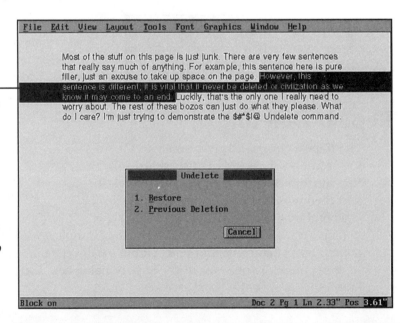

When you select the Undelete command, WordPerfect adds the last deletion back into the text and displays the Undelete dialog box.

3. If that's the text you want undeleted, select **R**estore. If it's not, select **P**revious Deletion until you see what you want and then select **R**estore. (Remember that WordPerfect only stores the last three things you deleted.)

TECHNO NERD TEACHES...

How does **U**ndelete perform its magic? Each time you delete something, it might appear as though it has gone off to some la-la land of deleted text—but that's not quite the case. WordPerfect sneakily saves each of the last three deletions in a special file called a *buffer* that stores not only the text itself, but its original location. Undeleting, then, is a simple matter of restoring the text from the buffer.

The Least You Need to Know

This compact little chapter gave you the scoop on deleting text (and undeleting it too, just in case). Here are a few pointers to take with you on your travels:

- ☞ To delete individual characters, use the **Delete** key (to delete whatever is to the right of the cursor or, if you use text mode, whatever is above the cursor), or the **Backspace** key (to delete whatever is to the left of the cursor).

- ☞ To delete a word, put the cursor inside the word and press **Ctrl+Backspace**.

- ☞ Press **Ctrl+End** to delete from the current cursor position to the end of the line.

- ☞ To delete from the current cursor position to the end of the page, press **Ctrl+Page Down**.

- ☞ You can speed up your deleting by using the Repeat command. Just press **Ctrl+R** to display the Repeat dialog box, enter a different number if

continues

continued

needed, and then press the appropriate deletion key or key combo.

☞ If you delete something by accident, immediately select Undelete from the Edit menu (or press **Esc**). Select Restore to undelete the highlighted text, or select Previous Deletion to see other deleted text.

Chapter 11

Block Partying: Working with Blocks of Text

In This Chapter

☛ How to select a block of text

☛ Making copies of text blocks

☛ Moving text blocks to different locations within a document

☛ Reversing errors with the Undo command

☛ Pleasurable prose chock-a-block with practical WordPerfect stuff

Blocs (as in "the Eastern bloc") may be out, but *blocks* are definitely in. I mean, we have block parents, block parties, block captains. Why, even the old "Gumby and Pokey" show (which featured the villainous Blockheads, of course) has made a bizarre comeback of sorts.

WordPerfect uses blocks, too. In this case, though, a *block* is just a section of text. It could be a word, a sentence, two-and-half paragraphs, or 57 pages. Whatever you need. The key is that WordPerfect treats a block as a single entity: a unit. And what does one do with these units? Well, you name it: you can copy them, move them, delete them, print them, format them, spell-check them, take them to lunch, whatever. Not only does this chapter show you how to select a block, but it also takes you through a few of these block tasks.

A **block** is a section of text of any length.

Selecting a Block of Text

WordPerfect, bless its electronic heart, gives you no less than three ways to select a block of text: you can use your keyboard, your mouse, or the handy Select command.

If you decide you don't want to select a block after all, just press **Esc** (in version 6) or **F1** (in version 5.1).

Selecting Text with the Keyboard

To select some text with your keyboard, begin by positioning the cursor at the beginning of the text. Now select **Block** from the **Edit** menu, or press either **F12** or **Alt+F4**. You'll see a **Block on** message in the status line. (The next step is optional: make a fist with your right hand, raise it over your head, and say "Block on, man!")

Once Block is on, you can use the arrow keys to move through the text you want to select. As you do, WordPerfect highlights the characters you're selecting (i.e., they appear white on a black background), as you can see here.

A block of text —

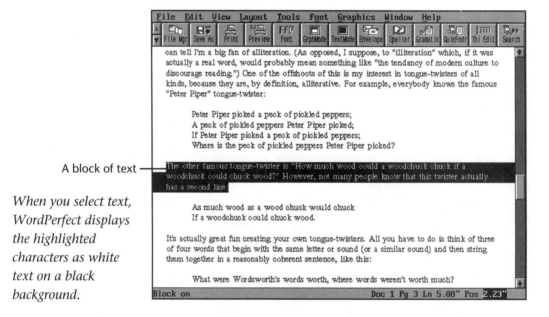

When you select text, WordPerfect displays the highlighted characters as white text on a black background.

Table 11.1 presents some key combos you can use for more fine-tuned selecting while Block is on.

Table 11.1   Key combinations to use while selecting text

Press	To select text to
Ctrl+right arrow	The next word
Ctrl+left arrow	The previous word
Home, right arrow or End	The end of the line
Home, left arrow	The beginning of the line
Ctrl+down arrow	The end of the paragraph
Ctrl+up arrow	The beginning of the paragraph
Home, down arrow	The bottom of the screen
Home, up arrow	The top of the screen
Page Down	The beginning of the next page
Page Up	The beginning of the previous page

You may have noticed that the key combinations in Table 11.1 bear a remarkable resemblance to the navigation keys you struggled through back in Chapter 8. Hey, you get an extra dessert tonight because, yes, they're exactly the same! In fact, you can use any of the stuff from that chapter (including **Ctrl+Home**—the handy **G**o to command) to select text.

Selecting Text with the Mouse

Once Block is on, just press any character and WordPerfect will extend the selection down to the next instance of that character. Pretty slick, huh? In particular, press period (.) to select to the end of the sentence, or press **Enter** to select to the end of the paragraph.

Mouse users, forget the keyboard—because selecting text with the little rodent guy is *way* easier. All you have to do is position the pointer at the beginning of the block, press and hold down the left button, drag the mouse over the text you want to select, and then release the mouse button. That's it! No unsightly key combinations! And if you need to cancel the block selection? No sweat: just click anywhere inside the typing area.

But wait, there's more! The mouse also makes it easy to select words, sentences, and even entire paragraphs. Table 11.2 gives you the fascinating details.

Table 11.2   Mouse actions for selecting text

If you do this	WordPerfect does this
Double-click inside a word	Selects the word
Triple-click inside a sentence	Selects the sentence
Quadruple-click inside a paragraph	Selects the paragraph

Triple-clicking, as you may have guessed by now, means you quickly press and release the left mouse button three times in succession. **Quadruple-clicking** is a real workout: you quickly press and release the left mouse button four—count 'em, four times—in succession. (Don't worry: there's no such thing as quintuple-clicking—yet.)

Using the Select Command

WordPerfect's Select command makes it easy to select single sentences, paragraphs, and pages. Just position the cursor in the sentence, paragraph, or page you want to select, and then choose the Edit menu's **Select** command. You'll see a cascade menu appear that includes the following entries: **Sentence**, **Paragraph**, and **Page**. Just select the appropriate command, and WordPerfect does the rest.

Copying a Block

One of the secrets of computer productivity is a simple maxim: "Don't reinvent the wheel." In other words, if you've got something that works, and you need something similar, don't start from scratch. Instead, make a copy of the original, and then make whatever changes are necessary to the copy.

Chapter 7, "Day-to-Day Drudgery I: Saving, Opening, and Closing," showed you how to use the Save As command to make a copy of an entire document. In most cases, though, your needs won't be so grandiose; you'll usually only need to make a copy of a few sentences or a few paragraphs. Happily, WordPerfect makes it easy to copy these smaller clumps of prose.

In fact (if you have version 6), you get not one but *two* copy methods: the regular two-command method (first Copy, then Paste) and the new one-command method (Copy and Paste).

In version 5.1, after you select **Paste** from the **Edit** menu, select **B**lock in the status line prompt.

Copying with Two Commands

With this method, once you've selected what you want to copy, just pull down the Edit menu and select the Copy command, or press **Ctrl+C**. You then position the cursor where you want to place the copy and then select **Paste** from the Edit menu, or press **Ctrl+V**. A perfect copy of your selection appears instantly. If you need to make other copies, just position the cursor appropriately, and select the Paste command again.

Copying with One Command

If you need to make only a single copy, version 6's new Copy and Paste command will do the job. To use it, select your text, pull down the Edit menu, and choose Copy and Paste or press **Ctrl+Insert**. Then position the cursor where you want the copy to appear and press **Enter**. If you decide you don't want to paste the copy after all, press **Esc** to cancel the operation.

Moving a Block

One of the all-time handiest word processor features is the capability to move stuff from one part of a document to another. This is perfect for rearranging everything from single sentences to massive chunks of text.

Now, you might think you'd do this by making a copy, pasting it, and then going back and deleting the original. Well, you *could* do it that way, but your friends would almost certainly laugh at you. Why? Because there's an easier way. WordPerfect lets you *cut* a selection right out of a document and paste it somewhere else. And (as with copying) version 6 gives you two methods.

Moving with Two Commands

Once you've selected what you want to move, pull down the Edit menu and select the Cut command, or press **Ctrl+X**. Your selection will disappear from the screen, but don't sweat it; WordPerfect is saving it for you in a secret location. Now position the cursor where you want to move the selection and then choose Paste from the Edit menu, or press **Ctrl+V**. Your text miraculously reappears in the new location. If you need to make further copies of the selection, just reposition the cursor and select **Paste** again.

If you cut a selection accidentally, immediately select the Edit menu's Undo command. For more Undo info, see the section titled "The Life-Saving Undo Command" later in this chapter.

Moving with One Command

For quick text moves, you can't beat version 6's new Cut and Paste command. Select your text, pull down the Edit menu, and choose Cut and Paste or press **Ctrl+Delete**. Again, WordPerfect plucks the text from the screen (but stores it in the secret location). Now position the cursor where you want the text moved, and press **Enter**.

Psst. Wanna know the name of the secret location that WordPerfect uses to keep the stuff you cut? It's called the *Clipboard*. Any time you cut or copy information, WordPerfect stores it in the Clipboard just in case you want it back. That's why, when you use the Cut and Paste command, the status line says **Press Enter to retrieve**; you're retrieving the text from the Clipboard.

Saving a Block

If you've just written some particularly breathtaking prose, you might want to save it in a file all its own. No problem. Just select the text, pull down the File menu, and choose the Save As command or press **F10**. WordPerfect displays the Save Block dialog box, shown here.

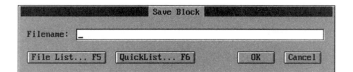

Use the Save Block dialog box to save a highlighted block to a file.

Enter a name for the file in the Filename text box and select **OK**.

Deleting a Block

Deleting a block of text is a no-brainer. Just make your selection and press either **Delete** or **Backspace**. Remember that if you delete anything accidentally, you can always fall back on WordPerfect's U**n**delete command. See Chapter 10, "Deleting Text (and Undeleting It, Too)," for the skinny on U**n**delete.

In version 5.1, enter a name for the file at the status line's **Block name** prompt, and then press **Enter**.

Appending a Block to a File

WordPerfect has a strange Append command that few people seem to know about. The idea behind it is that you might be working in one document and then suddenly decide that the

Version 5.1 displays a **Delete Block?** prompt in the status line after you press Delete or Backspace. Select **Y**es to continue with the deletion or **N**o to cancel.

sentence (paragraph, whatever) you just wrote *must* be included in yesterday's memo. Append lets you tack it on to that document without having to go through the whole rigmarole of opening it. (Although, in practice, you'll usually need to open the document eventually to position the added text appropriately.)

One common use for the Append feature is to add prose to a file of boilerplate text. For example, suppose you created a document called, say, BOILER.DOC, and you use it to store sentences and paragraphs you regularly include in your documents. Anytime you create a new boilerplate passage, you can use Append to add the text quickly and painlessly to the BOILER.DOC file.

To use this feature, all you do is select the appropriate block, pull down the Edit menu, choose Append, and then choose To File from the cascade menu that appears. In the Append To dialog box (shown below), enter the name of the file and select **OK**.

Use the Append To dialog box to add the highlighted text to the end of a file.

Make sure you select the Undo command *immediately* after you make a mistake. WordPerfect can only reverse your last action; so if you do anything else in the meantime, you may not be able to recover.

The Life-Saving Undo Command

Every WordPerfect user—from the rawest novice to the nerdiest expert—ends up at some time or other doing something downright silly. It may be a matter of cutting when you should have been copying, or just pasting a chunk of text in some absurd location.

Fortunately, WordPerfect has an Undo feature to get you out of these jams. The Undo command restores everything to the way it was before you made your blunder. (I've had some relationships where an Undo command would have come in *really* handy.) All you have to do is pull down the Edit menu and select Undo.

When I make mistakes (which is embarrassingly often, I have to tell you), I like to invoke the Undo command as quickly as I can. So, instead of the menus, I just use the **Ctrl+Z** key combination.

The Least You Need to Know

This chapter led you through the basics of working with WordPerfect's text blocks. We really only scratched the surface here, because there's plenty more you can do with blocks. However, I'll save all that rot for the chapters to come. For now, here's a rehash of what just happened:

☛ A block is just a selection of text that you can work with as a whole.

☛ To select text with the keyboard, choose the **Edit** menu's **B**lock command (or press either **F12** or **Alt+F4**), and then use WordPerfect's navigation keys to highlight the text you want.

☛ Selecting text with a mouse is even easier. Position the pointer at the beginning of the text, and then drag the mouse over the selection you need. You can also select a word by double-clicking on it, select a sentence by triple-clicking on it, and select a paragraph by quadruple-clicking on it.

☛ To copy a block, select **C**opy from the **E**dit menu (or press **Ctrl+C**), position the cursor, and then select **P**aste (or press **Ctrl+V**). Alternatively, select **C**opy and **P**aste (or press **Ctrl+Insert**), position the cursor, and then press **Enter**.

☛ To move a block, pull down the **E**dit menu and select Cu**t** (or press **Ctrl+X**), position the cursor, and then select **P**aste from the **E**dit menu. Or select Cu**t** and **P**aste (or press **Ctrl+Delete**), position the cursor, and then press **Enter**.

☛ To delete a block, just press **Delete** or **Backspace**.

☛ To reverse a blunder, immediately select **U**ndo from the **E**dit menu (or press **Ctrl+Z**). Make sure, however, that you run **U**ndo before performing any other action.

Yeah, this page is blank, but don't worry—you were only charged for the pages with stuff on them.

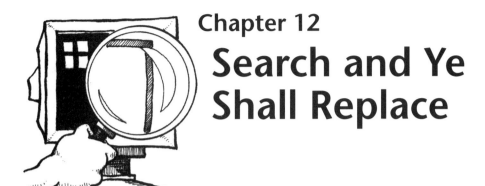

Chapter 12
Search and Ye Shall Replace

In This Chapter

- Searching for text, forwards
- Searching for text, backwards
- Search strategies
- Searching for and replacing text
- A sad little song, sure to bring a tear to your eye

Oh where, oh where has my little text gone?
Oh where, oh where can it be?

If you've ever found yourself lamenting a long-lost word adrift in some humongous mega-document, the folks at WordPerfect can sympathize (probably because it's happened to *them* a time or two). They were even kind enough to build a special Search feature into WordPerfect to help you find missing text. And that's not all: you can also use this feature to seek out and *replace* every instance of one word with another. Read on to find out how.

Searching for Text

If you need to find a certain word or phrase in a short document, it's usually easiest just to scroll through the text. But if you're dealing with more than a couple of pages, don't waste your time rummaging through the whole file. WordPerfect's Search feature enables you to search forward (toward the end of the document) or backward (toward the beginning) to find what you need.

Searching Forward

If you're pretty sure the text you want to locate is somewhere between the current cursor position and the end of the document, you can tell WordPerfect to search forward. Here are the steps you need to follow:

1. Pull down the Edit menu and select the Searc**h** command, or press **F2**. The Search dialog box appears, as shown here.

    You can also display the Search dialog box by clicking on the Search button in the WPMAIN Button Bar.

   Fill in the Search dialog box to hunt for text in a document.

   ```
   ┌──────────────────────── Search ────────────────────────┐
   │                                                         │
   │   Search For: │_                                      │ │
   │                                                         │
   │   ☐ Backward Search          ☐ Find Whole Words Only    │
   │   ☐ Case Sensitive Search    ☐ Extended Search (Hdrs, Ftrs, etc.)│
   │   ┌─────────┐ ┌──────────────────────┐  ┌─────────┐ ┌──────┐ │
   │   │Codes... F5│ │Specific Codes... Shft+F5│  │Search F2│ │Cancel│ │
   │   └─────────┘ └──────────────────────┘  └─────────┘ └──────┘ │
   └─────────────────────────────────────────────────────────┘
   ```

2. In the Search For text box, type the text you want to find (you can enter up to 80 characters).

3. Select the Search button or press **F2**. If WordPerfect finds a match, it places the cursor to the right of the text. If it doesn't find a match, WordPerfect displays a message to that effect, as shown below. You can remove this message from the screen by selecting **OK** or by pressing **Enter**.

WordPerfect displays this rather cryptic message if it can't find your search text.

Searching Backward

If you do a forward search and WordPerfect doesn't find a match, the darn program just bails out at the end of the document. If it was up to me, I'd make it wrap around and start checking from the beginning. However, they never asked for my opinion, so we're stuck with having to search backward, instead. Here are the steps to follow:

To search forward for text in version 5.1, pull down the **S**earch menu and select **F**orward. At the ← **Srch** prompt, type the search text (up to 80 characters) and press **F2**.

In 5.1, you search backward for text by pulling down the **S**earch menu and selecting **B**ackward. At the → **Srch** prompt, type the search text and press **F2**.

1. Pull down the Edit menu and select the Searc**h** command, or press **Shift+F2**, to display the Search dialog box. (In case you're confused, it *is* correct that both the **F2** and **Shift+F2** shortcut keys display the Search dialog box. However, as you'll see, pressing **Shift+F2** tells WordPerfect that you want to search backwards.)

2. In the Search For text box, type the text you want to find.

3. Activate the **B**ackward Search check box. (If you started Search by using the **Shift+F2** key combination, WordPerfect automatically activates the **B**ackward Search check box.)

4. Select the Search button or press **F2** to start searching.

Continuing the Search

Sometimes the text that WordPerfect finds is not the particular instance you want. To continue the search in the same direction, simply repeat the steps just mentioned. Note, however, that WordPerfect is smart enough to remember your last search text, and displays it automatically in the Search For text box. So once the Search dialog box is displayed, select the Search button to find the next example of the text. (The fastest way to continue searching is just to press **F2** twice: once to display the Search dialog box, and once to start the search operation.)

Using Search to Extend a Text Block

Version 5.1's Search menu contains two other commands—**Next** and **Previous**—that you can use to continue the search.

One handy use for the Search feature is to extend an existing text block down to the next occurrence of a word or phrase. (Head back to Chapter 11, "Block Partying: Working with Blocks of Text," if you need to learn more about text blocks.)

To try this out, first move the cursor to beginning of the text you want to select. Then start the text block by selecting some of the text (you can select a word or two, or even just a single letter). Now run the Search feature and look for the word or phrase you want to use to extend the block. If WordPerfect finds a match, it returns you to the document and extends the block to include the search text. To extend the block to the next instance of the search text, just continue the search, as described in the last section.

Searching Savvy

Searching for text is a relatively straightforward affair, but it wouldn't be WordPerfect if there weren't five thousand other ways to confuse the heck out of us. To makes things easier, here are a few plain-English notes that'll help you get the most out of the Search feature:

☞ For best results, keep your search text as short as possible (a word or two is all you'll usually need). Trying to match long phrases or even entire sentences can be a problem because you increase your chances of misspelling a word or accidentally leaving a word out of the search text. (For example, if you want to search for *It's a wonderful day in the neighborhood* and you enter *It is a wonderful day in the neighborhood*, WordPerfect will scoff at your efforts because the beginning of the two sentences don't match.) And besides, it just takes longer to type in a lengthy phrase or sentence.

☛ If you're not sure how to spell a word, just use a piece of it. WordPerfect will still find *egregious* if you search for *egre* (although, efficient beast that it is, it will also find words like *regret* and *degree*).

☛ As you can tell from the last point, WordPerfect will happily find a chunk of text that sits in the middle of a word (such as the *egre* in *regret* and *degree*). To find only words that *begin* with your search text, add a space before the text.

☛ Rather than fumbling around with searching both forward and backward, you can make sure you search the entire document by first positioning the cursor at the beginning (by pressing **Home**, **Home**, **up arrow**) and then searching forward. (If you're one of those people who likes to be different, you can accomplish the same thing by positioning the cursor at the bottom of the document—press **Home**, **Home**, **down arrow**—and then searching backward.)

☛ When your search is complete, you can return to your original position by pressing **Ctrl+Home** (to display the **G**o to dialog box), and then pressing **Ctrl+Home** again.

☛ If you need to differentiate between, say, *Bobby* (some guy) and *bobby* (as in a *bobby* pin or an English *bobby*), activate the Case Sensitive Search check box in the Search dialog box. This tells WordPerfect to match not only the letters, but also whatever uppercase and lowercase format you use. (In WordPerfect 5.1, if you type everything in lowercase, Search finds all occurrences of a word, regardless of case. If you add uppercase letters, Search will find only words that match the uppercase.)

☛ If you search for, say, *gorge*, WordPerfect may find not only the word *gorge*, but also *gorged*, *gorgeous*, and *disgorge* as well. If all you want is *gorge*, select the Find Whole **W**ords Only option in the Search dialog box. (To find whole words in 5.1, put a space on either side of the word in the search text.)

☛ Select the Search dialog box's Extended Search option to tell WordPerfect to search inside things like document headers, footers, and footnotes. (I show you how to work with headers and footers in Chapter 15, "Making Your Pages Look Good"; for footnotes, check out Chapter 17,

"Other Ways to Look Good.") To run an extended search in version 5.1, press **Home, F2** to search forward or **Home, Shift+F2** to search backward.

TECHNO NERD TEACHES...

WordPerfect litters your documents with bizarre hidden things called *formatting codes*. These codes are just WordPerfect's notes to itself about things like fonts and page layout. (If you're curious, you can see them by pulling down the **V**iew menu and selecting Reveal **C**odes, or by pressing **Alt+F3**; personally, these things give me the willies, so I prefer to keep them out of sight—and definitely out of mind. To send them back from whence they came, press **Alt+F3** again.) The Search dialog box's Codes (**F5**) and Specific Codes (**Shift+F5**) buttons enable you to search for these formatting codes, if you have the stomach for such things.

Searching and Replacing Text

If you do a lot of writing, one of the features you'll come to rely on the most is *search and replace*. This means that WordPerfect seeks out a particular bit of text and then replaces it with something else. This may not seem like a big deal for a word or two, but if you need to change a couple of dozen instances of *irregardless* to *regardless*, it can be a real timesaver.

Search and Replace: The Basic Steps

Searching and replacing is, as you might imagine, not all that different from plain old searching. Here's how it works:

1. Pull down the Edit menu and select the Replace command, or press **Alt+F2.** You'll see the Search and Replace dialog box shown here.

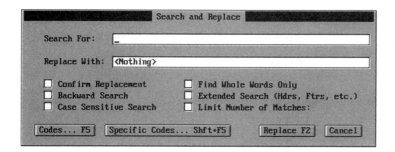

Use the Search and Replace dialog box to search for text and then replace it with something else.

2. In the Search For text box, enter the text you want to find (you can enter up to 80 characters).

3. In the Replace With text box, enter the text you want to use as a replacement. (Again, you have an 80-character limit.)

4. Select the Replace button, or press **F2**. WordPerfect races through the document, searching and replacing as it goes. When it's done, it displays a report on-screen of how many occurrences of the search text it found, and how many it replaced. (The picture below shows you an example. Select **OK**, or press **Enter**, to get rid of the report.)

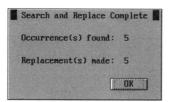

When WordPerfect finishes its search-and-replace chores, it displays a dialog box similar to this one to tell you how much havoc was wrought.

To keep your search-and-replace operations focused, you can first select a block (glance back at Chapter 11 "Block Partying: Working with Blocks of Text," if you need to learn block basics). This tells WordPerfect to search and replace *only* within the block. (Sorry, this doesn't work for plain searches.)

Search and Replace Options

To get the most out of this powerful search-and-replace stuff, you'll probably want to test-drive a few options. Many of the Search and Replace dialog box options are identical to those in the Search dialog box. In particular, you can search backward, perform case-sensitive searches, find whole words only, and extend the search into things like headers and footers. The rest of the options are explained below:

☛ Normally, WordPerfect just goes on a rampage through the document, replacing everything it finds. If you'd like a little more control over the process, activate the Confirm Replacement check box. Start the search, and each time WordPerfect finds a match, it displays the text highlighted, and you see the Confirm Replacement dialog box as shown below. To replace the highlighted text, select **Yes**; to move on without replacing, select **No**. If you get tired of the constant confirmations, you can either select **Replace All** to let WordPerfect go crazy, or **Cancel** to bail out of the operation altogether.

When you activate the Confirm Replacement check box, WordPerfect asks you for confirmation each time it's about to replace the search text.

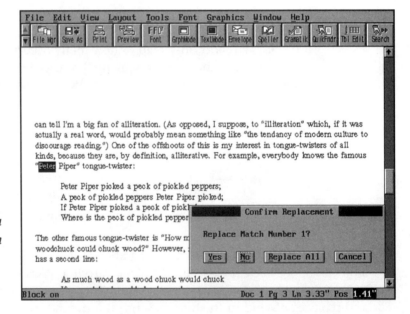

☛ Sometimes you want to replace only the first few occurrences of a piece of text. In this case, activate the Limit Number of Matches check box and enter the number of replacements you want in the text box that appears.

☛ If you want to search and *delete* text, just leave the Replace With text box blank and proceed normally (although, in this case, it's probably a good idea to turn on the Confirm Replacement option).

The Least You Need to Know

This chapter introduced you to WordPerfect's handy Search and Search and Replace features. Here's a fond look back:

- ☞ To search forward for some text, select Search from the Edit menu (or press **F2**), enter the search text, and then select the Search button (or press **F2** again).

- ☞ To search backward, select the Edit menu's Search command (or press **Shift+F2**), enter the search text, activate the Backward Search check box, and then select the Search button.

- ☞ If you're searching for proper names and other things where case matters, make sure you activate the Case Sensitive Search check box in the Search dialog box.

- ☞ To match entire words, activate the Find Whole Words Only check box in the Search dialog box.

- ☞ The Search and Replace feature is a great way to replace every instance of a word or phrase quickly. To use it, select Replace from the Edit menu (or press **Alt+F2**), enter your text in the Search For and Replace With boxes, and then select the Replace button (or press **F2**).

- ☞ Normally, WordPerfect doesn't ask you to confirm replacements in a Search and Replace operation. If you'd like the added safety of a confirmation, be sure to activate the Confirm Replacement check box before starting the replacement.

You could use this blank page as an opportunity to express your Inner Anarchist. You've always wanted to scrawl some desperate, futile slogan all over a page in a textbook, haven't you? Well, go crazy!
"CEASE THE OPPRESSION!"

Part III
Looking Good: Formatting Stuff

"The least you can do is look respectable." That's what my mother always used to tell me when I was a kid. This advice holds up especially well in these image-conscious times. If you don't look good up front (or if your work doesn't look good), you'll often be written off without a second thought.

When it comes to looking good—whether you're writing up a memo, slicking up a report, or polishing up your résumé—WordPerfect gives you a veritable cornucopia of formatting options. The chapters in this part give you the skinny on these various options, including lots of hints about how best to use them.

Chapter 13
Making Your Characters Look Good

In This Chapter

- Applying character attributes such as bold and italics
- Using different character sizes
- Converting letters between uppercase and lowercase
- Working with different fonts
- Adding WordPerfect's symbols to your documents
- Frighteningly fun formatting frolics

The first step on our road to looking good is the lowly character. I know, I know, you want to try out some really *big* stuff, but don't forget all that blather about the longest journey beginning with a single step. Besides, working with characters *can* make a big difference. Why, just a little bit of bold here, a couple of italics there, throw in a font or two, and suddenly that humdrum, boring memo is a dynamic, exciting thing of beauty.

Getting Graphic

The first order of business (for those of you who have version 6, anyway; 5.1 users are out of luck) is to remind you about that *graphics mode* thing. Graphics mode is a very slick new feature that lets WordPerfect users actually see what they're doing. In normal *text mode*, WordPerfect can't show things like italics or large characters; you just have to trust that everything is okay and wait until you get a printout to see how things look—or (shudder) try to decipher the bizarre colors WordPerfect uses for different formats.

For the curious, here's the difference between text mode and graphics mode: Text mode (it's also called *character-based mode*) operates by dividing your screen into 25 rows, with 80 columns in each row. Each of the resulting 2,000 screen positions can display only a single character from a pre-defined set of 254 so-called *ASCII* (American Standard Code for Information Interchange) characters. There's no room for bizarre things like italics or letters that are larger or smaller than the standard size. Graphics mode, on the other hand, divides your screen into tiny pinpoints of light called *pixels*. A basic graphics mode might have 480 rows divided into 640 columns, resulting in a whopping total of 307,200 pixels! This makes it easy to show different fonts and character attributes right on-screen.

Graphics mode changes all that because you can see everything right on the screen. Sure, it slows things down a tad, but it more than makes up for the time you'd otherwise spend printing out 57 copies trying to get things just right. It's also really easy to get to: just pull down the View menu and activate the Graphics Mode command.

 You can also click on this button in the WPMAIN Button Bar to head for graphics mode territory.

 If, for some reason, you prefer text mode, just click on this button to crank it up.

Changing Character Attributes

My *Concise Oxford Dictionary* defines an *attribute* as a "characteristic quality." So this means that a *character attribute* would be a "characteristic character quality." Hmm. In any case, WordPerfect lets you alter the attributes of your document's characters to get things like bold, underlining (single and double), and italics, as you can see in the picture below.

In order to use graphics mode, you need to have a monitor and something called a *video card* that can handle it. If WordPerfect won't switch to graphics mode, you know you don't have the proper equipment.

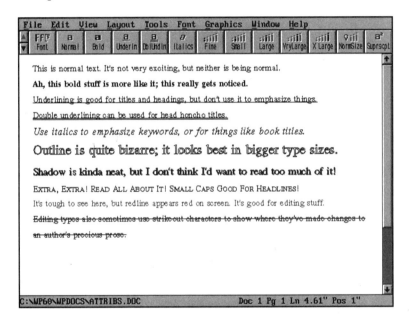

Some of the character attributes you can play with.

The good news is that WordPerfect makes it easy to mess around with these attributes. You begin by selecting the block of text you want to change (by pressing **Alt+F4** and using the arrow keys, or by dragging the mouse over the text; see Chapter 11, "Block Partying: Working with Blocks of Text," for more info). Then just pull down the **Font** menu and select the attribute you want.

If you're short on time, you can also set the character attributes by using the buttons in the Fonts Button Bar. (As a reminder, you display this Button Bar by pulling down the **View** menu, choosing Button Bar Setup, and then choosing Select. In the dialog box that appears, double-click on FONTS.) The following table shows you the appropriate buttons to use (to keep you keyboardists happy, I've also thrown in a few shortcut keys).

Click on	Or Press	To get
Normal	Ctrl+N	Normal text
Bold	F6	Bold text
UnderIn	F8	Underlined text
DblUndIn		Double underlined text
Italics	Ctrl+I	Italic text
Outline		Outline text
Shadow		Shadow text
SmallCap		Small caps text
Redline		Redline text
Strkeout		Strikeout text

Instead of changing existing text, you might prefer to have any new text you type appear with a certain attribute. This is even easier, as the following steps show:

1. Select the attribute from the Font menu, or click on the appropriate button in the Fonts Button Bar.

2. Type the text. WordPerfect displays subsequent characters with the attribute you chose.

3. When you're done, turn off the attribute either by reselecting it from the Font menu, or by clicking on its button again in the Fonts Button Bar.

For even more formatting fun, you can *combine* attributes to get, say, **bold italic** text or S̶m̶a̶l̶l̶ ̶C̶a̶p̶s̶ ̶S̶t̶r̶i̶k̶e̶o̶u̶t̶ characters. All you do is rehighlight the block and select whatever you need from the Font menu (or Fonts Button Bar). To get rid of multiple formats, you can either reselect the options from the Font menu (or the Fonts Button Bar) or select the Normal command.

An even easier way to apply multiple attributes is to use the Font dialog box. See the section "Working with Fonts," later in this chapter, to get the details.

In version 5.1, select the **A**ppearance command from the **F**ont menu, and then select an attribute from the cascade menu that appears. In most cases, you won't see the attribute on the screen (you *will* see bold, and— if you have a mono-chrome monitor— underlining). Instead, WordPerfect uses all the colors of the rainbow to represent the formatting.

Rehighlighting a block can be a pain, but here's a nifty trick that makes it easy. Once you've added some formatting, press **Alt+F4** (or **F12**) to turn Block mode back on. Now press **Ctrl+Home** *twice*. Voilà! Your block is rehighlighted instantly!

Changing Character Size and Position

You can also format the size of your charac-ters. You can make characters really big to scare the heck out of people, or really small so that no one can read them. You can even change the relative *position* of characters to get superscripts (characters slightly higher than normal) or subscripts (characters slightly lower than normal). The following picture illustrates different text sizes, superscripts, and subscripts.

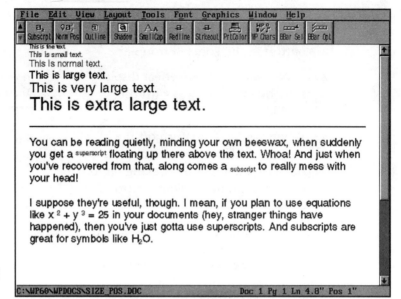

WordPerfect lets you use different text sizes. It also lets you change the relative position of characters to get superscripts and subscripts.

To change the size or position of existing text, first select the block you want to work with. Then pull down the Font menu and select the Size/Position command (in version 5.1, just pull down the Font menu). In the cascade menu that appears, select the command you need. You can also use our old buddy the Fonts Button Bar to work with this stuff. The following table summarizes the available buttons.

Click on	To get
Fine	Fine text
Small	Small text
Large	Large text
VryLarge	Very large text
X Large	Extra large text

Click on	To get
NormSize	Normal size text
Suprscpt	Superscript text
Subscrpt	Subscript text
Norm Pos	Normal position text

State Your Case: Converting Uppercase and Lowercase Letters

On most keyboards, the Caps Lock key is just above the Shift key. In the heat of battle, I usually end up hitting Caps Lock by mistake a few times a day. The result: anything from a few words to a few lines appears all in uppercase! Fortunately, WordPerfect lets me off the hook easily with its case-conversion feature. You can change uppercase to lowercase, lowercase to uppercase, and you can even get it to convert only the initial letter in each word to uppercase (to change *alphonse* to *Alphonse*, for example).

To convert case, select the appropriate text block, pull down the Edit menu, and then select the Convert Case command. In the cascade menu that appears, select Uppercase, Lowercase, or Initial Caps (the latter is only available in version 6).

Working with Fonts

Until now, you may not have given much thought to the individual characters that make up your writings. After all, an *a* is an *a*, isn't it? Oh, sure, you can (as you've just learned) make it bold or italic or big or small, but it still looks more or less the same. However, when you start working with different *fonts*, you'll see that not all *a*'s are the same (or *b*'s or *c*'s for that matter).

Just What the Heck is a Font, Anyway?

Fonts are to characters what architecture is to buildings. In architecture, you look at certain features and patterns; if you can tell a geodesic dome from a flying buttress, you can tell whether the building is Gothic or Art Deco or whatever. Fonts, too, are distinguished by a set of unique design characteristics that can make them wildly different, as you can see here.

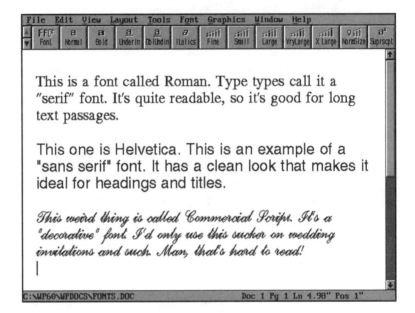

As these examples show, fonts can be very different.

Fonts come in three flavors: *serif*, *sans-serif*, and *decorative*. A serif font contains fine cross-strokes—typographic technoids call them *feet*—at the extremities of each character. These subtle appendages give the font a traditional, classy look. Roman (the first font in the picture above) is an example of a serif font.

A sans-serif font doesn't contain these cross-strokes. As a result, serif fonts usually have a cleaner, more modern look (check out Helvetica in the picture).

Decorative fonts are usually special designs used to convey a particular effect. So, for example, the Commercial Script font shown above would be ideal for fancy-shmancy invitations or certificates, but you wouldn't want to use it for a novel.

Selecting Different Fonts

Okay, enough theory. Let's get down to business and see how you go about selecting different fonts for your documents. To begin with, pull down the Font menu and select the Font command, or press **Ctrl+F8**. You see the Font dialog box, shown below.

You can also display the Font dialog box by clicking on the Font button in either the WPMain or Fonts Button bar.

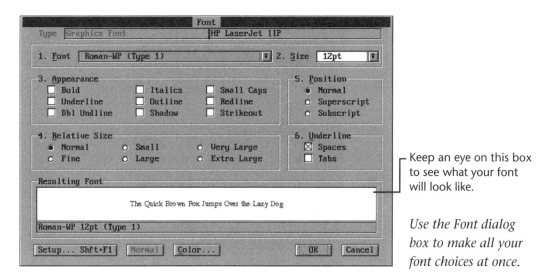

Keep an eye on this box to see what your font will look like.

Use the Font dialog box to make all your font choices at once.

From here, selecting the font you want is easy: just open the Font drop-down list (by selecting Font or by clicking on the downward-pointing arrow) and then select the one you want. While you're here, you can also pick out any other character attributes you want to set. Just activate the appropriate check boxes or radio buttons, or use the Size drop-down list to set the character size. As you're selecting your formatting options, keep your eyes on the **Resulting Font** box; it'll give you an idea of what your font will look like. When you're done, select **OK** to return to the document.

You can also select a font by using this drop-down list in the Ribbon.

12pt ▼ To set the type size, use this drop-down list in the Ribbon.

TECHNO NERD TEACHES...

The various radio buttons in the **R**elative Size group are equivalent to the sizing options on the Font, Size/Position cascade menu. These just change the character size relative to the normal size (or *base font,* as it's called). Use the **S**ize list when you want an explicit type size. The numbers you see are measured in *points*; there are 72 points in an inch.

Avoiding the "Ransom Note" Look

The downside to WordPerfect's easy-to-use character attributes and fonts is that they can sometimes be too easy to use. Flushed with your newfound knowledge, you start throwing every formatting option in sight at your documents. This can turn even the most profound and well-written documents into a real dog's breakfast. (It's known in the trade as the "ransom note" look.) Here are some tips to avoid overdoing your formatting:

- Never use more than a couple of fonts in a single document. Anything more looks amateurish, and will only confuse the reader.

- If you need to emphasize something, bold or italicize it in the same font as the surrounding text. Avoid using underlining for emphasis.

- Use larger sizes only for titles and headings.

- Avoid bizarre decorative fonts for large sections of text. Most of those suckers are hard on the eyes after a half dozen words or so. Serif fonts are usually very readable, so they're a good choice for long passages. The clean look of sans serif fonts makes them a good choice for headlines and titles.

Adding Silly Symbols

Were you stumped the last time you wanted to write "Dag Hammarskjöld" because you didn't know how to get one of those *ö* thingamajigs? I thought so. Well, you'll be happy to know that your documents aren't restricted to just the letters, numbers, and punctuation marks you can eyeball on your keyboard. WordPerfect comes with all kinds of built-in characters that will supply you not only an *ö*, but a whole universe of weirdo symbols.

To start, position the cursor where you want to insert the symbol. Then pull down the Font menu and select the **W**P Characters command, or press **Ctrl+W**. The WordPerfect Characters dialog box appears on-screen.

 You can also click on this button in the Fonts Button Bar to display the WordPerfect Characters dialog box.

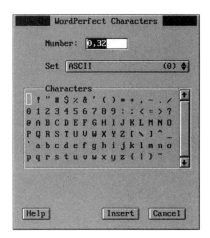

The layout of this dialog box is pretty simple: the Characters area shows you all the symbols available for whatever character set is selected in the **S**et pop-up list. If you select a different character set, a whole new set of symbols is displayed.

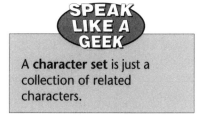

SPEAK LIKE A GEEK

A **character set** is just a collection of related characters.

To use a symbol from a character set, move into the Characters area, use the arrow keys to highlight a symbol, and then press **Enter**. If you have a mouse, just double-click on the symbol. The dialog box closes, and WordPerfect inserts the character at the current cursor position.

The Least You Need to Know

This chapter was the first stop on your journey towards looking good on paper. You learned how to format characters by making them bold or italic, giving them larger or smaller sizes, or using different fonts. Here's the condensed version of what happened:

- ☞ If you have version 6 (and you have a system that can handle it), select the **G**raphics Mode command from the **V**iew menu. Graphics mode lets you see your formatting right on-screen so you don't have to wait for the document to be printed.

- ☞ To alter the attributes of your characters, select the block you want to work with, and then choose the appropriate command from the **F**ont menu.

- ☞ Select the **F**ont menu's Size/Position command to get a menu of sizing and position choices.

- ☞ If you need to convert a block of text from uppercase to lowercase (or vice versa), select Convert Case from the **E**dit menu, and choose the appropriate command from the cascade menu that appears.

- ☞ Fonts are distinctive character designs. To select a different font, choose **F**ont from the **F**ont menu (or press **Ctrl+F8**) and pick out what you need from the Fonts dialog box.

- ☞ WordPerfect comes with various character sets built-in. These sets can give you international characters, scientific symbols, and more. Select the **WP** Characters command from the **F**ont menu, or press **Ctrl+W**.

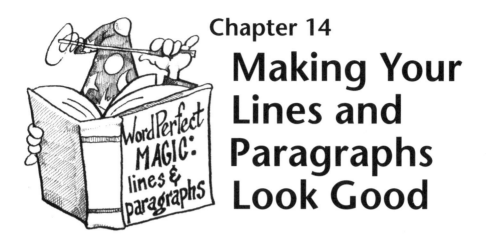

Chapter 14

Making Your Lines and Paragraphs Look Good

In This Chapter

- ☛ Setting and deleting tab stops in a paragraph
- ☛ Left-justifying, centering, and right-justifying text
- ☛ Adjusting the line spacing
- ☛ Indenting paragraph text
- ☛ Working with paragraph margins
- ☛ The usual motley collection of trenchant tips and topical tirades

The last chapter showed you how to format characters, so now this chapter'll bump things up a notch and look at formatting lines and paragraphs. How will this help you look good on paper? Well, all the character formatting in the world won't do you much good if your lines are all scrunched together, and if the various pieces of text aren't lined up like boot-camp recruits. Documents like this look cramped and uninviting—and will often get tossed in the old "circular file" without a second look. This chapter will help you avoid this sorry fate.

If you want to arrange text or numbers in a tabular format, it might be easier to set up a *table*. See Chapter 25, "Techniques for Terrific Tables," to find out what tables are all about.

If things somehow go haywire and your document ends up all askew, you need to do two things. First, start chanting the following mantra in your head: "This is not my fault; this is WordPerfect's fault. This is not my fault...." Second, select **Undo** from the **Edit** menu (or press **Ctrl+Z**) to reverse the mayhem.

To Block or Not to Block: How WordPerfect Formats Paragraphs

The way WordPerfect formats lines and paragraphs can be hopelessly confusing, even for experienced word processing hacks. So, to soften the blow a little, here are a couple of points to keep in mind when working with this chapter's formatting options:

☞ If you select a formatting option *without* selecting a block, WordPerfect formats everything from the current paragraph to the end of the document.

☞ If you select a block (even just a single character), WordPerfect formats only the paragraph that contains the block.

Working with Tab Stops

Documents look much better if they're properly indented and if their various parts line up nicely. The best way to do this is to use tabs instead of spaces whenever you need to create some room in a line. Why? Well, a single space can take up different amounts of room, depending on the font and size of the characters you're using. So your document can end up looking pretty ragged if you try to use spaces to indent your text. Tabs, on the other hand, are fastidiously precise: when you press the **Tab** key, the insertion point moves ahead exactly to the next tab stop—no more, no less.

To begin, pull down the **Layout** menu and select the **Tab Set** command. (If you're using version 5.1, select the Layout menu's **Line** command, and then select the **Tab Set** command.) This displays the Tab Set dialog box (shown on the following page).

 Another way to display the Tab Set dialog box is to click on the Tab Set button in the Layout Button Bar.

The ruler across the top of this dialog box shows you where the current tabs are set. (The measurements represent the distance from the left edge of the page. So, for example, 1" represents the horizontal position that is 1

inch from the left edge.) Each **L** you see represents a tab stop (the "L" indicates that it's a *left* tab; I'll explain what this means in a second). By the way, it's often best to start with a clean slate and just set your own tabs. See the section titled "Deleting Tabs," later in the chapter.

Checking Out WordPerfect's Tab Types

WordPerfect, you'll be happy to know, has a tab to suit your every mood. Here's a quickie summary of the available types:

Left   Text lines up with the tab on the left. These tab types are represented by L's in the Tab Set ruler.

Right   Text lines up with the tab on the right. The Tab Set ruler shows these tab types as R's.

Center   Text is centered on the tab. These tab types are represented by C's in the Tab Set ruler.

Decimal   Numbers line up with the tab at their decimal places. These tab types are shown as D's in the Tab Set ruler.

Dot Leader   In this tab type, the tab space for a left, right, center, or decimal tab is filled with a bunch of dots. The Tab Set ruler identifies dot leader tabs by adding a highlight to the normal tab symbol (L, R, C, or D).

Here's a picture that illustrates each of these tab types.

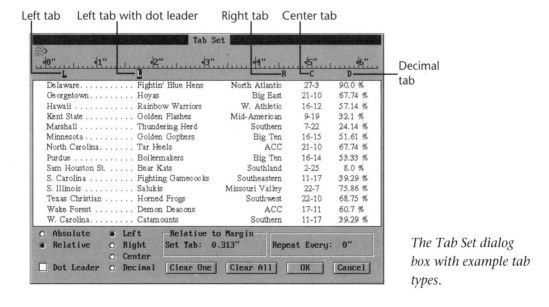

The Tab Set dialog box with example tab types.

TECHNO NERD TEACHES...

You can also make your tab stops *absolute* or *relative*. Absolute tab stops are measured from the left edge of the page. They're rock-solid; they wouldn't change position in a hurricane. Relative tab stops are more laid back. They're measured from the left margin, so if you change the margin position (which I'll show you how to do in the next chapter), they're happy to move right along. In general, it's best to stick with relative tab stops.

Setting Tabs in Version 6

Once you've displayed the Tab Set dialog box, WordPerfect gives you umpteen different ways to actually set the little beasts. Here are the easiest ones:

- ☛ Move the ruler's cursor to the position you want (either by clicking inside the ruler or by using the left and right arrow keys) and then press either **L** (for a left tab), **R** (for right), **C** (for center), or **D** (for decimal).

- ☛ With the mouse, click on the tab type (using the Left, **Right**, Center, or Decimal radio buttons), and then double-click on the ruler position you want.

- ☛ Activate the **Set Tab** text box, enter the position where you want the tab to appear (for example, to place a tab at 2", enter **2**) and press **Enter**.

- ☛ To move an existing tab, place the cursor under the tab, hold down **Ctrl**, and use the left and right arrow keys to move it. When you've got it positioned just right, let go of **Ctrl** and press **Enter**.

- ☛ To set a bunch of tabs at a regular interval, select the Repeat Every text box, enter a number for the interval (in inches), and then press **Enter**.

Setting Tabs in Version 5.1

To set tabs in version 5.1, select Line from the Layout menu and then choose Tab Set from the menu that appears. A ruler with the current tab stops appears near the bottom of the screen. Use the arrow keys to move the cursor to the tab position you want. Then select Left, **Right**, Center, or Decimal from the bottom line of the screen. Press period (.) to add a dot leader. When you're done, press **F7** twice.

Deleting Tabs

If you'd like to get rid of a tab or two, just position the ruler's cursor under the tab stop and either press **Delete** or click on the Clear **One** button in the Tab Set dialog box. If you'd like a fresh start, select the Clear **All** button to delete all the existing tabs.

For version 5.1, display the tab ruler, position the cursor under the tab you want to remove, and then press **Delete** or **Backspace**. To delete all tabs, move the cursor to the beginning of the ruler and press **Ctrl+End**.

Justifying Your Text

Justifying your text has nothing to do with defending your ideas (luckily for some of us!). Rather, it's all about lining up your paragraphs so they look all prim and proper. Here's an example document, showing the various justification options.

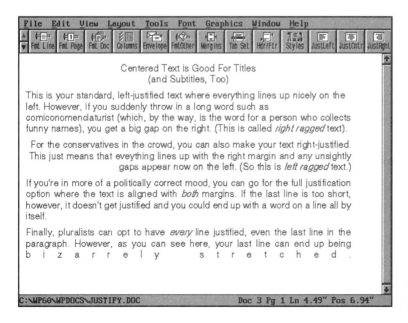

Some text justification examples.

SPEAK LIKE A GEEK

Left-justified text is said to be **right ragged** because the right side of each line doesn't line up. Similarly, right-justified text is called **left ragged**.

If you try to do any of this stuff on a typewriter, you just end up adding to your stomach's ever-growing ulcer population. On a computer, though, it's a walk in the park. All you do is pull down the Layout menu, select Justification, and then choose the command you want from the cascade menu that appears. The following table summarizes the available commands and shows you the corresponding buttons to select from the Layout Button Bar. (To display the Layout Button Bar, pull down the View menu, choose Button Bar Setup, choose Select, and then double-click on LAYOUT in the dialog box that appears.)

Command	Button	What It Does
Left	JustLeft	Justifies each line on the left margin.
Center	JustCntr	Centers each line between both margins.
Right	JustRght	Justifies each line on the right margin.
Full	JustFull	Justifies each line on both margins. Ignores the last line in a paragraph if it's too small.
Full, All Lines	None	Justifies every line in a paragraph on both margins.

 You can also use this drop-down list in the Ribbon to select a Left, Center, Right, or Full justification.

5.1

In version 5.1, select the Layout menu's Line command, and then select Justification from the menu that appears. In the status line prompt, select the justification option you want, and then press **F7**.

Just to make things confusing, WordPerfect also gives you a way to justify individual lines. To check this out, place the cursor anywhere in the line, and select Alignment from the Layout menu. If you want to center the line, select the Center command from the cascade menu (you can also center a line by pressing **Shift+F6**). To right-justify the line, select the Flush Right command (or press **Alt+F6**).

 You can also center a line by clicking on this button in the Layout Button Bar.

You can also right-justify a line by clicking on this button in the Layout Button Bar.

Changing the Line Spacing

Typewriters have little levers or buttons you can maneuver to alter the line spacing. Well anything a typewriter can do, WordPerfect can do better. So, while a typewriter usually only lets you set up double- or triple-spacing, WordPerfect can handle just about any number of spaces—and even takes things to two decimal places! By the way, the maximum value you can use for line spacing is 65,516!

To set your line spacing, pull down the Layout menu and select the Line command. WordPerfect displays the Line Format dialog box, shown below. Use the Line Spacing spinner to enter the number of spaces you want. (Note, as well, that you can use this dialog box to set your tabs by using the **Tab Set** option or that you can adjust the paragraph justification by using the radio buttons in the Justification group.) When you're ready, select **OK**.

 Click on this button in the Layout Button Bar to display the Line Format dialog box.

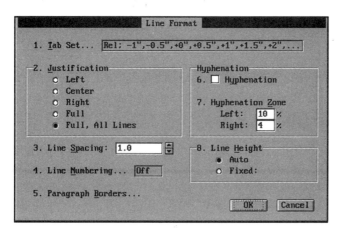

In the Line Format dialog box, use the Line Spacing spinner to enter the number of spaces you want between lines.

Indenting Text

If you need to indent a whole paragraph from the margin, don't do it with tab stops. Instead, WordPerfect will indent an entire paragraph for you.

You have four options: indenting from the left margin; indenting from both margins; indenting all but the first line from the left margin (this is called a *hanging indent*); outdenting the first line of the paragraph (*outdenting* means to move something outside the margin) to create a *back tab*. (You can also indent the first line of a paragraph; see "Setting Paragraph Margins," later in this chapter, to find out how it's done.) The picture below shows examples of each type of indentation; the next few sections show you how to format each type.

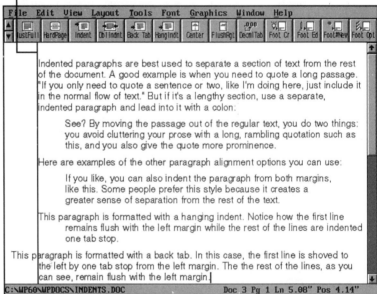

This line represents the left margin.

Examples of the four kinds of indentation.

Indenting a Paragraph from the Left Margin

To indent a paragraph from the left margin, place the cursor at the beginning of the paragraph (you don't need to select a block this time—didn't I tell you this was confusing?), pull down the Layout menu, select Alignment, and then select the Indent → command from the cascade menu (you can also just press **F4**). WordPerfect indents each line in the paragraph to the first tab stop.

 Click on this button in the Layout Button Bar to indent the current paragraph from the left margin.

Indenting Text from Both Margins

If you need to indent a paragraph from *both* margins, place the cursor at the beginning of the paragraph, select Alignment from the Layout menu, and then choose the Indent →← command (or you can avoid the menus altogether by pressing **Shift+F4**).

 Click on this button in the Layout Button Bar to indent the current paragraph from both margins.

Creating a Hanging Indent

Hanging indents are useful for a series of point-form paragraphs, or for the items in a bibliography. To create a hanging indent, place the cursor at the beginning of the paragraph, pull down the Layout menu, select Alignment, and then select the Hanging Indent command.

 You can also click on this button in the Layout Button Bar to create a hanging indent.

Creating a Back Tab

Back tabs are similar to hanging indents, except that the first line is outdented to the left of the left margin by one tab stop; the other lines in the paragraph remain flush with the left margin. To create a back tab indent, pull down the Layout menu, select Alignment, and then select Back Tab (or you can press **Shift+Tab**).

 Clicking on this button in the Layout Button Bar will also create a back tab.

Setting Paragraph Margins

Every page in a document has a margin around each side. I'll show you how to work with these in the next chapter, but as a warm-up, let's see how you format a paragraph's margins. A *paragraph's* margins? Yup. This just refers to the white space above and below a paragraph (i.e., the spacing between paragraphs) and to the left and right of a paragraph (i.e., between the paragraph and the left and right page margins). As an added bonus, you can also indent the first line of a paragraph.

Here's how you do it:

1. Select a block in the paragraph you want to work with.

2. Pull down the Layout menu and select the **Margins** command. You'll see the Margin Format dialog box on the screen.

   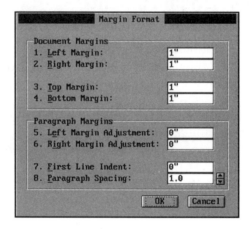 You can also click on this button in the Layout Button Bar to display the Margin Format dialog box.

3. Use the options in the Paragraph Margins group to make your adjustments. You should note three things here:

Use the Margin Format dialog box to specify paragraph margins, spacing, and the first line indent.

- ☛ The Left Margin Adjustment and Right Margin Adjustment are relative to the current page margins. So if you enter 1" and the page margins are 1 inch, the paragraph will be indented 2 inches.

- ☛ The First Line Indent is relative to the left paragraph margin.

- ☛ The Paragraph Spacing refers only to the number of spaces above and below the paragraph. Don't confuse this with the line spacing we looked at earlier in this chapter.

4. When you're done, select **OK** to return to the document.

The Least You Need to Know

This chapter walked you through some of WordPerfect's line and paragraph formatting options. It is, as I said, somewhat confusing at times, so I think a brief recap is in order:

- ☛ If you want to format just a paragraph, block off some text in the paragraph (a letter or two will do). Otherwise, WordPerfect formats everything from the cursor position on down.

- ☛ To set tab stops, select the Tab Set command from the Layout menu and use the Tab Set dialog box to enter your tabs.

- ☛ To justify text, pull down the Layout menu, select the Justification command, and then choose the justification option you need from the cascade menu that appears.

- ☛ To change the spacing between the lines in a paragraph, select the Layout menu's Line command. In the Line Format dialog box, enter the number of spaces you want in the Line Spacing text box.

- ☛ You can indent text either from the left margin or from both margins. Position the cursor at the beginning of the paragraph, select the Alignment command from the Layout menu, and select the appropriate option from the cascade menu.

- ☛ To set paragraph margins, pull down the Layout menu and select the Margins command. Enter your new margin values in the Margin Format dialog box.

OK people, move it along. Nothing to see here.

Chapter 15
Making Your Pages Look Good

In This Chapter

- Making adjustments to the page margins
- Creating your own page breaks
- Using WordPerfect's new page mode
- Adding and formatting page numbers
- Defining headers and footers
- Sad stories of widows and orphans

So far in Part 3 we've looked at formatting characters, lines, and paragraphs. Since logic is an occasionally useful tool that I succumb to from time to time, we'll now graduate to full-fledged *page formatting*. This is the stuff that can add a certain *je ne sais quois* to your documents. (Of course, adding fancy foreign terms in italics also helps, but I'll leave that up to you.) This chapter takes on the topics of margin adjustments, page numbers, headers, footer, and more.

As usual, if any of this formatting stuff gets out of hand, immediately select the **Edit** menu's **Undo** command (or press **Ctrl+Z**) to bring everything back in line.

Adjusting Page Margins

The *page margins* refer to the white space that surrounds your text on a page. There are, then, four margins altogether: at the top and bottom of the page, and on the left and right sides of a page. By default, WordPerfect decrees each of these margins to be one inch, but you can override that. Why would you want to do such a thing? Here are a few good reasons:

☞ If someone else is going to be making notes on the page, it helps to include bigger left and right margins (to give them more room for scribbling).

☞ Smaller margins all around mean that you get more text on a page. On a really long document, this could save you a few pages when you print it out.

☞ If you have a document that's just slightly longer than a page (say by only a line or two), you could decrease the top and bottom margins just enough to fit the wayward lines onto a single page.

TECHNO NERD TEACHES...

When the last line of a paragraph appears by itself at the top of a page, it's called, sadly, a *widow*. If you get the first line of a paragraph by itself at the bottom of a page, it's called an *orphan*. (No, I don't know who comes up with this stuff.) WordPerfect, mercifully, lets you prevent these pathetic creatures from inhabiting your documents. Just pull down the **Layout** menu and select **Other** to display the Other Format dialog box. Activate the **Widow/Orphan Protect** check box and select **OK**.

 You can also display the Other Format dialog box by clicking on this button in the Layout Button Bar.

Before changing the margins, you need to decide how much of the document you want affected. You have two choices:

☞ To adjust the margins from a particular paragraph to the end of the document, position the cursor inside the paragraph. So, for example, if you want to adjust the margins for the entire document, place the cursor at the top of the first page (by pressing **Home**, **Home**, **up arrow**).

☞ To adjust the margins for only certain (consecutive) paragraphs, select a block that includes some text from each paragraph. (If you just want to change the left and right margins for a single paragraph, refer back to Chapter 14, "Making Your Lines and Paragraphs Look Good," for the appropriate steps.)

When you're ready, pull down the Layout menu and select the **Margins** command. The Margin Format dialog box appears, as shown here.

 Clicking on this button in the Layout Button Bar will also display the Margin Format dialog box.

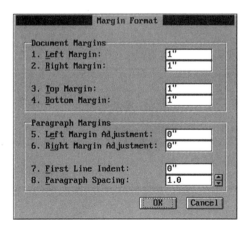

Use the Margin Format dialog box to set your page margins.

You use the text boxes in the Document Margins group to set your margins. For example, to adjust the top margin, enter a number in the **Top** Margin box. (Note that these numbers are measured in inches from the edge of the page. You don't have to bother with the inch sign (") though; WordPerfect adds it for you.) When you're done, select **OK** to return to the document and put your new settings into effect.

If you plan to print a document on a laser printer, keep in mind that most lasers can't print anything that's closer to the edge of the page than a quarter of an inch or so.

When you adjust your margins, you'll notice that the status line's Ln and Pos indicators are affected as well. For example, if you set the top margin to a half an inch, the Ln indicator will display **0.5"** when you're at the top of a page.

Dealing with WordPerfect's Page Breaks

As you may know by now, WordPerfect signals the start of a new page by running a line across the screen (it's called a *page break*). Text that appears above the line prints on one page, and text below the line prints on the next page. This text arrangement is not set in stone, of course. If you insert a new paragraph or change the margins, the text on both sides of the page line moves accordingly.

Page breaks that adjust themselves automatically are **soft page breaks**. A page break that doesn't move is called a **hard page break**.

But what if you have a line or paragraph that *has to* appear at the top of a page? You could fiddle around by pressing Enter enough times, but WordPerfect gives you an easier way. Just position the cursor where you want the new page to begin, pull down the Layout menu, select the Alignment command, and then select the Hard **Page** command (or you can simply press **Ctrl+Enter**). WordPerfect creates a new page and marks the break with a double line. Now, no matter how much stuff you insert on the previous pages or how much stuff you insert on the previous pages or how you adjust the margins, the text just below the double line always remains at the top of that page.

 You can also insert a hard page break by clicking on this button in the Layout Button Bar.

If you need to delete a hard page break, you have two options:

- ☞ Position the cursor at the beginning of the line below the break and press **Backspace**.

- ☞ Position the cursor at the end of the line above the break and press **Delete**.

Pages à la Mode: Version 6's Page Mode

Many of the formatting options you'll learn about in the rest of this chapter won't actually appear on your screen. Things like page numbers, headers, and footers only appear once you've printed the document. If you'd like to take a look at these before you print out (and you use version 6), switch to *page mode*. This mode shows you just what your page will look like when it's printed, including the otherwise-hidden formatting options. All you do is pull down the View menu and select the Page Mode option.

Another way to see what your page looks like is with WordPerfect's Print Preview feature. Head back to Chapter 9, "Getting It Down on Paper: Printing Documents," for the Print Preview particulars.

If you're using WordPerfect 5.1, you can take a look at page numbers, headers, and such by pulling down the File menu, selecting the **P**rint command, and then selecting View Document from the Print menu. Note, however, that you can't make changes to the document while viewing it in this manner.

Adding Page Numbers

WordPerfect's status line tells you which page you're on when you ramble through a document on screen, but what happens when you're looking at the printed version? To avoid getting lost in large printouts, you should add page numbers that'll appear on the hard copies. Once you tell WordPerfect that you want page numbers, the program tracks everything for you.

Everything happens inside the Page Numbering dialog box, so you need to display that first. Begin by pulling down the Layout menu and selecting the **Page** command. In the Page Format dialog box that appears, select the Page Numbering command.

 Click on this button in the Layout Button Bar to display the Page Format dialog box.

Positioning the Page Numbers

The first decision you have to make is where you want your numbers to appear on the page. WordPerfect, ever eager to please, gives you no less than eight possibilities. To check them out, select the Page Number Position command at the top of the Page Numbering dialog box. This displays the Page Number Position dialog box, shown below.

WordPerfect's Page Number Position dialog box gives you all kinds of ways to position your page numbers.

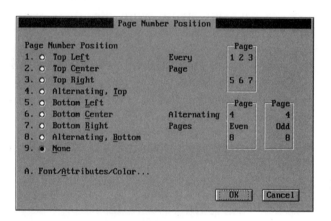

Most of the options are straightforward. You can position the numbers on the top or bottom of the page, and in each case you can choose from the left, center, or right side of the page. Two other choices—Alternating, Top and Alternating, Bottom—may require a bit more explanation. These options mean that WordPerfect will switch the position of the numbers depending on whether the page is odd or even. For example, the Alternating, Top option places the numbers on the top right for odd pages and the top left for even pages (which is, you'll notice, the way this book is formatted).

After you've marveled at the sheer wealth of choices available to you, pick the one you want, and then select **OK** to return to the Page Numbering dialog box. (In version 5.1, once you have the Page Numbering menu displayed, press the number that corresponds to the position you want, and then press **F7** to exit.)

Rather than just using a number all by itself, you can add some text to go along with your page numbers. So, for example, you could add the word "Page" or even something like "My Great American Novel." All you do is type what you want in the Page Number Format text box. (It's usually best to insert the text before the [page #] code that's already in there.)

Setting the Page Number

Most of the time you'll just begin your page numbers at 1 and go from there. However, you're free to start the page numbers at whatever number you like. This is great if your document is a continuation of an existing project (such as a new chapter in a book). If the rest of the project has 100 pages, you'd start this document at page 101.

In the Page Numbering dialog box, select the Page Number option to display the Set Page Number dialog box (shown below). Enter the starting number in the New Number text box.

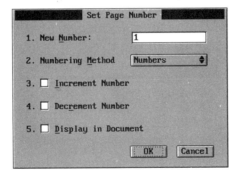

Use the Set Page Number dialog box to specify your starting page number.

You're not restricted to using plain old numbers on your pages. If you check out the Numbering Method pop-up list, you'll see that you can use letters (uppercase or lowercase) or even Roman numerals. When you finish setting page number options, select **OK** to return to the Page Numbering dialog box.

To set the page number in version 5.1, select Page Numbering from the Page Numbering menu, and then select New Page Number. Enter the number you want, and then press **F7** to exit.

TECHNO NERD TEACHES...

In general, you shouldn't work with documents any larger than a couple of dozen pages or so. Not only might you run out of memory, but humongous documents are just a pain to work with. Ideally, you should break monster projects into manageable chunks—a chapter per document is usually okay.

Happily, WordPerfect includes lots of page numbering options that are great for keeping track of these large projects. In the Page Numbering dialog box, place the cursor in the Page Number Format text box, and then either press **F5** or click on the **Number Codes** button. In the Page Number Codes dialog box that appears, select either **Second-ary Page Number**, **Chapter Number**, or **Volume Number**, and then press **Enter**. A new code—such as [chpt #] for a chapter number—appears. Add some text so you know which number is which, like so:

Chapter [chpt #] Page [page #]

WordPerfect won't increment chapter or volume numbers automatically, so you'll need to use either the **Chapter** or **Volume** command to adjust them yourself.

Centering Text Between the Top and Bottom

If you've read Chapter 14, "Making Your Lines and Paragraphs Look Good," then you know how to center text between the left and right margins. WordPerfect also lets you center text between the top and bottom margins, which is great for things like title pages, résumés, and short business letters.

First move to the page you want to center, and then select **Page** from the Layout menu. To center only the current page, activate the Center Current Page check box. If you want every page in the document centered, activate the Center Pages check box. (Inconveniently, version 5.1 will center only one page at a time. Select **Page** from the Layout menu, choose the Center Page option, and then press **F7** to exit.)

Setting Up Headers and Footers

Take a look at the top of the page you're reading now. Above the line that runs across the top you'll see a page number and some text (on the even pages, you see the part number and part name; on the odd pages, it's the chapter number and chapter name). These are examples of *headers*— sections of text that appear at the top margin of every page.

WordPerfect lets you include headers in your own documents, just like the pros. You can put in the usual stuff—page numbers (as described in the last section), chapter titles, and so on—but you're free to add anything you like: your name, your company's name, your dog's name, whatever. And you can even do *footers*, as well. A footer is the same as a header, only it appears at the bottom of each page (makes sense). When you add a header or footer, WordPerfect uses it for all the pages from the current page to the end of the document.

To add a header or footer, follow these steps:

1. Position the cursor somewhere in the first page on which you want to have a header or footer.

2. Pull down the Layout menu and select the Header/Footer/Watermark command. (If you're using WordPerfect 5.1, select the Layout menu's Page command.) The Header/Footer/Watermark dialog box appears, as shown here.

    You can also display the Header/Footer/Watermark dialog box by clicking on this button in the Layout Button Bar.

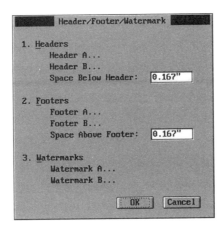

The Header/Footer/Watermark dialog box.

3. Select Headers to add a header or Footers to add a footer.

4. You can define up to two headers or footers (A and B) per page, so you now need to select which header or footer to add. For example, to define header A, select Header **A**.

5. The dialog box that appears lets you choose whether to place your headers or footers on all pages, or only on odd or even pages. Select the appropriate option from the dialog box, and then select the Create button.

6. WordPerfect then presents you with a blank editing screen. Just type in the header text you want to use. Feel free to use any character or line formatting options (fonts, bold, justification, page numbers, and so on). You can, if you like, add several lines of text. Just remember that the bigger the header or footer, the less room you'll have for your regular text.

7. When you're done, press **F7** to return to the document.

A *watermark*, in case you're wondering, is a translucent image or section of text that prints "underneath" existing text on a page. You can use them to add logos or descriptive comments. If you'd like to check them out, follow the same basic steps that you use for a header or footer.

The Least You Need to Know

This chapter walked you through some of WordPerfect's page formatting options. Here's a recap of what you really need to know to make your life complete:

- ☞ To adjust the page margins, pull down the Layout menu, select the Margins command, and then enter the new margin values in the Margin Format dialog box.

☛ A *soft page break* is a page separator that WordPerfect adds automatically to your documents. It's based on the current margin settings. A *hard page break* is a break you enter yourself. It remains in position even if you enter text above it or change the margins. To add a hard page break, position the cursor and press **Ctrl+Enter**.

☛ To add page numbers to a document, first select the **Layout** menu's **Page** command, and then select the Page **N**umbering option. In the Page Numbering dialog box, select Page Number **P**osition to position the page numbers and Page **N**umber to set a starting page number and format.

☛ Centering text between the top and bottom margins is a breeze. Just select **P**age from the **L**ayout menu, and then activate either the **C**enter Current Page or Center **P**ages check box.

☛ If you need to add headers or footers to a document, select the **H**eader/Footer/Watermark command from the **L**ayout menu, and run through the options in the dialog box that appears.

☛ To see formatting options such as page numbers, headers, and footers, switch to *page mode* by selecting the **P**age Mode command from the **V**iew menu.

Fix your eyes on the center of this page and wait for a 3-D image to appear. Be patient.

Chapter 16
Looking Good with Envelopes and Labels

In This Chapter

- ☛ Defining an envelope
- ☛ Printing an envelope
- ☛ Working with envelope options such as POSTNET bar codes
- ☛ Defining labels and entering label text
- ☛ Envelope and labels basics and some smart shopping tips

While waiting in a bookstore checkout line a few years ago, I happened to notice a woman standing in the paperback best-sellers section. She had a book in each hand and was clearly trying to figure out which one to buy. She stared intently at the covers, read the blurbs on the back, and checked out the price, but she just couldn't decide. Finally, she put the two books spine-to-spine and chose the thicker one!

I recall this story to remind you that most people look at the whole package when they evaluate something. If you're going to be mailing your documents, applying all the fancy formatting techniques we've been looking at is only the start. Your package might not even be opened if it arrives in a sloppily addressed envelope—and if it does get opened, your careful prose will almost certainly be read with a jaundiced eye.

This chapter shows you how to avoid such a sorry fate by showing you how easy it is to create great-looking envelopes and labels in WordPerfect. (It's also a lot faster than trying to type an address directly on an envelope using that rickety old Selectric you keep hidden in the corner.)

Printing Addresses on Envelopes

For a true professional touch, you can persuade WordPerfect to print mailing and return addresses on an envelope of just about any size. Just think how impressed your recipients will be when they see their name and address all slick and neat, smack-dab in the middle of an envelope. Is it hard? Not a chance! All you do is tell WordPerfect the mailing and return addresses you want to use, print the envelope, and then shove the envelope into your printer. It's all quite civilized, really. The next few sections take you through the basic steps for creating an envelope: setting up, defining the envelope, and printing the darn thing.

"In theory, theory and practice are the same thing; in practice, they're not." I'm not sure who said that, but he or she must have been a computer user. Why? Well, because in theory, printing envelopes is a breeze; in practice, well, you usually need to try a few experiments to make sure things come out right. Not to worry, though: I'll be showing you how to fine-tune your envelope printing later on in this chapter.

Getting Your Document Ready for This Envelope Stuff

Getting your document ready for creating an envelope is pretty straightforward. In fact, there are only two things you need to do: select a printer and enter the mailing address.

The first order of business is to make sure you've selected the printer you're going to use to print the envelope. For each printer you've installed, WordPerfect comes with one or more *envelope definitions* that ensure the envelope is printed like an envelope (and not like, say, an 8 1/2" by 11" sheet of paper). To check which printer is currently selected, pull down the

File menu and select the Print/Fax command (or press **Shift+F7**). In the Print/Fax dialog box that appears, the **Current Printer** box at the top shows you the name of the currently selected printer. If this isn't the one you'll be using for your envelope, go ahead and select the correct one. (If you're not sure how to go about this, trudge back to Chapter 9, "Getting It Down on Paper: Printing Documents," to learn everything you need to know.)

TECHNO NERD TEACHES...

In case you're wondering, each envelope definition covers a number of characteristics. These include the dimensions of the envelope, the *orientation* of the text (either *landscape*, in which the text runs along the long side of the envelope, or *portrait*, in which the text runs along the short side of the envelope), where you'll be loading the envelope into the printer (this is usually "manual feed"), and any position adjustments that are needed for the addresses to print correctly.

With your printer selected, the only other task you need to perform is to add the mailing address to the document. (If you like, you can bypass this step; WordPerfect also lets you enter the mailing address when you define the envelope, as you'll see in the next section.) This is no big deal: you can plop the address just about anywhere that makes sense. Remember, however, that what you type is exactly what will appear on the front of the envelope. So make sure the address is complete (including the ZIP or postal code) and contains no spelling mistakes (see the following figure).

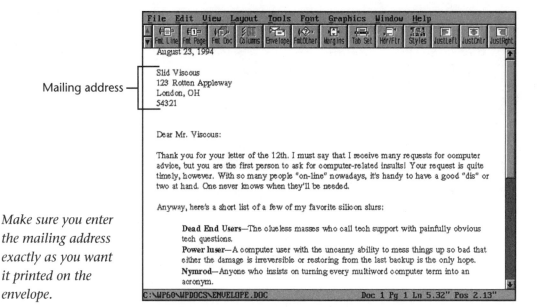

Mailing address ⎯

Make sure you enter the mailing address exactly as you want it printed on the envelope.

Defining the Envelope

The next step is to define the envelope itself. This includes entering the return address, selecting the envelope size you'll be using, and a couple of other things. The following steps show you what to do:

If you press **Enter** twice after the mailing address when you enter it, WordPerfect will find the address automatically; you don't have to select it. The only exception to this is if your document contains more than one address, in which case, you need to select the address you want to use.

1. If you entered the mailing address in the document, select it.

2. Pull down the Layout menu and select the Envelope command, or press **Alt+F12**. WordPerfect displays the Envelope dialog box, shown below.

    You can also click on this button in either the WPMain or Layout Button Bar.

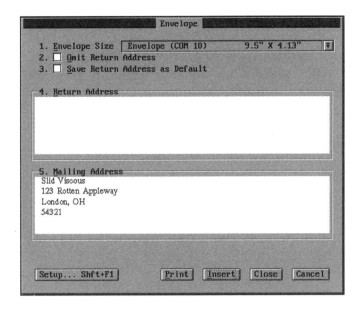

Use the Envelope dialog box to define your envelope.

3. If necessary, use the Envelope Size drop-down list to select the appropriate envelope size. (The default size is 9.5" x 4.13".)

4. If you want to include a return address on the envelope, select the **R**eturn Address text box and enter the address. When you're done, press **F7** to exit the text box. You can also use the following two check boxes to control the return address:

> **S**ave Return Address as Default If you activate this check box, WordPerfect saves the return address and displays it each time you open the Envelope dialog box.

> **O**mit Return Address If you've saved a default return address, activate this check box to tell WordPerfect not to use the return address for this envelope.

5. If you didn't enter a mailing address in the document, use the **M**ailing Address text box to enter it. Again, press **F7** when you're done.

Printing the Envelope

With your envelope defined, you can either print it out right away, or insert it into the current document for later use. Here are the options you have:

☞ If you want to print the envelope, first make sure your printer is up and running. Then you need to load the envelopes into the printer. (How you do this varies depending on the type of printer you have; your printer manual should tell you.) When you're ready to go, select the Print button in the Envelope dialog box.

☞ If you want to print the envelope later, you can insert it into the document by pressing the Insert button in the Envelope dialog box. WordPerfect adds a new page to the end of the document (by inserting a hard return) and displays the return and mailing addresses. To print this envelope later, select the mailing address, display the Envelope dialog box, and then select **Print**.

Depending on the printer you have, the envelopes you're using, and WordPerfect's mood that day, getting your envelopes to print correctly is not always easy. If things don't look right, see the next section, "Changing the Envelope Setup," for some ways to make adjustments. Also, rather than waste good envelopes on trial runs, try printing a few on regular paper until all is well.

Changing the Envelope Setup

As usual, WordPerfect gives you all kinds of bells and whistles to make sure you get exactly the kinds of envelopes you need. The next few sections take you through the various setup options that are available for envelopes.

Adding POSTNET Bar Codes to Envelopes

The U.S. Postal Service (USPS) uses POSTNET bar codes to computerize their mail sorting and speed up mail delivery. If you do bulk mailings, you can save on postal rates by presorting the envelopes and including the USPS POSTNET bar code as part of the mailing address. (See the following figure.)

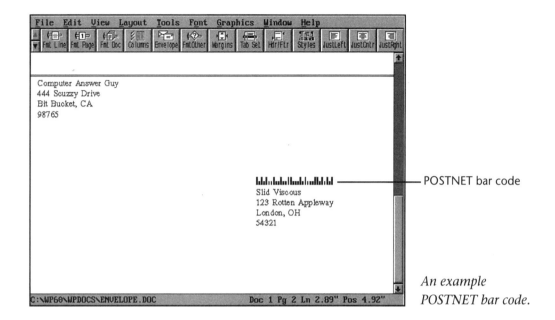

An example POSTNET bar code.

Follow these steps to add a POSTNET bar code to an envelope:

1. Display the Envelope dialog box and define your envelope, as described earlier in this chapter.

2. Click on the **Setup** button or press **Shift+F1**. WordPerfect displays the Envelope Setup dialog box.

3. In the **Bar Code Creation** group, select one of the following options:

   Automatically Create Bar Code   When you select this option, WordPerfect automatically extracts the ZIP code from the mailing address and inserts it in the POSTNET **B**ar Code text box that it adds to the Envelope dialog box.

I know it's a pain, but when you first activate the Automatically Create Bar Code radio button, WordPerfect doesn't fill in the POSTNET **B**ar Code text box. You have to exit the Envelope dialog box and then come back in.

Manually Enter Bar Code   When you select this radio button, WordPerfect adds a POSTNET **Bar** Code text box to the Envelope dialog box, but doesn't fill it in for you. When you want to print the bar code, enter the ZIP code in the POSTNET **Bar** Code text box.

Remove Bar Code Option   Select this radio button to remove the POSTNET **Bar** Code text box from the Envelope dialog box.

4. Select **OK** to return to the Envelope dialog box.

5. If you elected to have WordPerfect automatically create the bar code, exit the dialog box (by selecting the **Close** button) and come back in to put this feature into effect. If you're entering the bar code manually, type the mailing address ZIP code in the POSTNET **Bar** Code text box.

6. Print or insert the bar code.

Changing the Address Position

One of the most common problems with envelopes is that the addresses often don't print where they're supposed to. For example, the mailing address might be too far down or the return address might be too far to the left. If you don't like where WordPerfect is printing the return and mailing addresses on the envelope, you can adjust the address positions. Here's how:

1. Pull down the Layout menu and select the Envelope command, or press **Alt+F12** to display the Envelope dialog box.

2. Select the **Setup** button or press **Shift+F1** to display the Envelope Setup dialog box.

3. In the Envelope Size group, highlight the envelope size you're working with and then select the Address Positions command. WordPerfect displays the Envelope Address Positions dialog box, shown below.

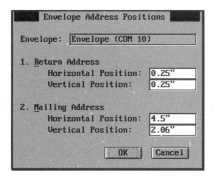

Use the Envelope Address Positions dialog box to adjust where your addresses print on the envelope.

4. Use the **Return** Address and **Mailing** Address text boxes to adjust the address positions. For the Horizontal Position text boxes, enter a value in inches from the left edge of the envelope. For the Vertical Position text boxes, enter a value in inches from the top edge of the envelope.

5. Click on **OK** to return to the Envelope Setup dialog box.

6. Click on **OK** to return to the Envelope dialog box.

7. Print or insert the envelope.

Working with Labels

Instead of printing an address directly on an envelope, you can instead place the address on a label and then stick the label on the envelope. This is handy if you're using envelopes that are too big to fit in your printer, or if you're using padded envelopes that could cause a printer to choke. Of course, there are many other uses for labels: name tags, floppy disks, file folders, your neighbor's cat....

The next couple of sections show you how to define labels and enter text into them.

Defining Your Labels

Labels, of course, come in all shapes and sizes, from the relatively small file folder labels that hold only a line or two, to the much larger "full sheet" labels that can hold a short story. Whatever your needs, WordPerfect is up to the challenge, because it comes equipped to handle literally dozens of different labels.

So the first thing you need to do is tell WordPerfect what kind of labels you'll be using. Start by pulling down the Layout menu and selecting the **Page** command to display the Page Format dialog box. Then select the Labels command. WordPerfect displays the Labels dialog box, as shown below.

 You can also display the Page Format dialog box by clicking on this button in the Layout Button Bar.

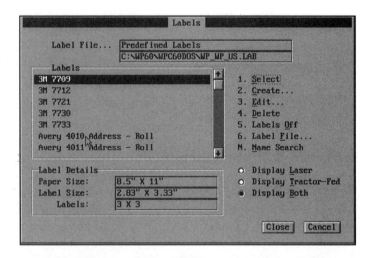

Use the Labels dialog box to let WordPerfect know what kind of labels you'll be using.

Use the Labels list to select the type of labels you're using. (Handily, WordPerfect's label names are the same as those used by the label companies.) To make sure you select the right labels, keep an eye on the boxes in the **Label Details** group; they'll tell you the size of each label and how many you can fit on a single page.

When you're done, choose the **S**elect option. If this is the first time you've selected these labels with the current printer, WordPerfect (ever

eager for more data) will display the
Labels Printer Info dialog box with the
following options:

Location   Use this command to tell
WordPerfect how you'll be feeding the
label sheets into your printer.

To make the **Labels** list
easier to navigate, you can
reduce the number of labels
displayed by selecting either
Display **L**aser (to only
display labels designed for
laser printers), or Display
Tractor-Fed (to only display
labels designed for dot-
matrix printers).

Prompt to Load   If you activate this
check box, WordPerfect will remind
you to load the labels into the printer.

Use **R**otated (Landscape) Font   Activate
this check box to have Word-Perfect
print along the long side of the label.

Adjust Text   Use these controls to adjust where WordPerfect prints the
label text. For example, if you find your labels are printing too far to the
left, enter a value in the **R**ight text box to move the labels to the right.

Select **OK** to return to the Page Format dialog box, and then select **OK** to
return to the document. WordPerfect displays a single label, ready for you
to type in your text.

Typing Text in Labels

With your first label displayed, you can go ahead and enter your label text.
A label is really just a mini-page, so you can enter and format your text as
you normally would. When you want to start a new label, press **Ctrl+Enter**
to insert a hard page break. When you're done, you can print the labels
just like a regular document. (See Chapter 9, "Getting It Down on Paper:
Printing Documents," to get the poop on printing.)

As with envelopes, you'll likely have to monkey around with
your labels to make sure they print properly. One highly
useful feature to use with labels is the Center Pages option
(discussed in Chapter 15, "Making Your Pages Look Good").
This feature will center your labels between the top and
bottom margins.

The Least You Need to Know

This chapter showed you how to send your documents in style by using envelopes and labels. Here's a rehash of the main events:

☞ Before defining an envelope, make sure you've selected the printer you'll be using.

☞ You can either enter the mailing address in the document, or wait until you display the Envelope dialog box. If you do put the address in the document, press **Enter** twice after the last line to make sure WordPerfect will find the address automatically. Alternatively, you can select the address.

☞ To define the envelope, pull down the Layout menu and select the Envelope command (or you can press **Alt+F12**). In the Envelope dialog box, select an envelope size and enter the return address and the mailing address (if necessary).

☞ Select the **P**rint button to print the envelope. To insert the envelope in the current document, select the **I**nsert button, instead.

☞ To reduce costs in bulk mailings, include a USPS POSTNET bar code on your envelopes.

☞ To define labels, pull down the Layout menu, select **P**age, and then select **L**abels. Highlight the labels you're using in the Labels list and choose **S**elect.

Chapter 17
Other Ways to Look Good

In This Chapter

- ☛ Adding and formatting dates and times in a document
- ☛ Creating footnotes, endnotes, and comments
- ☛ Using hyphenation for fun and profit
- ☛ Working with different paper sizes
- ☛ Miscellaneous ways to fool people into thinking you know what you're doing

This chapter will be your formatting graduate school. Earlier chapters covered grade school (formatting characters), high school (formatting lines and paragraphs), and college (formatting pages). Now you get to do graduate work with things like dates, footnotes, and hyphenation. Believe me, people will be *very* impressed. Will this be as hard as graduate school? No way. You'll still just be learning the basics in the same non-technical fashion that you've come to know and love.

Inserting the Date and Time into a Document

If you need to add a date to a document (if you're just starting a letter, for example), don't bother typing it yourself—let WordPerfect do it for you.

The first thing you need to do is select the date format you want to use. WordPerfect has no less than a dozen date and time formats, one of which is sure to satisfy your needs. To select one of these formats, pull down the Tools menu, select the Date command, and then select Format. You'll see the Date Formats dialog box, shown below. Select the format you want to use and then select **OK**.

 You can also display the Date Format dialog box by clicking on this button in the Tools Button Bar.

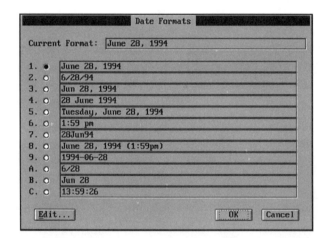

Use the Date Formats dialog box to select one of WordPerfect's umpteen date or time formats.

With your format selected, you're ready to insert the date or time. Position the insertion point where you want the date or time to appear in your document, pull down the Tools menu, select Date, and then select one of the following commands from the cascade menu:

☛ Text   This command inserts the date just as though you typed it yourself.

 Click on this button in the Tools Button Bar to insert the current date as text.

☛ Code   This command inserts a special code that tells WordPerfect to always display the current date. This means the date will change if you open the document tomorrow, next week, or next month.

 Click on this button in the Tools Button Bar to insert a date code that always displays the current date.

If the date or time that appears is wrong, don't blame WordPerfect; your computer is supposed to keep track of these things. If it's fallen down on the job, there's a way to fix it—if you don't mind attempting a DOS command or two. (Yes, a shudder *is* the appropriate reaction at this point.) The next time you're at the DOS prompt, type **date** and press **Enter**. DOS shows you the current date and prompts you for a new one. Type in the date, with the **mm-dd-yy** format that DOS uses (you need to include the dashes) and press **Enter**. To fix the time, type **time**, press **Enter**, and enter the correct time in DOS's **hh:mm** format.

Take a Note: Adding Footnotes and Endnotes

One of the best ways to make people think you worked *really* hard on a document is to include *footnotes* at the bottom of the page. Footnotes say "Hey, this person took the time and effort to write this little parenthetical note for my edification or amusement. I think I'll take her out to lunch."

To make sure we're on the same page (so to speak), here are some concepts to keep in mind as you work through this section:

☛ A *footnote* is a section of text placed at the bottom of a page. Footnotes are convenient for the reader, but too many on one page can make your text look cluttered.

☛ An *endnote* is a section of text placed at the end of a document. They're less convenient than footnotes, but they're good for longer entries that would otherwise usurp too much space on a page.

☛ Both footnotes and endnotes usually contain asides or comments that embellish something in the regular document text.

☛ Each footnote is numbered, and each number appears in the document beside the text to which the footnote refers.

If you've ever tried adding footnotes to a page with a typewriter, you know what a nightmare it can be trying to coordinate the size of the note with the regular page text. And if you need to change your footnote numbers? Forget about it.

WordPerfect changes all that by making footnotes as easy as typing text. The program arranges things so your pages accommodate any size footnote perfectly, and it'll even manage the footnote numbers for you—automatically!

Creating Footnotes and Endnotes

Since a footnote or endnote always refers to something in the regular text, your first task is to position the cursor where you want the little footnote/endnote number to appear. Once you've done that, pull down the **Layout** menu and select either the Footnote or Endnote command. In the cascade menu that appears, select Create. WordPerfect displays the footnote or endnote editing screen with the note's number. Enter your text (feel free to use any character or line formatting options, too), and press **F7** when you're done. WordPerfect returns you to the document and displays the same number at the cursor position (see the picture below).

 Click on this button in the Layout Button Bar to create a footnote.

 Click on this button in the Layout Button Bar to create an endnote.

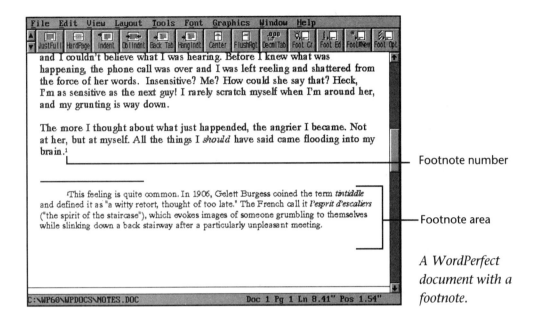

Footnote number

Footnote area

A WordPerfect document with a footnote.

If you want to see your footnotes or endnotes, put WordPerfect in page mode by activating the View menu's Page Mode command (you need version 6 for this). Alternatively, you can use the Print Preview feature (see Chapter 9, "Getting It Down on Paper: Printing Documents").

Editing Footnotes and Endnotes

If you need to make changes to a footnote or endnote, pull down the Layout menu, select Footnote or Endnote, and then choose Edit from the cascade menu. In the dialog box that appears, enter the number of the footnote or endnote that you want to edit, and then select **OK**. WordPerfect displays the appropriate edit screen for you to make your changes. Press **F7** when you're done.

 You can also edit your footnotes by clicking on this button in the Layout Button Bar.

 Click this Layout Button Bar button to edit your endnotes.

Adding Snide Comments to a Document

When you're writing, you may need to make a quick note to yourself about something related to the text. Or, other people may be reading your work on-screen, and they might want to make some snarky remarks for you to see. In either case, you can use WordPerfect's document comments feature to handle the job. A *comment* is text that appears in a box on-screen but doesn't print out.

To add a comment, first position the cursor where you want the comment to appear. Then pull down the Layout menu, select Comment, and select Create from the cascade menu. WordPerfect displays the comment editing screen where you can type your text (and add some formatting options, if you like). Press **F7** when you're done, and you'll see the comment displayed inside a box, as you can see here.

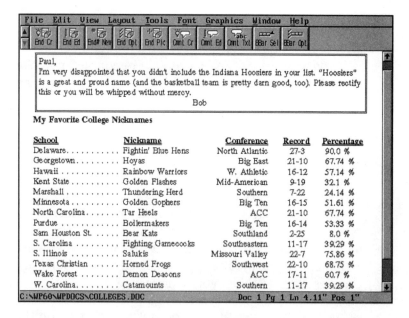

WordPerfect places document comments inside a box. These comments don't appear when you print the file.

 You can also create a comment by clicking on this button in the Layout Button Bar.

If you need to edit a comment, position the cursor on the first line below the comment, select Comment from the Layout menu, and then select Edit from the cascade menu. When the editing screen appears, make your changes, and then press **F7** to exit.

 Clicking on this button in the Layout Button Bar will also display the comment editing screen.

Here's my writing tip of the day. Count yourself lucky. It's at no charge. One of the keys to productive writing is to build up some momentum. If you're on a roll, but you get stuck on a particular idea or phrase (or if you come across a fact you need to check), don't get bogged down trying to solve it. Ignore it for now and keep going; you can always come back later on and fix things up.

Before moving on, though, you should probably make a quick note or two, just to get your ideas down so you don't forget them. The WordPerfect comments feature, of course, is perfectly suited for this.

Using Hyphenation to Clean Up Your Documents

As you've seen by now, WordPerfect's word wrap feature really makes typing easier, because you don't have to worry about a looming right margin the way you do on a typewriter. If you're in the middle of a word when the margin hits, WordPerfect just moves the whole thing to a new line. While this is convenient, it can make your document look ragged if the word is a large one.

For example, take a look at the first paragraph in the following picture.

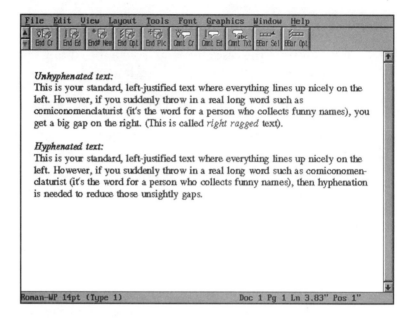

Hyphenation can reduce the gaps produced by some longer words.

As you can see, the second line has a large gap on the right because the next word—*comiconomenclaturist*—was too long to fit. One solution would be to use full justification (where text is aligned with both the left and right margins; see Chapter 14, "Making Your Lines and Paragraphs Look Good"). This often works, but you sometimes end up with lines that look unnatural.

Often a better solution is *hyphenation*, where WordPerfect takes any long words that won't fit at the end of a line, splits them in two, and adds a hyphen. The second paragraph above is hyphenated.

Follow these steps to add hyphenation to your document:

1. WordPerfect adds hyphenation from the current paragraph down to the end of the document. Position the cursor appropriately or, if you only want to hyphenate the current paragraph, select a block inside the paragraph (a letter or two will do).

2. Select the Layout menu's Line command to display the Line Format dialog box.

3. Activate the Hyphenation check box and then select **OK**. WordPerfect examines the text, and if it finds any candidates suitable for hyphenation, it displays the Position Hyphen dialog box (see figure) that shows you where the hyphen will go.

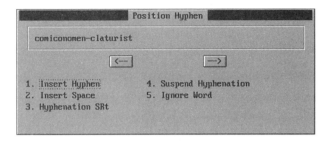

When WordPerfect finds a word that needs hyphenating, it displays the word in the Position Hyphen dialog box.

4. If you don't like where WordPerfect will break up the word, you can move the hyphen location by using the left or right arrow keys or by clicking on the new location with your mouse.

5. Select the **Insert Hyphen** command to, well, insert the hyphen.

6. If WordPerfect finds any more words to hyphenate, you'll have to keep repeating steps 4 and 5.

You may have noticed that the Hyphenation group in the Line Format dialog box also included a Hyphenation Zone option. You don't need to know about this to use hyphenation, but I'll give a quickie explanation for the curious.

Basically, these zones just control the amount of hyphenation in a document. The left zone is the space immediately to the left of the right margin. The right zone, then, is the space to the right of the right margin (are you sure you want to know this?). The size of each zone is a percentage of the line length. For example, the left zone is usually 10%. So if the line is 6.5 inches long, the left zone is .65 inches.

If a word begins before the left zone and continues past the right zone, WordPerfect will try to hyphenate it. If it begins after the left zone, it gets wrapped to the next line, no matter what. So, if you want more hyphenation in a document, decrease the size of each zone.

If you just have a word or two that you want to hyphenate, forget all this rigmarole. Instead, position the cursor where you want the word broken up, and press **Ctrl+−**. This adds a so-called *soft hyphen*; if you alter the position of the word, the hyphen disappears.

Trying Out Different Paper Sizes

You'll probably do most of your work on good old 8 1/2-by-11-inch paper. However, should the mood strike you, WordPerfect lets you set different paper sizes. For example, you could switch to 8 1/2-by-14-inch legal size, or just about anything you want. You can also select a different *orientation*. Normal orientation has the lines running across the short side of the page, but if you prefer to have the lines run across the long side of the page, WordPerfect can handle it.

Having the lines run across the short side of a page is called **portrait orientation**. When you turn things around and have the lines run across the long side of the page, it's called **land-scape orientation**.

To change the paper size or orientation, select Page from the Layout menu to display the Page Format dialog box. Select the Paper **S**ize/Type option, and you'll see the Paper Size/Type dialog box, shown below. Use the **P**aper Name list to highlight the paper you'll be using. The Paper Details group tells you everything you need to know about the highlighted paper. When you've got the one you want, choose the **S**elect command to return to the Page Format dialog box, and then choose **OK** to return to the document.

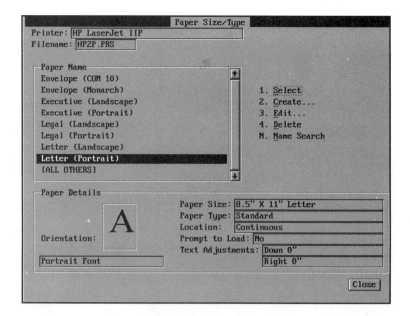

Use the Paper Size/ Type dialog box to select a different paper size.

The Least You Need to Know

This chapter took you on a quick graduate course of some other WordPerfect formatting options. Here's a review before the final exam:

- ☞ If you want to add the date or the time to a document, first choose a format by pulling down the **T**ools menu, selecting **D**ate, and then selecting **F**ormat. Pick out the format you want from the Date Formats dialog box and select **OK**.

- ☞ To insert the date or time, pull down the **T**ools menu and select the **D**ate command. In the cascade menu, select **T**ext to insert a date that won't change or select **C**ode to tell WordPerfect to insert a date that changes to the current date whenever you open or print the document.

- ☞ Footnotes and endnotes are handy ways to add information to a document without cluttering the text. Select either **F**ootnote or **E**ndnote from the **L**ayout menu, select **C**reate, and then fill in the note. Press **F7** when you're done.

- ☞ Comments are an easy way to include notes to yourself or others in a document. Select Comment from the **L**ayout menu, and then select **C**reate from the cascade menu. When the editing screen appears, add your text, and then press **F7** to exit.

- ☞ Use hyphenation to clean up some of the gaps caused by long words. Select the **L**ayout menu's **L**ine command and activate the Hyphenation check box. If WordPerfect finds a suitable hyphenation candidate, it displays a dialog box. Move the hyphen if necessary, and then select **Insert Hyphen**.

- ☞ To work with a different paper size, select the **P**age command from the **L**ayout menu, and then select the Paper **S**ize/Type option. Pick out the paper you want to use from the dialog box that appears.

Attention Star Rangers:
Wipe this page with lemon juice and
wait for this week's Captain Space
Commander Clue to appear!

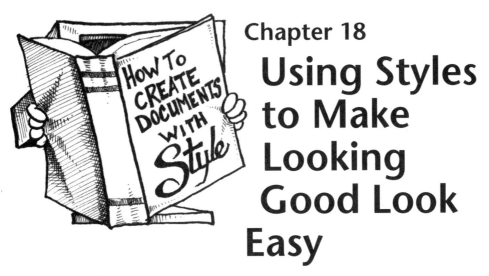

Chapter 18

Using Styles to Make Looking Good Look Easy

In This Chapter

- ☛ The advantages of using styles
- ☛ Creating your own personal styles
- ☛ Applying styles to document text
- ☛ Checking out WordPerfect's built-in styles
- ☛ Working with the handy style libraries
- ☛ Tip-top techniques that'll have you styling in no time

In the last few chapters, we've been looking at the progression of your formatting knowledge as being akin to working through the various levels of school. Since I enjoy beating a metaphor to death as much as the next person, we'll do the same in this chapter. However, you know enough by now that your formal formatting "education" is over; you're in the real world now (or the "RW" as business school types like to call it), where practical concerns outweigh theory. The real world has looming deadlines and meetings in 10 minutes, so you don't want to be fumbling around with lengthy formatting chores.

To that end, this chapter is presented in the spirit of books such as *"What They Don't Teach You in Harvard Business School."* In our case, though, it'll be more like *"What They Don't Teach You in Beginner WordPerfect Books."* Specifically, we'll be looking at *styles* and how they can knock even the most complex formatting task down to size. We'll begin by examining styles and learning just what the heck they are. I'll then show you the easy way to create your own styles, how to apply styles to any document text, and more.

What Is a Style and Why Should You Bother?

As you've seen throughout the chapters here in Part III, formatting is essential if you want to produce good-looking documents that get noticed. The problem is that formatting always seems to take up so much time (especially in WordPerfect).

For example, suppose you want to add a title to a document. Titles usually appear in a larger, sans-serif font, so you type in the text, select it, and then use the Font command to set up the appropriate formatting (as explained back in Chapter 13, "Making Your Characters Look Good"). For good measure, you also center the title. It's not bad, but you decide the text needs to be bold. So, you rehighlight the text and select **Bold** from the Font menu. Things are looking good, but now you decide to use a larger type size. Once again, you highlight the text and make the size adjustment. After fiddling with a few more options (maybe underlining or small caps would look good), you finally get the title exactly right. You've just wasted 10 minutes out of your busy day—but, hey, that's the reality of working with WordPerfect, right?

Wrong. You don't have to stand for this! By learning how to use styles, you can accomplish the same chore in 10 seconds, instead of 10 minutes. How is that possible? Well, you see, a *style* is nothing more than a predefined collection of formatting and layout settings. WordPerfect comes with quite a few styles built-in, but it's also easy to create your own. For example, you could create a "Title" style that consists of, say, an 18-point, bold, underlined Helvetica font, that's centered between the left and right margins. You'd then enter your document title, select it, and apply the Title style. In the blink of an eye, WordPerfect formats the text as 18-point, bold, underlined Helvetica, centered between the left and right margins. That's right: with a single command, WordPerfect can throw any number of character, line, or paragraph formatting options at the selected text.

Here's a short list of just some of the advantages to using styles:

☛ The most obvious, of course, is the time you'll save. Once you've invested the initial few minutes to create a style, applying any style takes only a few keystrokes or mouse clicks.

☛ You eliminate the trial and error that goes into many formatting chores. Once you've decided on a look that you like, you can capture it in a style for all time.

☛ If you change your mind, a style can be easily edited. Does this mean you have to go back and reapply the style throughout the document? No way. Any text formatted with that style is *automatically* reformatted with the revised style. This feature alone is worth the price of admission.

☛ You can create many different kinds of styles to handle all your needs. Whether it's document titles, subtitles, headings, indented paragraphs, special text, whatever. WordPerfect places no practical restrictions on the number of styles you can create.

☛ Styles make it easy to create documents that have a consistent look and feel. In fact, it's not hard to set up an entire *style library*—a separate file that contains one or more style definitions. You can then access the library styles from any document.

☛ Styles reduce the number of keystrokes and mouse clicks you need to get your job done. In this age where repetitive strain injuries such as carpal-tunnel syndrome are reaching almost epidemic proportions, anything that reduces the wear-and-tear on our sensitive anatomy is a welcome relief.

If it all sounds too good to be true, well, there is a downside: styles can save you so much time that you may run out of things to do during the day (pause while the laughter dies down).

Creating a Style the Easy Way

Well, since fine words butter no parsnips, as they say (no, they really do), let's get down to business and see how you create a style. The simplest way to go about this is to *create a style by example*: first you format a section of text exactly the way you want it, and then you create the style based on this formatting. Here are the steps you need to follow:

1. Using some existing text, enter the formatting options you want to include in the style. (You can use any of the formatting features we've looked at in the last few chapters.) When you're done, make sure the cursor is inside the formatted text.

2. Pull down the Layout menu and select Styles, or press **Alt+F8**. WordPerfect displays the Style List dialog box.

    You can also display the Style List dialog box by clicking on this button in the Layout Button Bar.

3. Select the Create command. The Create Style dialog box appears, as shown below.

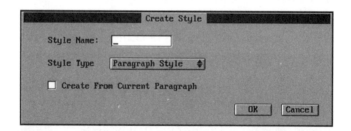

The Create Style dialog box appears when you select the Create command.

4. In the Style Name text box, enter a name for the style using up to 12 characters. To avoid conflicts, don't give your style the name of an existing style.

5. In the Style Type pop-up list, select the type of style you want. (WordPerfect 5.1 only gives you two choices in the Type list: Paired, which is similar to version 6's Character Style, and Open.)

    Paragraph Style   When you apply this type of style, the formatting affects the entire paragraph containing the cursor (or the paragraphs containing the currently selected text).

Character Style   When you apply this type of style, the formatting affects only the selected text or any text typed from the current cursor position.

Open Style   When you apply this type of style, the formatting affects all the text from the current cursor position to the end of the document.

6. Activate either the Create From Current Paragraph check box (if you selected the Paragraph Style in the last step) or the Create From Current Character check box (if you selected the Character Style). This tells WordPerfect to include in the style the existing formatting in effect at the cursor.

7. Select **OK**. WordPerfect displays the Edit Style dialog box.

8. Use the **D**escription text box to enter a brief description for the style. (This description appears in the Style List dialog box; it can make it easier to select the style you want later on.)

TECHNO NERD TEACHES...

If you chose the Open Style in step 5, WordPerfect doesn't let you create the style by example. In this case, select the Style Contents box, use the menus to select the formatting you want to include in the style, and then press **F7** to exit the box.

9. Select the Enter Key Action command and choose one of the following radio buttons from the Enter Key Action dialog box that appears (see the figure which follows):

Insert a **H**ard Return   This option (it's only available for character styles) inserts a hard return and leaves the style turned on (this is the normal Enter key behavior).

Turn Style Off   This option turns the style off when you press **Enter**.

Turn Style Off and Back **O**n   This options restarts the style in the next paragraph when you press **Enter**. (This is useful for styles where the first line of the paragraph is indented.)

Turn Style Off and Link to: This option turns the style off when you press **Enter**, and then begins a different style. For example, you might have a Title style and a Subtitle style. In most cases, you'd probably want the Subtitle style to immediately follow the Title style. When you select this radio button, WordPerfect displays a drop-down list of styles you can link the current style to.

*Use the Enter Key Action dialog box to decide what happens to your style when you press **Enter**.*

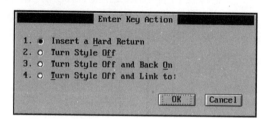

10. When you're done, select **OK** to return to the Edit Style dialog box.

11. Select **OK** to return to the Style List dialog box.

12. Select **Close** to return to the document.

The Easy Part: Applying a Style

Once you've defined a style, you can then apply it to any text in the same document. (I'll show you later on how to use styles from other documents.) Here's how it's done:

1. If you're applying a paragraph style, position the cursor inside the paragraph you want to format. (If you want to apply the style to multiple paragraphs, select a block that includes some text from each paragraph.) If you're applying a character style, select the text you want to format.

2. Pull down the Layout menu and select Styles, or press **Alt+F8** to display the Style List dialog box. (See the following page.)

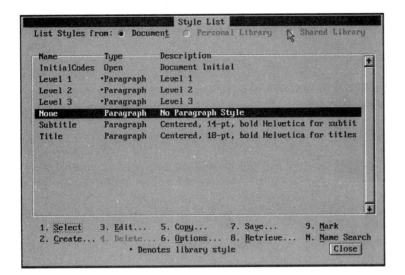

Use the Style List dialog box to select the style you want to apply.

3. In the Name list box, highlight the style you want to apply.

4. Choose the Select command. WordPerfect applies the style.

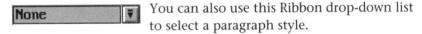 You can also use this Ribbon drop-down list to select a paragraph style.

Making Changes to a Style

Hey, nobody's perfect, so occasionally you'll need to edit a style to either add new formatting, change the existing formatting, or delete a format or two. The following steps show you what to do:

1. Display the Style List dialog box by pulling down the Layout menu and selecting the **S**tyles command, or by pressing **Alt+F8**.

2. Use the Name list box to highlight the style you want to edit, and then select the Edit command. WordPerfect displays the Edit Style dialog box, as shown on the following page.

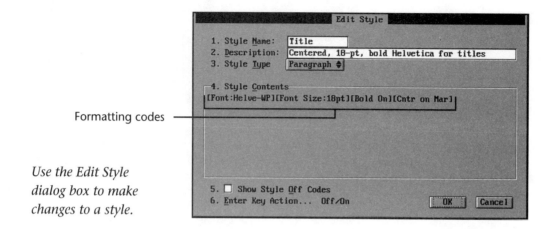

Formatting codes ——

Use the Edit Style dialog box to make changes to a style.

3. Use the Style **Name**, **Description**, and Style **Type** controls to modify the style's name, description, and type.

4. The Style Contents box shows the codes that correspond to the style's formatting options. For example, the code [Font Size: 18pt] represents a type size of 18 points. Similarly, the [Cntr on Mar] code represents the Center alignment. Select the Style Contents box and use the following techniques to modify these codes:

   ☞ To add formatting to the style (that is, to insert a new code in the Style Contents box), use the pull-down menus to select the appropriate formatting options (just as though you were formatting document text).

   ☞ To delete formatting, select the appropriate code (either by clicking on it with your mouse or by using the left and right arrow keys), and then press **Delete**. Note that you can't edit a style code directly; you have to delete the existing code first, and then insert a new one to replace it.

5. When you're done, press **F7** to exit the Style Contents box.

6. Select **OK** to return to the Style List dialog box.

7. Choose **Select** to apply the revised style (remember, though, that WordPerfect automatically reformats any text that was previously formatted with the style); otherwise, select **Close** to return to the document.

Using System Styles to Avoid Reinventing the Wheel

Before you go off on some kind of style-creating frenzy, you should first check out WordPerfect's *system styles*. The system styles (as opposed to the *user styles* that you create yourself) are built-in styles that come with WordPerfect. They cover everything from headers and footers to headings and footnotes.

To see these styles for yourself, display the Style List dialog box (by selecting **Styles** from the **Layout** menu, or by pressing **Alt+F8**), and then select the **Options** command. In the Style Options dialog box that appears (see below), activate the List System Styles check box, and then select **OK**. WordPerfect returns you to the Style List dialog box and displays a seemingly endless list of new styles.

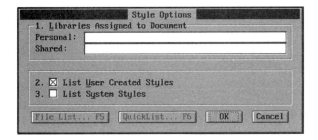

WordPerfect displays the Style Options dialog box when you select the Options command.

You're free to use these system styles just like any other style (by applying them to your documents, or even by editing them to suit your taste). If you want to examine a system style before using it, highlight it and select the **Edit** command. When you've seen what havoc the style will wreak upon your text, select **Cancel** to return to the Style List dialog box.

Working with Style Libraries

When you create your own styles, they're only available to the current document. If you close the document, the styles disappear along with it. (WordPerfect does save the styles, however; the next time you open the document, the styles will reappear.) There are a number of different ways to make your styles available to all your documents, but the easiest is to save them in a *style library*. A style library is a special file that exists on this earth only to store styles. Once you've created a library, you can then *assign* it to a document and, like magic, all the stored styles become instantly available. The next couple of sections show you how to save your styles in a library and how to access library styles.

To make it easier to work with your style libraries, make sure you give them an extension different from what you normally use for your documents. Most people use the extension .STY (e.g., STYLES.STY).

Depositing Styles In a Library

To save the styles you've created in a library, display the Style List dialog box (by selecting the Layout menu's Styles command, or by pressing **Alt+F8**), and then select the Save command or press **F10**. In the Save Styles dialog box that appears (shown below), use the Filename text box to enter a name for the file. Make sure the Save User Created Styles check box is activated (but not the Save WP System Styles check box), and then select **OK**.

Use the Save Styles dialog box to enter a name for your style library.

Check Out Time: Accessing Library Styles

The whole purpose of style libraries, of course, is to access your carefully defined styles in other documents. To do this, display the Style List dialog box (as described umpteen times earlier in this chapter), and then select the Options command to display the Style Options dialog box. Select either the **Personal** or **Shared** text box (it doesn't matter which) and enter the name of the style library you want to use (be sure to include the extension, if you specified one when you created the library). Select **OK** to return to the Style List dialog box.

Depending on how you opened the library (either as personal or shared), you'll notice the following differences in the Style List dialog box:

☞ If you entered the library name in the **Personal** text box, the Personal Library radio button will become available. Activating this button will display the library styles.

☞ Similarly, if you entered the library name in the **Shared** text box, the Shared Library radio button will become available. Activating this button will display the library styles.

WordPerfect comes with its own library of styles (called LIBRARY.STY) that includes an even greater variety of styles than the system styles. To check them out, open the Style Options dialog box, type **C:\WP60\LIBRARY.STY** in either the **Personal** or **Shared** text box, and then select **OK** to return to the Style List dialog box. Select either Personal Library or Shared Library (as appropriate) to see the styles.

Since it doesn't matter whether you open a library as shared or personal, many people like to use both. For example, you can get the best of both worlds by using the **Personal** text box to enter the name of your own style library, and by using the **Shared** text box for LIBRARY.STY.

The Least You Need to Know

This chapter showed you how to use styles to make formatting a breeze. Here's a quick review of your newfound know-how:

☞ A style is a predefined collection of formatting and layout options.

☞ Styles save time by reducing formatting chores to a few keystrokes or mouse clicks. They also allow you to produce consistently formatted documents, and they make it easy to modify a document's formatting.

☞ To display the Style List dialog box, pull down the Layout menu and select the **Styles** command, or press **Alt+F8**.

continues

continued

☞ To create a new style, add the appropriate formatting to the document, and then select **C**reate in the Style List dialog box.

☞ To apply a style, position the cursor or select a text block, highlight the style you want in the Style List, and then choose **S**elect.

☞ To save styles in a style library, choose Save (or press **F10**) in the Style List dialog box, and then enter a name for the library file (be sure to include an extension such as .STY).

Part IV
Fiddling with Your Files

This part looks at the "forest" of your files as a whole, rather than the "trees" of the individual characters, words, and pages. From this bird's-eye view, you'll learn how to work with multiple files and document windows (Chapter 19), WordPerfect's File Manager (Chapter 20), and the ever-so-handy QuickFinder feature (Chapter 21).

Chapter 19
Working with Multiple Documents

In This Chapter

- ☞ The fastest ways to switch between open documents
- ☞ Using version 6's window frames
- ☞ Using frames to move, size, close, and arrange windows
- ☞ Fascinating juggling lore to think about while playing with all those documents

Remember the minor juggling craze that bounced around the country a few years ago? Well, your faithful scribe was one of many who jumped on that strange bandwagon. No, I didn't become any kind of expert (or run off and join the circus), but I did learn the basic three-ball pattern. I've kept it up to this day—and will, on a dare, attempt to juggle three of just about anything (which, believe me, has scared the heck out of many a party hostess).

If you missed that particular craze, WordPerfect lets you do some juggling of your own. In version 5.1, you can open two documents at once, but in version 6, you can open as many as nine documents at the same time. (Nine is a lot of documents, but it's still short of the official world's record for juggling, which is a mind-boggling eleven rings at once.) This not only lets you work with several documents at once, but it's great for quickly comparing two or more documents or pasting info between files. And it's easy too!

Switching Among Multiple Documents

Opening several documents is easy: for each one, just use the File menu's Open command (or press **Shift+F10**), enter the name of the file in the dialog box, and then select **OK**. WordPerfect sets up a new work area for the file and updates the Doc number on the status line. Once you have your documents open, however, you need some way of switching among them. As you might expect by now, WordPerfect has about a million ways to do this. Here's a sampling:

☛ To cycle through the documents, pull down the **Window** menu and select Next (or press **Ctrl+Y**) to cycle through the documents in the order you opened them. To cycle backwards through the open documents, select the **Window** menu's Previous command.

☛ To switch between the current document and the last one you worked with, select the **Window** menu's Switch command, or press **Shift+F3**.

☛ To switch to a specific document number, press **Home** and then the number. For example, to display document 2 on the screen, press **Home, 2**.

☛ To see a list of all the open documents, pull down the Window menu and select the Switch to command, or press **F3**. WordPerfect displays the Switch to Document dialog box. As you can see in the figure, each document is listed, along with its number. Just press the appropriate number to switch to the file you need.

If you have two open documents in version 5.1, you can switch between them by selecting **S**witch Document from the **E**dit menu, or by pressing **Shift+F3**. You can also split the screen and display both documents at once. Just select **W**indow from the **E**dit menu, or press **Ctrl+F3**.

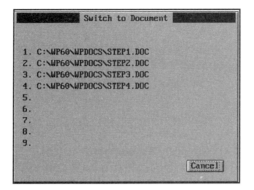

The Switch to Document dialog box displays a list of all the open documents. Select a number to see the document on-screen.

One of the benefits of multiple open documents is that you can share text among them. There are endless uses for this capability, but here's a sampler:

☞ You could take sections of a report and use them in a memo or letter.

☞ If you have one or more files organized as a project, you could take chunks out and use them to create a summary document.

☞ You could create a document to hold boilerplate (bits of often-used text), and keep it open all the time. You could then copy stuff from the file (or add more things to it) at will.

The good news is that this is all extremely simple to do. Here are the basic steps:

1. Open the appropriate files and display the document that has whatever text you need.

2. Block the text (if you need some blocking basics, refer to Chapter 11, "Block Partying: Working with Blocks of Text").

3. Use the appropriate Edit menu command to cut or copy the text (this was also covered in Chapter 11).

4. Switch to the document that you want to receive the text.

5. Position the cursor where you want the text to appear, and then paste it.

WordPerfect's Adjustable Windows

As I've said, every time you open a document, WordPerfect sets up and displays the file in a new work area. In WordPerfect parlance, these work areas are called *windows*. This makes some sense, I suppose. After all, at any one time, the screen can only show you a part of a document, so it's like looking through a window at your text.

If you have version 6, you can think of your computer as a room with nine different windows. As you've just seen, you can display a document in any of these windows and just switch among them.

The window you're currently working in is called the **active window**.

Framing a Window

The problem with windows is that normally you can look through only one at a time on your screen. It would be nice, on occasion, to be able to see maybe a couple of documents at the same time. Sound impossible? With version 6's new *window frames*, it's easier than you think. What does framing do? Well, it puts a border around a window that lets you do all kinds of crazy things:

- Change the size of the window.
- Move the window to a different location.
- Make the window really small so it's out of the way.
- Make the window really big so you can't see anything else.

To access this voodoo, just pull down the **Window** menu and select the Frame command. As you can see in the next figure, your window will suddenly sprout a border with various funny symbols on it.

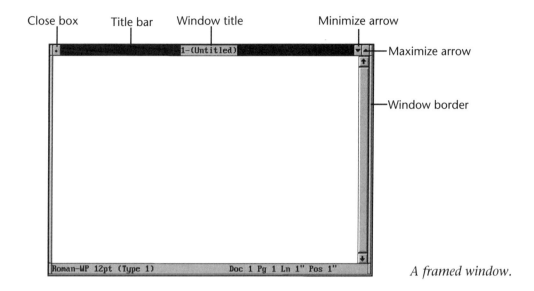

A framed window.

Anatomy of a Window

Here's a summary of the new features you get when you frame a window (I'll talk about things like moving and sizing windows later in the chapter):

Window title   This shows you the name of the document and the document number.

Title bar   You can use this area to move the window with a mouse.

Border   You can use the side and bottom borders to change the size of the window with a mouse.

Maximize arrow   This arrow is used to increase the window to its largest extent (i.e., the normal window view you get when you open a document).

Minimize arrow   This arrow decreases the window to its smallest size.

Close box   This button closes the document. (It acts just like the **File** menu's Close command.)

Adjusting Your Windows

Now that you know how to frame a window, you may be wondering why you would want to do such a thing. It's quite simple, really: a framed window is an *adjustable* window, which means you can move it around, make it different sizes, and more. In other words, you have control over what you see on your screen. The next few sections show you how to wield that control.

A final reminder before you start scattering windows willy-nilly about the screen: the active window is the window that has the blinking cursor and the title bar with the darker color.

Sizing Up Your Windows

If you'd like to see a couple of windows on-screen at the same time, one way to do it is to change the size of each window so they both fit. This is (by far) easiest with a mouse, but the keyboard will do in a pinch.

The secret to sizing a window with the mouse is to use the borders that appear when you frame the window. Follow these steps:

1. Position the mouse pointer over one of the window borders according to the following guidelines:

    ☞ If you want to change the width of the window, move the pointer over the left or right border.

    ☞ If you want to change the height of the window, move the pointer over the window's status bar.

    ☞ If you want to change the width and height at the same time, move the pointer over one of the window corners.

    In each case, you'll know the mouse pointer is positioned correctly when it changes to a two-headed arrow (see the picture below).

2. Hold down the left mouse button and then move the mouse to drag the border. As you're dragging, WordPerfect displays a dotted line to show you the new size.

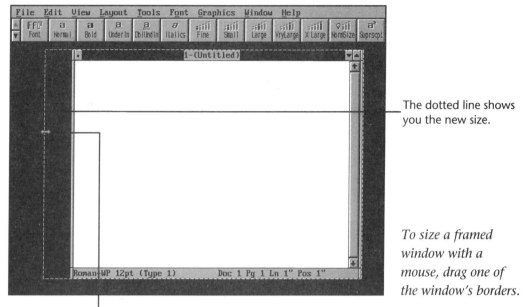

The dotted line shows you the new size.

To size a framed window with a mouse, drag one of the window's borders.

Mouse pointer for sizing a window

3. When things look about right, release the mouse button. WordPerfect dutifully redraws the window in the new size.

If you prefer to use the keyboard, you need to follow these steps:

1. Switch to the window you want to size.

2. Press **Ctrl+F3** to display the Screen dialog box, and then select the **W**indow option. WordPerfect displays the Window dialog box.

3. Select the **S**ize option. A dotted outline appears around the window.

4. Use the arrow keys to size the window outline.

5. Once the outline is the size you want, press **Enter**. WordPerfect redisplays the window in the new size.

If you decide you don't want the window resized after all, just press **Esc.**

Windows on the Move

One of the problems with having several windows open at once is that they have a nasty habit of overlapping each other. And, of course, it never fails that what gets overlapped in a window is precisely the information you want to see. (Chalk up another one for Murphy's Law, I guess.) Instead of cursing WordPerfect's ancestry, you can try moving your windows around so they don't overlap (or so they overlap less).

Things are, once again, *way* easier with a mouse:

1. Position the mouse pointer over the window's title bar. The pointer will change to a four-headed arrow this time.

2. Hold down the left mouse button and drag the window's title bar. As you do, WordPerfect displays a dotted outline of the window.

3. When you've got the outline where you want it, release the mouse button, and WordPerfect redisplays the window in the new location.

For the diehard keyboard mavens in the crowd, here are the steps to follow:

1. Switch to the window you want to move.

2. Display the Screen dialog box by pressing **Ctrl+F3**, and then select the **Window** option. The Window dialog box appears.

3. Select the Move option. A dotted outline appears around the window.

4. Use the arrow keys to move the window outline.

If you change your mind about moving the window, you can press the **Esc** key at any time.

5. Once the outline is in the location you want, press **Enter**. WordPerfect redisplays the window in the new location.

Letting WordPerfect Do the Work: Cascading and Tiling

All this moving and sizing stuff is fine for people with time to kill. The rest of us just want to get the job done and move on. To that end, WordPerfect includes Cascade and Tile commands that will arrange your windows for you automatically. (Speaking of having time to kill, did you know that the world's record for the longest time juggling three objects without a drop is a mind-numbing 8 hours, 57 minutes?)

The Cascade command arranges your open windows in a diagonal pattern that puts the active window on top and shows only the title bars of the other open windows (see the picture, below). This is good for those times when you want things nice and neat, but you don't need to see what's in the other windows. To cascade your windows, pull down the Window menu and select the Cascade command. (The basic three-ball pattern that you see most jugglers using is also called a *cascade*. Just a coincidence? I wonder.)

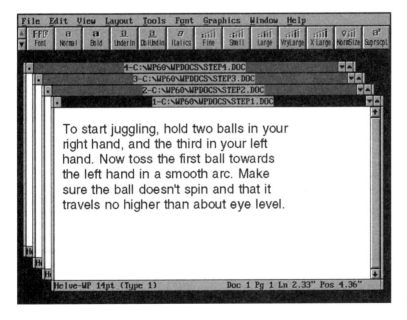

Windows arranged in a cascade pattern.

The **Tile** command divides up your screen and gives equal real estate to each window, as shown below. This pattern enables you to work in one window and still keep an eye on what's happening in the other windows (you never know what those pesky little devils might be up to). To tile your windows, pull down the **Window** menu and select the **Tile** command.

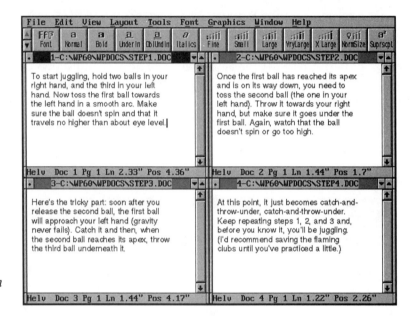

Windows arranged in a tile pattern.

The Minimalist Approach: Minimizing Windows

You'll often find you have some windows you know you won't need for a while. You could move them out of the way or make them smaller, but that takes time—and our goal is always to make things as easy as possible. Fortunately, there's an alternative: you can *minimize* the window down to a minuscule rectangle. The picture below shows several windows minimized at the bottom of the screen.

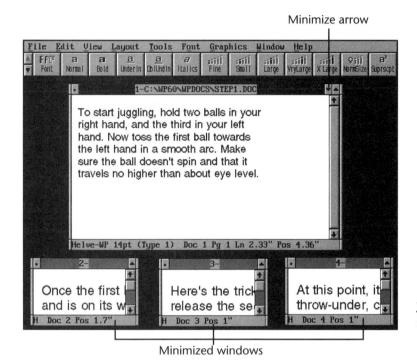

Minimize arrow

Minimized windows

You can minimize your windows to get them out of the way.

If you use a mouse, you can minimize a window in no time at all by clicking on the frame's minimize arrow (the one pointing down). It takes a teeny bit more effort if you're using the keyboard. In this case, you need to pull down the Window menu and select the Minimize command.

Taking It to the Max: Maximizing a Window

If you get tired of all this "frame" monkey business, you can *maximize* a window to its normal size.

If you use a mouse, all you have to do is click on the window's maximize arrow (the one pointing up). From the keyboard, pull down the Window menu and select the Maximize command.

Closing a Window

When a window is framed, you'll see a dot in the upper left corner. This is called the *close box* and, if you have a mouse, you can close the window simply by clicking on the close box. (To close a window from the keyboard, of course, you pull down the File menu and select the Close command.) If you've made changes to the document, WordPerfect will, of course, ask whether you want to save them as it normally does.

The Least You Need to Know

This chapter gave you the lowdown on using multiple documents in WordPerfect. You learned some basic techniques for switching among open documents and for using WordPerfect's window frames. Here's the highlight film:

☞ To switch between windows, you can use the various **Window** menu commands (Next, **Previous**, **S**witch, or Switch To) or you can press **Home** and then the document number.

☞ Select **F**rame from the **W**indow menu to display a frame around a document window.

☞ To size a framed window, drag the left, right, or bottom border. You can also press **Ctrl+F3, 1, S,** and use the arrow keys.

☞ To move a framed window, drag the title bar to the location you want. From the keyboard, press **Ctrl+F3, 1, M,** and use the arrow keys.

☞ If you'd prefer WordPerfect to arrange your windows for you, select either the **C**ascade or the **T**ile command from the **W**indow menu.

☞ To reduce a window to its smallest size, click on the minimize arrow or select **M**inimize from the **W**indow menu. To increase a window to its largest size, click on the maximize arrow or select the **W**indow menu's Maximize command.

☛   To close a window, click on the close box in the upper-left corner or pull down the **File** menu and select **C**lose.

Get some crayons and draw a nice picture with some trees and mountains and birds and flowers on this page. It'll make you feel good, I bet.

Chapter 20

Using WordPerfect's File Manager

In This Chapter

☞ Starting and navigating File Manager

☞ A quick briefing on files and directories

☞ Using File Manager to open, retrieve, and view documents

☞ Other file fun: copying, moving, renaming, and deleting

☞ A snappy analogy designed to knock some sense into all this DOS mumbo-jumbo

What I'm about to tell you is explicit and unexpurgated, and may therefore be offensive to some. You may want to remove small children from the room before continuing. Okay, here it is: WordPerfect is a DOS program; WordPerfect documents are, in fact, DOS files; these files exist in DOS directories. You cannot escape DOS; it knows where you live and where you work. DOS, death, and taxes: the three constants in life.

Why the scaremongering? Because, sooner or later (hopefully later), you're going to have to deal with DOS in some way. You're going to need to copy or rename a file, or create a directory, or delete the hard disk detritus that has accumulated over the years.

But friends, I'm here today to tell you there's good news. I'm here to tell you that, yes, you have to deal with DOS—but, no, you don't have to deal with DOS *directly*. WordPerfect's File Manager tames the DOS beast, and while it may not make this stuff any more pleasant, it *does* make it easier. This chapter tells you everything you need to know.

Starting File Manager

To start File Manager, pull down the File menu and select the **File Manager** command, or press **F5**. You'll see the Specify File Manager List dialog box, as shown below.

 You can also start File Manager by clicking on this button in the WPMain Button Bar.

When you select the File Manager command, WordPerfect first displays the Specify File Manager List dialog box.

This dialog box prompts you about something called a *directory*. I'll be explaining directories a little later on, so if you're not sure what to do, just select **OK**. (If you're familiar with directories, all the better: use the **Directory** text box to enter the directory you want to work with in File Manager.) Eventually, you'll see the File Manager screen, which will look something like (but not exactly like) the one shown on the next page.

The File Manager screen looks pretty complicated, but it all boils down to just two areas: the File Manager commands on the right, and a list of files in the current directory on the left. Before moving on, let's take a closer look at these *file* and *directory* things.

Subdirectories
Current directory

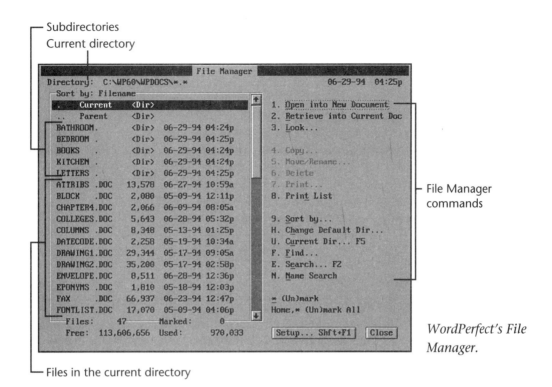

Files in the current directory

WordPerfect's File Manager.

Files and Directories: A Brief Primer

When people ask me to explain files and directories to them (well, no, it doesn't happen *that* often), I always tell them to think of their computer as their house. Not just any old house, mind you, but one with all kinds of servants waiting to do their bidding. (People usually start warming up to the analogy at this point.) The inside of the house—you can think of this as the computer's hard disk—has maids, valets, cooks, and so on; these are the programs (such as WordPerfect) that are installed on the hard disk. Outside the house there are gardeners, landscapers, and chauffeurs; these are the devices attached to the computer (such as the keyboard, printer, or modem).

In the simplest possible terms, your computer's *files* are equivalent to the various elements in the house. As I've said, the people (the servants) are the files that run your programs. The inanimate objects in the house—the furniture, appliances, utensils, and so on—are the data files (such as a WordPerfect document) used by you or your software.

Imagine, for a moment, that this house had no rooms, and that all the stuff inside was just scattered randomly throughout. Clearly, trying to *find* anything in such a place would be, if not impossible, at least frustrating. The problem, of course, is that there's no organization. A normal house has many different rooms, and usually everything in one room is related in one way or another. So, if you were looking for either cooking utensils or food, you'd probably look in the kitchen instead of the bedroom.

Your computer's hard disk also contains a number of "rooms," and these are called *directories*. In a properly organized hard disk, each directory normally contains a number of related files. For example, your WordPerfect directory contains all the files that WordPerfect uses (and, possibly, some of your documents). You may also have separate directories for other programs installed on your computer.

Let's extend the analogy a little further. Some rooms in a house have a smaller room attached to them (such as a walk-in closet in a bedroom, or a dining room in a living room). Even storage spaces such as pantries and cupboards are "room-like" because they store objects. All of these are examples of what we could call "subrooms." Directories can also have "subrooms," and these are called—you guessed it—*subdirectories*. Your main WordPerfect directory has a number of subdirectories. In particular, it probably has a WPDOCS subdirectory that you've been using to store all your documents; this is the default directory displayed by File Manager.

TECHNO NERD TEACHES...

If File Manager's default directory is named WPDOCS, how come we see something like **C:\WP60\WPDOCS*.*** at the top of the File Manager dialog box? Well, the C: part is the letter of the disk drive where WordPerfect is stored (drive C, in this case; if you installed WordPerfect in a different drive, you'll see a different letter). The WP60 part is the name of the main WordPerfect directory. (If you're using version 5.1, the main directory is called WP51.) The WPDOCS part is, as I've said, the subdirectory where WordPerfect stores your documents. The *.* (it's pronounced *star-dot-star*) is a computer short form that means "everything." In this case, it means that File Manager is displaying every file in the WPDOCS subdirectory. (Check out Chapter 21, "Finding Files Quickly with QuickFinder," to get more dirt on this shorthand notation.)

Figuring Out the File List

So, to apply all this to File Manager, the file listing on the left is really just an inventory of objects in one of your hard disk's rooms (in the default case, it's your WPDOCS subdirectory). You'll see all kinds of items listed, but each one falls into one of two categories: subdirectories and files.

The Subdirectory Items

If the current directory has any subdirectories, they'll be displayed near the top of the list. As you can see below, a typical subdirectory entry has a <Dir> identifier, as well as the date and time the subdirectory was created.

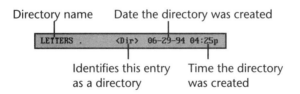

A subdirectory entry from the File Manager list.

What's with the dot (.) and double-dot (..) deals at the top of the list? Well, these are just more DOS shorthand symbols. The dot represents the current directory, and the double dot represents the so-called *parent* directory: the directory out of which the current directory has sprung. For example, we

continues

continued

know the WP60 directory has a WPDOCS subdirectory. WP60
would then be the parent directory of WPDOCS (and
WPDOCS would be the *child* directory of WP60; and no, I
don't know who the heck makes up this stuff).

The File Items

The rest of the list displays the files in the current directory. The following
figure is a typical entry that shows the file's name and extension, its size in
bytes, and the date and time it was last modified. (For more info on file
names, refer to Chapter 7, "Day-to-Day Drudgery I: Saving, Opening, and
Closing.")

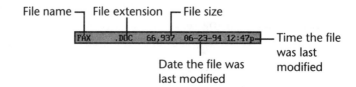

*A file entry from the
File Manager list.*

Navigating the File List

The basic idea behind File Manager is that you highlight a file in the file
list, and then do something to it (copy it, delete it, whatever). The following table lists some of the keys you can use to navigate the file list.

Press	To Move
Up or down arrow	Up or down one file
Page Up or Page Down	Up or down one screenful
Home, Home, up arrow	To the top of the list
Home, Home, down arrow	To the bottom of the list
N+letter	To the first file that starts with *letter*
Enter on a directory	To the directory

If you have a mouse, you can use three methods to navigate the list:

- To highlight a file on the screen, click on the file name.

- To move to another part of the list, use the scroll bars. (If you need some scroll bar basics, trek back to Chapter 8, "Day-to-Day Drudgery II: Navigating Documents," to get the scoop.)

- Double-click on a directory name to move to the directory.

SPEAK LIKE A GEEK

A **byte** is computerese for a single character of information. For example, the phrase "This phrase is 28 bytes long" is, yes, 28 bytes long (you count the spaces too, but not the quotation marks, silly).

What You Can Do with File Manager

Yeah, I know what you'd *like* to do with File Manager, but I'll let you handle that on your own. Otherwise, File Manager can be quite useful. The following sections take you through some of the more common tasks that'll crop up from time to time.

Opening and Retrieving Documents

You normally open a document by selecting the File menu's **O**pen command and then entering the name of the file. But what if you don't remember the name of the file? Or what if it's in a different directory? Or what if you're not sure how to spell it? The solution to these problems is simple: use File Manager to

If you have a mouse, you can open a document quickly just by double-clicking on it.

highlight the document you need, and then select the **O**pen into New Document command. If you want to retrieve the document instead, you need to select the **R**etrieve into Current Doc command. (Chapter 7, "Day-to-Day Drudgery I: Saving, Opening, and Closing," explains the difference between opening and retrieving.)

In 5.1, highlight the file you need, and then select **R**etrieve. If you already have a file open, you'll see the following prompt in the status line:

Retrieve into current document? No (Yes)

Press **N** to open the document in a new work area, or **Y** if you want to combine the files.

Looking at a Document

I *hate* opening the wrong document. It means that not only have I wasted the time it took to open the file, but now I have to close it and go hunting around for the correct one. What a bother. Happily, you can avoid this fate by using File Manager's Look feature. Look lets you examine a document first and *then* decide whether you want to open it.

To try out this feature, highlight the file you want to view and then select the Look command. WordPerfect puts the document on-screen and displays a menu of commands at the bottom (see the following picture). If the file is the one you want, select Open. To view other files in the list, use the Next and Previous commands. If you just want to return to File Manager, select **Close**.

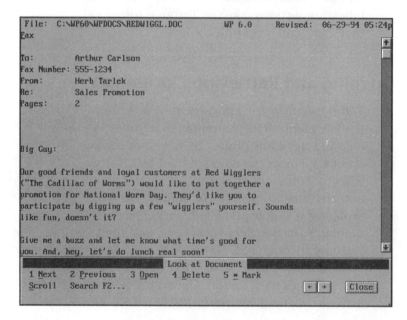

The Look feature in action.

If you want to see more of a file displayed by Look, just use the usual WordPerfect navigation keys or, if you have a mouse, the scroll bar. (This is all covered in Chapter 8, "Day-to-Day Drudgery II: Navigating

Documents.") Look also has a neat Scroll feature: just select the Scroll command, and WordPerfect scrolls through the file. Press **Esc** to stop the scrolling.

Copying Files

If you need to make a copy of a file to a floppy disk or to another directory, File Manager's Copy option will do the job. Just highlight the file and then select Copy. You'll see the Copy dialog box, shown below.

The Look feature is designed mostly for displaying WordPerfect documents. If you happen to select a different type of file accidentally, you may end up with a royal mess on-screen. But don't worry; just select **Close** to get the heck out of there.

Use the Copy dialog box to specify the destination for the copy.

Enter the destination for the file in the Copy Highlighted File to text box. To be safe, you should always include the drive and directory. When you're ready, select **OK** to start copying. If a file with the same name already exists in the destination directory, WordPerfect will ask if you want to replace it. If you're sure you don't need the other file, select **Yes**. (Make sure you're sure, however; once you overwrite a file, it's gone for all time.)

Selecting the **C**opy option in version 5.1's File Manager produces the following prompt at the bottom of the screen:

Copy this file to:

Type in the name of the destination and press **Enter**.

Moving and Renaming Files

If you want to move a file to a new location, or if you want to just give it a different name, highlight the file and select File Manager's **M**ove/Rename command. This displays the Move/Rename dialog box, and all you do is enter the new name or the new location in the New Name text box. When you're done, select **OK**.

Don't move or rename any of the files in your main WordPerfect directory (unless it's a document that you created yourself). WordPerfect expects things to be named a certain way and if something is off by even a letter, the program will complain and moan something fierce (or it may refuse to run altogether). The safest course is to move or rename only those files that you know you've created yourself.

Deleting Files

As you're learning WordPerfect, you'll probably create all kinds of garbage files while you practice the program's features. This is fine, but after awhile these files can really clutter up your hard disk, which makes finding stuff in File Manager a real needle-in-a-haystack exercise. You can use File Manager's Delete option to do periodic housecleanings. Just highlight a file you want to scrap, and then select the Delete command. WordPerfect will ask you to confirm that you want to delete the file. Select **Yes** to delete or **No** to cancel.

Unless you have special "undelete" software (or at least version 5 of DOS), deleted files are gone for good, so you should be absolutely sure you can live without a file before expunging it. If you have *any* doubts whatsoever, use the Look command to take a peek at the file's contents. (If you have DOS 5 or later and you do happen to delete a file accidentally, you may be able to recover it. To learn how, I'd suggest picking up a copy of *The Complete Idiot's Guide to DOS* by the most excellent Jennifer Fulton.)

Once you've highlighted a file, you can select the **Delete** option quickly just by pressing the **Delete** or **Backspace** key.

Selecting Multiple Files

You can perform many File Manager operations (such as opening, copying, and deleting) on a single file or on multiple files. Although you can only highlight one file at a time, you can *mark* other files and File Manager will include them in the operation.

To mark a file, just highlight it and press asterisk (*) or the **Spacebar**. You'll see an asterisk appear beside the file name. To unmark a file, just highlight it and press * or **Spacebar** again. If you need to mark *every* file, press **Home, ***. To unmark all files, press **Home, *** again.

If you have multiple files marked and you select a File Manager command, WordPerfect will usually ask you to confirm that you want to perform the operation on the marked files. Just select Yes to use the marked files or No to perform the operation on only the currently highlighted file.

The Least You Need to Know

This chapter gave you a quick tour of File Manager—WordPerfect's answer to DOS. Here's a brief rundown of what was important:

☞ To start File Manager, select **File Manager** from the File menu (or press **F5**), enter the directory you want to see, and then select **OK**.

☞ File Manager shows you a list of the files in the current directory. This is analogous to looking at a list of the inventory in the room of a house.

☞ To work with a file, highlight it and then select one of File Manager's commands (**C**opy, **M**ove/Rename, **D**elete, and so on).

☞ To select multiple files, you need to mark each one individually. Just highlight each file in turn and press asterisk (*) or the **Spacebar**. Press * or **Spacebar** again to unmark a file.

Exciting Sno-Globe Page!
Draw a picture of your favorite
celebrity, athlete, or political figure,
then shake the book around and watch
them become engulfed in a blizzard of
media attention or public outrage!
Better than CNN, and there's no
monthly service charge!

Chapter 21

Finding Files Quickly with QuickLists and QuickFinder

In This Chapter

- ☛ A brief primer on wild-card characters
- ☛ How to create a QuickList
- ☛ Using a QuickList to display a subset of your documents
- ☛ How to create a QuickFinder index
- ☛ Using QuickFinder to find a file
- ☛ Gaining the upper hand on your documents (before they gain the upper hand on you)

If you use WordPerfect regularly, you probably create at least a few documents a week, if not a few documents a day. Although this doesn't sound like much, over time you can easily end up with dozens or even hundreds of WordPerfect files littering your computer's hard disk. Before things get completely out of hand, you need to start thinking about how you're going to handle all that verbiage.

You can use the File Manager to separate the wheat from the chaff by deleting old files or moving unnecessary files to different locations (see Chapter 20, "Using WordPerfect's File Manager," for details), but it's not a total solution. This chapter examines two features that can make it easier to keep a handle on your files: QuickList and QuickFinder.

File Name Flexibility: Understanding Wild-Card Characters

Before you check out what QuickList and QuickFinder can do, you should know what *wild-card characters* are. If you've ever played poker, you know you can designate one or more cards to be "wild," and they can then assume any value during the game. WordPerfect's wild-card characters operate in a similar fashion, only they're designed to give you more flexibility when dealing with file names.

Why do we need such flexibility? Well, as shown later in this chapter, both QuickList and QuickFinder deal with subsets of the files on your hard disk. With wild-card characters, it's easy to specify exactly the file names you want to work with. (Don't sweat it if this isn't all that clear to you now; things should come nicely into focus as we go along.)

WordPerfect has two wild-card characters: the question mark (?) and the asterisk (*). The question mark matches a single character. When you insert a question mark in a file name, you're saying "I wanna deal only with certain files that have any character at this position." For example, *letter?.doc* would cover any file name where the first six characters are *letter*, the seventh character is anything at all, and the extension is *.doc* (such as LETTER1.DOC, LETTER2.DOC, LETTERS.DOC, and so on).

The asterisk matches multiple characters. For example, **.doc* covers all files that have any primary name (the part to the left of the dot) and the extension *.doc* (such as CHAPTER.DOC, WORF.DOC, or WHATS_UP.DOC).

To help this stuff sink in, here are a few examples that show wild cards in action:

File specification	What you get
?o?ato.doc	All file names where the first and third characters are anything, the second character is *o*, the fourth through sixth characters are *ato*, and the extension is *.doc* (such as TOMATO.DOC and POTATO.DOC, but not POTATOE.DOC).

File specification	What you get
letter?.*	All file names that begin with *letter*, have anything for the seventh character, and have any extension (such as LETTER5.DOC or LETTERS.WP). This example shows that it's perfectly okay to combine the two wild-card characters.
c*.txt	All file names that begin with *c* and have the extension *.txt* (such as CHAP_1.TXT and CRIMINY.TXT).
memo.*	All file names where the primary name is *memo* and any extension (such as MEMO.DOC and MEMO.TXT).
.	Files with any primary name and any extension (i.e., every file).

When you combine names such as **.wp*, *letter?.doc*, and **.** with the drive and directory of the files, you end up with something called a **file specification**, because it specifies exactly which files you want to work with. (The cognoscenti, however, almost always abbreviate this to "file spec" and pronounce it *file speck*.) For example, consider the following file specification:

c:\wp60\wpdocs*.doc

This refers to all files with the .DOC extension in the \WP60\WPDOCS directory on the C drive. (If you're a little leery of directories, take a look at Chapter 20, "Using WordPerfect's File Manager," to learn the basics.)

Working with QuickLists

A QuickList is a file listing narrowed down to only those files with certain names. If you recall the computer house analogy (you know, the one from Chapter 20, "Using WordPerfect's File Manager," where your computer is like a house, and the files on your hard drive are like the objects inside the house; yeah, *that* computer house analogy), a normal directory list would be like looking at a complete inventory of, say, the kitchen's contents. A QuickList for the kitchen, however, might include only the appliances or utensils.

Suppose you write a quarterly report for your company, and you always name the report something like 3RDQTR94.DOC, 1STQTR95.DOC, and so on. You could create a QuickList of, say, only those reports from 1994 (???QTR94.DOC). Then, instead of wading through all your other documents to find the report you want, you could narrow things down by displaying the QuickList.

Creating a QuickList

Before you can use a QuickList, of course, you need to create one. Here are the steps you have to follow:

1. Pull down the File menu and select the File Manager command, or press **F5** to display the Specify File Manager List dialog box.

   You can also display the Specify File Manager List dialog box by clicking on this button in the WPMain Button Bar.

2. Select the **QuickList** button or press **F6**. The QuickList dialog box appears.

3. Select the Create command. WordPerfect displays the Create QuickList Entry dialog box, as shown below.

Use the Create QuickList Entry dialog box to enter a description and file specification for your QuickList.

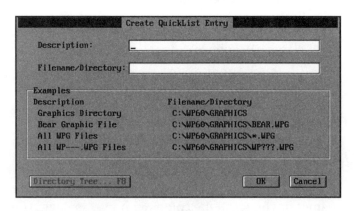

4. Use the **Description** text box to enter a brief description of the files that will appear in the QuickList (e.g., **My 1994 Quarterly Reports**). You can enter up to 40 characters, so there's lots of room to be creative (which also makes it easier to find your QuickLists).

5. Use the **Filename/Directory** text box to enter the file specification for the files you want to appear in the QuickList. Here are some guidelines to follow:

    ☞ Always begin the file specification with the letter of the disk drive that contains the files (this is almost always the drive you used to install WordPerfect; usually C) followed by a colon (:).

    ☞ After the colon, enter the name of the directory where the files can be found. Be sure to include backslashes (\) between the directory names.

    ☞ (Optional) Finish the specification with the file name/wild card combination that defines the files you want to see. If you want to see all the files in the directory, however, just leave off the file name part; WordPerfect will assume you want to see every file in the directory.

6. When you're done, select **OK** to return to the QuickList dialog box.

7. If you want to display a QuickList, skip to the next section. Otherwise, select **Close** to return to the Specify File Manager List dialog box, and then select **Cancel** to return to the document.

Displaying the QuickList Files

Once you've created a QuickList, you can use it to display the subset of files you defined. First, follow steps 1 and 2 from the last section to display the QuickList dialog box, if necessary (see the following figure).

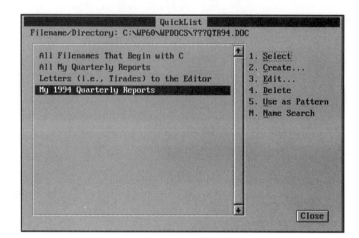

The QuickList dialog box contains a list of all your QuickLists.

Now highlight the QuickList description you want to work with and choose the Select command. WordPerfect opens the File Manager and displays only your QuickList files.

If you need to make changes to a QuickList, just display the QuickList dialog box, highlight the QuickList you want to modify, and then select the Edit command. The Edit QuickList Entry dialog box that appears is identical to the Create QuickList Entry dialog you saw earlier.

If you're sick and tired of a particular QuickList entry and you want to get rid of it, all you need to do is highlight it in the QuickList dialog box and select Delete. When WordPerfect asks if you're sure you want to delete it, select Yes.

Trying QuickFinder On for Size

Way back in Chapter 12, "Search and Ye Shall Replace," I showed you how to hunt down text in the current document using WordPerfect's Search feature. A slightly different scenario might occur when you want to find (and usually open) a document, and you can't remember the name but you're sure it contains some specific words or a particular phrase. For example, you may be trying to find your Christmas list from last year, and you know it contains the word "Super Soaker." You can't use Search, of course, because the document isn't open yet; you could use File Manager's Look command to take a sneak peek at each of your documents, but I assume you've got better things to do over the next week or so. So what's a body to do?

I'm glad you asked. WordPerfect's QuickFinder feature can create an alphabetical index of every word contained in your documents. It's then an easy matter to search this index for, say, "Super Soaker," and WordPerfect displays a list of every file containing this phrase. Pretty slick, huh? The next few sections show you how to work with QuickFinder.

Creating a QuickFinder Index

The first step is to create the alphabetical index of words from your documents. QuickFinder is quite flexible about the whole thing, because it lets you create different indexes for different subsets of files.

Before you create your first index, you need to tell WordPerfect where you want to store your index files. The following steps tell you everything you need to know:

1. Display the Specify File Manager List dialog box by selecting the File menu's File Manager command or by pressing **F5**.

2. Select the Use QuickFinder button or press **F4**. The QuickFinder File Indexer dialog box appears.

   You can combine steps 1 and 2 by clicking on this button in the WPMain Button Bar.

3. Select the **Setup** command or press **Shift+F1**. WordPerfect now displays the QuickFinder File Indexes Setup dialog box.

4. Select the Location of **Files** command to display the QuickFinder Index Files dialog box, as shown in the following figure.

Use the QuickFinder Index Files dialog box to enter the directory where you want to store your index.

QuickFinder Index Files

1. **P**ersonal Path: [   ]

2. **S**hared Path: [   ]

[Directory Tree... F8]   [QuickList... F6]   [OK]   [Cancel]

5. In the **Personal Path** text box, enter the directory where you want your index stored, and then select **OK**. I suggest entering your main WordPerfect directory (usually **c:\wp60**). WordPerfect drops you back at the QuickFinder File Indexes Setup dialog box.

With that malarkey over with, you can now proceed to define your QuickFinder index. Here are the steps to follow:

1. In the QuickFinder File Indexes Setup dialog box, select the Create Index Definition command. The Create Index Definition dialog box appears.

2. Use the Index **Description** text box to enter a brief description for the index. For example, if you want to include all your documents in the index, enter **All My Documents**. When you're done, press **Enter** twice.

3. Select the Add command. The Add QuickFinder Index Directory Pattern dialog box appears. (Are you as sick of these dialog boxes as I am?)

If the files you want to use are already defined by a QuickList, select the **QuickList** button or press **F6**, and then select the QuickList you want from the QuickList dialog box that appears.

4. In the **Filename Pattern** text box, enter a file specification that defines which files you want to include in the index. For example, to include every file in WordPerfect's WPDOCS subdirectory, type **C:\WP60\WPDOCS**. When you're ready, select **OK** to return to the Create Index Definition dialog box. The file specification appears in the Directories and Files to Index list (see the following figure).

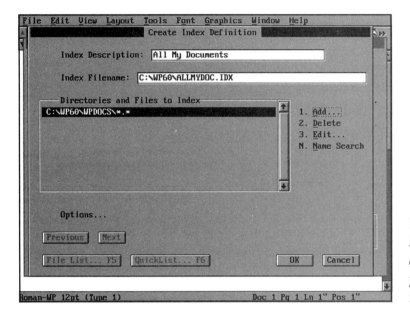

You use the Create Index Definition dialog box to define your QuickFinder index.

5. If you want to add other directories and files to the index, repeat steps 3 and 4. When you've completed the definition, select **OK** to return to the QuickFinder File Indexes Setup dialog box.

6. Select the **Generate Marked Indexes** command. WordPerfect then creates the indexes by marching through each of your documents and alphabetizing each word it finds. (Depending on the number of files you're using and the speed of your computer, this may take as little as a few seconds, or as much as a few minutes.)

7. Select **Close** to return to the QuickFinder File Indexer dialog box.

8. If you want to perform a search, skip to the next section. Otherwise, select **Cancel** to return to the document.

Using a QuickFinder Index to Find a File

Once you've created a QuickFinder index, you can use it to search for documents that contain specific words or phrases. Here are the steps to follow:

1. If necessary, display the QuickFinder File Indexer dialog box, as described in the last section.

2. If you've defined multiple QuickFinder indexes, use the **Index** drop-down list to select the one you want to use.

3. In the **Word** pattern text box, enter the text you want to find.

TECHNO NERD TEACHES...

You can add a bit of sophistication to your searches by inserting one of the five QuickFinder operators in your search text. The And operator (&) finds files that contain one word *and* another. For example, the search text *ben&jerry* finds those files that contain the word *ben* and the word *jerry*. The Or operator (|) finds files that contain one word *or* another. For example, the search text *ben|jerry* finds those files that contain either the word *ben* or the word *jerry*. The Not operator (!)—like the overused expression from "Wayne's World"—finds files that do not contain a word. For example, if you enter *!ben* as the search text, QuickFinder finds those files that don't contain the word *ben*. The other two operators are already familiar to you: the question mark (?), which matches a single character, and the asterisk (*), which matches multiple characters.

4. Select **OK**. WordPerfect scours the index and then displays the File Manager with a list of all the files that contain the text you specified, as shown in the following figure. (If the search text was not found, a different dialog box appears to let you know. In this case, select **OK** to return to the QuickFinder File Indexer dialog box.)

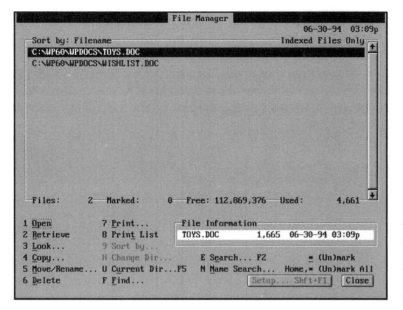

If WordPerfect finds any files that contain your search text, it displays them in the File Manager.

5. If you want to open one of the files, highlight it and select Open. (You can also use the other File Manager commands to work with the selected file; see Chapter 20, "Using WordPerfect's File Manager," for details on these commands.) Otherwise, select **Close** to return to the document.

Updating a QuickFinder Index

Life goes on, of course, after you create a QuickFinder index. In particular, you still create new documents and edit existing ones. This is fine, but it means that your QuickFinder indexes will no longer accurately reflect the words in your documents. To fix this problem, you need to update the index. First display the QuickFinder File Indexer, as described earlier in this chapter, and then use one of the following methods:

☛ If you want to update all your indexes, the fastest way is to select the Update Indexes button. WordPerfect updates all your indexes and returns you to the dialog box. Select **Cancel** to return to the document.

☞ If you don't want every index updated, select **Setup** (or press **Shift+F1**) to display the QuickFinder File Indexes Setup dialog box. For each index you want to update, highlight it and press the **Spacebar**. When you're ready, select the **Generate** button. WordPerfect regenerates each index and then returns you to the QuickFinder File Indexer dialog box. Select **Cancel** to return to the document.

The Least You Need to Know

This chapter showed you the basics of two of WordPerfect's handiest tools: QuickLists and QuickFinder. Let's take a fond look back at some of the chapter's more memorable moments:

☞ Understanding wild-card characters is crucial for getting the most out of QuickLists and QuickFinder. The question mark (?) matches individual characters, and the asterisk (*) matches multiple characters.

☞ A QuickList is a listing of files that has been narrowed down so it includes only files with names that match a particular file specification.

☞ To start a QuickList, select the **File** Menu's **File Manager** command (or press **F5**), select the **QuickList** button (or press **F6**), and then select **Create**.

☞ Before creating your first QuickFinder index, tell WordPerfect where you want to store your index files by selecting the Location of **Files** command in the QuickFinder File Indexes Setup dialog box.

☞ To create an index, select the **Create Index Definition** command in the QuickFinder File Indexes Setup dialog box.

☞ To use a QuickFinder index to find a file, display the QuickFinder File Indexer dialog box, enter your search text in the **Word** pattern text box, and then select **OK**.

Part V
Wielding WordPerfect's Tools

At this stage of your WordPerfect wanderings, you know enough to create and print reasonably polished documents that will look good in just about any setting. But if that was all there is to WordPerfect, it wouldn't be as popular as it is (and nowhere near as expensive, either!). No, this baby is brimming with fancy-shmancy features, most of which are for hard-core word jockeys, and so have little to do with you and me. However, there are a few of these features that can not only add an extra level of sophistication to your documents, but can even make it easier to work with WordPerfect. Too good to be true? Nah. Just try on the eight chapters in this section for size, and you'll see!

Chapter 22

Using the Spell Checker and Thesaurus

In This Chapter

- ☛ Checking your spelling with Speller
- ☛ Handling unusual capitalizations and duplicate words
- ☛ Looking up words you don't know how to spell
- ☛ Trying out WordPerfect's Thesaurus
- ☛ A downright fascinating collection of word words

Words. Whether you're a logophile (a lover of words) or a logophobe (one who has an aversion to words), you can't leave home without 'em. Whether you suffer from logomania (the excessive use of words) or logographia (the inability to express ideas in writing), you can't escape 'em. So far, you've seen ways to edit words, ways to organize them, and ways to get them all dressed up for the prom, but when it comes down to using them, well, you're on your own. But now that changes, because in this chapter you learn about a couple of tractable tools—Speller and Thesaurus—that help you become word-wise (or perhaps even word-perfect). Who knows? With these tools in hand, you may become a full-fledged logolept (a word maniac).

Checking Out WordPerfect's Speller

Nothing can ruin the image of your finely crafted documents more than a few spelling mistakes. In the old days, we could just shrug our shoulders and mumble something about never being good at spelling. With WordPerfect, though, you have no excuses because the darn program comes with a utility called Speller—a built-in spell checker. Speller's electronic brain is stuffed with a 100,000-word strong dictionary that it uses to check your spelling attempts. If it finds something that isn't right, it lets you know and gives you a chance to correct it. You can even look up words that you haven't the faintest idea how to spell, and you can make Speller smarter by adding your own words to its dictionary.

You should save your document before running Speller. Not only might you be making a lot of changes to the document, but it takes time—and if a power failure should hit, you lose all your changes.

To check your spelling in version 5.1, pull down the **Tools** menu and select **Spell** (or just press **Ctrl+F2**). In the prompt at the bottom of the screen, select **Word**, **Page**, or **Document**.

Cranking Up Speller

Speller can check a single word, a text block, a page, everything from the cursor to the end of the document, or the entire document. So the first thing you need to do is position the cursor appropriately:

- ☞ If you're checking a word or page, place the cursor anywhere inside the word or page.

- ☞ If you're checking a block, select the block.

- ☞ If you want Speller to check everything from the cursor to the end of the document, position the cursor where you want WordPerfect to start checking.

To use Speller, pull down the Tools menu, select the **Writing Tools** command, and then, in the Writing Tools dialog box that appears, select **Speller** (you can also simply press **Ctrl+F2**).

You can also start Speller by clicking on this button in either the WPMain or the Tools Button Bar.

At this point, one of two things happens:

☞ If you selected a block, Speller begins checking the block.

☞ Otherwise, the Speller dialog box appears, as shown below. In this case, just tell Speller what you what you want to check (**W**ord, **P**age, **D**ocument, or **F**rom Cursor), and the checking begins.

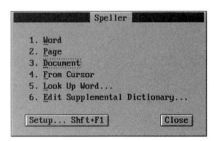

Use the Speller dialog box to specify how much of the document you want to check.

Correcting Spelling Mistakes

If Speller finds something amiss in your document, it highlights the word in the text and displays the Word Not Found dialog box on your screen, as shown here.

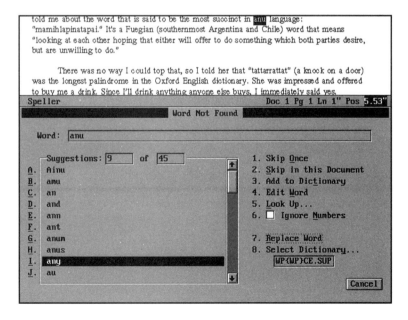

The Word Not Found dialog box appears when Speller finds a word that's not in its vocabulary.

Not only does Speller point out misspelled words, but it's even kind enough to lay out a few suggested alternatives. If you want to use one of these words, highlight it in the Suggestions list and then select the **Replace Word** command.

There are times, however, when a word that Speller doesn't recognize is perfectly legitimate (such as your name, your company's name, or an overly hip word like *cowabunga*). For these cases, Speller gives you four options:

- ☞ Select **Skip Once** to skip this instance of the word.

- ☞ Select **Skip in this Document** to skip all instances of the word in the document.

- ☞ Select Add to Dictionary to include the word in Speller's vocabulary.

- ☞ If the word has a number in it (such as *Fireball XL-5*), activate the Ignore Numbers check box to tell Speller not to flag these sorts of words.

Speller is good, but it's not *that* good. In particular, it won't flag words that are merely misused (as opposed to misspelled). For example, Speller is perfectly happy with either "we're going wrong" or "were going wrong," since everything is spelled correctly. For this grammatical stuff, see Chapter 23, "Painless Grammar Checking."

Editing Words

If Speller flags a word but you don't see the correct spelling in the suggestions (or if you string two words together accidentally, likethis), you can edit the text to make the correction yourself. Just select the Edit **Word** command in the Word Not Found dialog box, and Speller puts the cursor beside the word. Make your changes, and then press **F7** or **Enter**.

Handling Weird Capitalizations

If you leave the Shift key down a split second too long when capitalizing, you end up with words like "SHift" and "TIerra del FUego." Speller will flag these unusual capitalizations and display the Irregular Case dialog box shown in the following figure. You can choose Skip Word to move on, or you can highlight one of the suggestions and select Replace Word. If you'd like to just edit the word, there's also an Edit Word command.

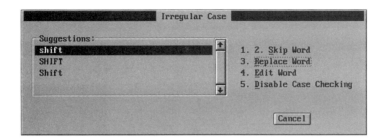

If Speller finds some unusual capitalization, it displays the Irregular Case dialog box.

Handling Duplicate Words

Another blunder that Speller looks out for is when you use the same word twice in in a row (like that). In this case, Speller highlights the second word and displays the Duplicate Word Found dialog box (see the figure below). Select Delete Duplicate Word to fix it. If the duplication is okay (e.g., Pago Pago or "Tora, Tora, Tora!"), select the Skip Duplicate Word command instead. If you have millions of legitimate duplicates in your text, select the Disable Duplicate Word Checking command to get on with your life.

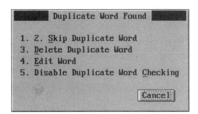

If Speller finds the same word twice in a row, it displays the Duplicate Word Found dialog box.

Looking Up Words

If you're really not sure how to spell a word, you can use Speller to look it up in the dictionary. I know, I know, it's the old story: how do you look up a word that you can't spell? Well, that's the beauty of Speller: all you have to do is take a stab at it, and it displays any word that's even close.

To look up a word, start Speller and select the Look Up Word command to display the Look Up Word dialog box. Type how you think the word *might* be spelled in the Word or Word Pattern text box, and then press

Enter. Speller consults its dictionary and produces a list of suggestions, as shown here.

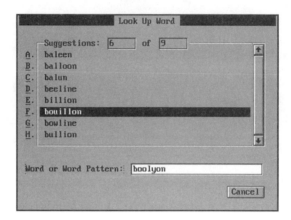

Speller lists every word in its dictionary that is even close to the word you entered.

If you see the word you want, highlight it and press **Enter** to add it to the text. If the word isn't among the suggestions, press **Tab** and enter a new word, or just select **Cancel**.

While Speller is a handy tool, its big problem, of course, is that it won't tell you the meaning of a word. For that you're going to have to rely on a good old-fashioned dictionary. And since Speller isn't infallible, don't treat it as a substitute for a thorough proofreading.

You can even use the wild cards we looked at back in Chapter 21, "Finding Files Quickly with QuickLists and QuickFinder." To refresh your memory, there are two wild-card characters: the question mark (?) and the asterisk (*). The question mark substitutes for individual letters. So, for example, *?oof* finds all the words that begin with any letter and end with *oof* (such as *goof*, *hoof*, and *woof*). The asterisk substitutes for a group of letters. For example, if you can never remember the order of the last four letters of *onomatopoeia*, just look up *onomatop** to find out.

Using the Splendiferous Thesaurus

Did you know that the English language boasts well over 600,000 words (plus about another 400,000-or-so technical terms)? So why use a boring word like *boring* when gems such as *prosaic* and *insipid* are available? What's that? Vocabulary was never your best subject? No problem-o. WordPerfect's built-in Thesaurus can supply you with enough synonyms (words with the same meaning) and antonyms (words with the opposite meaning) to keep even the biggest word hound happy.

Starting the Thesaurus

To see what the Thesaurus can do, place the cursor inside a word, pull down the Tools menu, select **Writing Tools**, and then select **Thesaurus** from the dialog box. WordPerfect highlights the word and displays the Thesaurus dialog box shown below.

 You can also start the Thesaurus by clicking on this button in the Tools Button Bar.

Headword

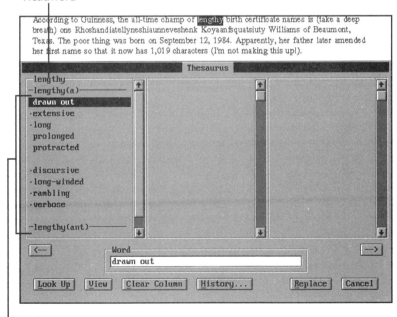

The Thesaurus dialog box.

References

The word at the top of the column is called the **headword**. The words in the list are called **references**.

The Thesaurus displays your word at the top of the first column and displays a list of words beneath it. Depending on the word you used, the list will be divided in up to four different sections: adjectives (a), verbs (v), nouns (n), and antonyms (ant). You can use the up or down arrow keys or the scroll bar to navigate the list. If you see a word you'd like to use instead of the original, highlight it, and then select the Replace button.

Displaying More Words

Not all of the reference words will have exactly the same meaning as the headword. You can often get more ideas by asking the Thesaurus to display the synonyms for one of the reference words. To do this, just highlight the reference word and press **Enter**, or double-click on it. The Thesaurus displays a new list of words in the next column.

If you like, you can keep repeating this process to get new lists of words in other columns as well. To navigate between the columns of words, use the left and right arrow keys, or click on the left and right arrows in the Thesaurus dialog box.

If you get lost among all the columns, select the **History** button to see a list of the headwords. Highlight the column you want and choose the **Select** button. If you want to remove a column from the screen, highlight a word in the column and select the Clear Column button.

The Least You Need to Know

This chapter showed you how to get control of your words with WordPerfect's Speller and Thesaurus utilities. Here's a quick review for the logofascinated:

☞ To start Speller, select **Writing Tools** from the **Tools** menu, and then select **S**peller from the dialog box. (You can also just press **Ctrl+F2**.) Once the Speller dialog box appears, select how much of the document you want to check.

☞ To correct a spelling mistake found by Speller, highlight the word you want to use and select **R**eplace Word.

☞ If a word flagged by Speller is actually spelled correctly, you can select the Add to Dictionary option to include the word in Speller's vocabulary.

☞ If you're not sure how to spell a word, start Speller and select the **L**ook Up command. Type the word as you think it is spelled and press **Enter**. Speller displays a list of possible words. If you see one you want to use, highlight it and press **Enter**.

☞ WordPerfect's Thesaurus can give you a list of synonyms and antonyms for a word. Just place the cursor inside the word, select the **Tools** menu's **Writing Tools** command, and then select **Thesaurus**.

This page unintentionally left blank.

Chapter 23
Painless Grammar Checking

In This Chapter

- About Grammatik, WordPerfect's grammar checker
- Using Grammatik to check your documents interactively
- Fixing (or ignoring) grammatical errors
- Allowing for different writing styles
- Idiot-proof grammar checking that absolutely *doesn't* require you to know a thing about predicates or prepositions

Grammar ranks right up there with root canal and tax audit on most people's Top Ten Most Unpleasant Things list. And it's no wonder, either: all those dangling participles, passive voices, and split infinitives. One look at that stuff and the usual reaction is "Yeah, well split *this*!"

If, like me, you couldn't tell a copulative verb from a correlative conjunction if your life depended on it, help is just around the corner. WordPerfect 6 comes with a tool that will check your grammar for you. That's right, this utility—it's called Grammatik—will actually analyze your document phrase by phrase, sentence by sentence, and tell you if things aren't right. It'll even tell you how to fix the problem and often will be able to do it for you at the press of a key. It's about as painless as grammar gets, and it's the subject of this chapter.

Starting Grammatik

Before starting Grammatik, open or switch to the document you want to check. (You can open files in Grammatik, but it's easier just to display the file first in WordPerfect.) Now pull down the Tools menu, select the **Writing Tools** command, and then select the Grammatik command from the Writing Tools dialog box that appears. In a few moments, the main Grammatik screen will appear, as shown in the picture below.

 You can also start Grammatik by clicking on this button in either the WPMain or Tools Button Bar.

Menu bar ——

Work area —

Grammatik's main screen.

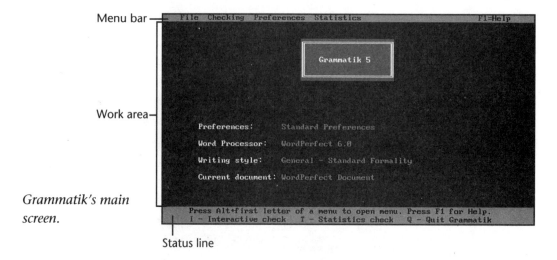

Status line

The Grammatik screen is not unlike the WordPerfect screen in text mode (Grammatik doesn't have a graphics mode). You have a menu bar across the top (it works just like WordPerfect's menu bar) that contains Grammatik's pull-down menus; there's a large work area where everything happens; and there's a status line (actually, the bottom *two* lines) that displays Grammatik's messages and shortcut keys.

The Basic Interactive Check

Grammatik has a number of ways to check your document, but the most straightforward is the *interactive* check. In this case, Grammatik scans your document and stops each time it thinks it has found a problem. It then shows you what's wrong and gives you a chance to correct it on the spot. (Just because Grammatik says something is a problem, doesn't mean it actually *is* a problem. See the section "A Word About Grammatik's Accuracy," later in the chapter.)

To start the interactive check, pull down the Checking menu and select the **Interactive** command (you can also just press I). Whenever Grammatik finds a potential error, you'll see a screen like the one shown here.

For quicker checks, you can narrow Grammatik's focus a little. For example, selecting the Grammar and Mechanics command (shortcut Key: **G**) from the **Checking** menu tells Grammatik to ignore style errors (for example, clichés, passive voice, and wordiness). If you only want to check your spelling, choose the Checking menu's Spelling only command (shortcut key: **E**).

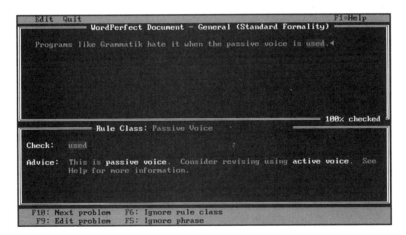

You'll see this screen each time Grammatik finds a possible error.

Grammatik divides the work area into two boxes. The top box shows a section from your document, with the offending word or phrase high-lighted. The bottom box is Grammatik's commentary on the problem, and it usually contains the following parts:

Rule Class   Grammatik divides grammar problems into 72 different types or *classes*. This line tells you which class the current problem falls under.

Check   This is the word or phrase in your document that caused Grammatik to go "tsk, tsk."

Advice   This is what Grammatik thinks you ought to do about the problem.

Replacement   This is Grammatik's suggested replacement for the errant prose. You'll see this only on certain types of problems.

Some of Grammatik's explanations can get pretty technical. If you feel brave enough, you can look up some of the more arcane terms in Grammatik's glossary. Just press **F1** to pull down the **Help** menu, and select the **Glossary** command. In the list that appears, highlight a word or phrase and press **Enter**. When your mind is sufficiently messed up with all that grammar gobbledygook, press **Esc** twice to bail out and return to the checking screen.

Handling Grammatik's Errors

Once Grammatik displays an error, you need to decide what the heck to do with it. The Edit menu lists all your possible courses of action. (Not all of these commands will be available for each problem.) Here's a rundown of the more common ones:

- **Skip to next problem**   This command (one of my favorites) just ignores the problem altogether and tells Grammatik to move on.

  Shortcut key: F10

- **Edit this problem**   Selecting this command places a cursor in the document area so you can make changes to the document yourself. When you're done, press **Esc**.

  Shortcut key: F9

- **Replace problem**   This command tells Grammatik to fix the problem using its suggested replacement. If the problem is a spelling error, you'll see a list of possible words. In this case, highlight the word you want and press **Enter**.

  Shortcut key: F2

☞ **Replace problem, skip to next**   This is the same as above, except that Grammatik moves on to the next problem once it has finished the replacement.

Shortcut key: F3

☞ **Mark this problem**   If you don't want to fix the problem, but you don't want to ignore it either, this command will insert Grammatik's advice into the document at the point of the error.

Shortcut key: F8

☞ **Ignore class from now on**   This command instructs Grammatik to ignore any other instances of this rule class.

Shortcut key: F6

☞ **Learn misspelled word**   For words that Grammatik flags as misspelled or unusual capitalization, use this command to add the word to Grammatik's dictionary.

Shortcut key: F7

☞ **Ignore phrase from now on**   This command tells Grammatik not to flag any other instances of the highlighted phrase.

Shortcut key: F5

TECHNO NERD TEACHES...

The grammar hounds in the audience might want to check out the **Edit** menu's **Show parts of speech info** command (the shortcut key is **F4**). This displays the various parts of speech (nouns, verbs, conjunctions, and so on) that Grammatik has assigned to the words in the problem sentence.

Quitting Interactive Check

Grammar checking is a complex business, so Grammatik can take a while to go through a large document. If important duties beckon (such as lunch), you can quit the interactive check at any time by selecting one of the following four Quit menu commands:

☞ **Quit, Save work so far**   This command quits the interactive check and saves any changes you've made so far.

Shortcut key: S

☛ **Quit, place Bookmark**   Select this command if you want to pick up where you left off later on. (You can do that by selecting the Checking menu's **Resume interactive** command in the main Grammatik screen.)

Shortcut key: B

☛ **Quit, mark rest of document**   This command continues checking, but just marks up the document with Grammatik's sage advice.

☛ **Cancel, ignore work so far**   Use this command to quit and restore the document to its original state. Grammatik will ask if you're sure you want to quit. Select **Yes**.

Shortcut key: Ctrl+C

A Word About Grammatik's Accuracy

Grammatik is probably one of the most sophisticated software programs on the market today. As you've seen, it can do some pretty amazing things—but in the end, it's no match for the English language. There are just too many strange rules and too many ways to throw sentences together. As a result, Grammatik will often either miss some obvious problems or flag things that are okay.

Here's an example where Grammatik missed a glaring error, but flagged something that was fine.

Grammatik is good, but it's no match for the complexity of English.

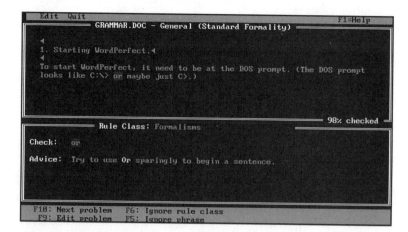

The phrase "it need to be" is bad English in anyone's book (except, possibly, for the bogus Indians in Grade-B westerns), but Grammatik missed it completely. On the other hand, it thinks that the "or" is starting a new sentence. (It was probably thrown off by the prompt symbol C:\>. It seems DOS messes with *everyone's* head!)

The lesson here is not that Grammatik is a lousy program, because it's not. It's just that you shouldn't lean on it too heavily. Take Grammatik's advice with a grain of salt—and always proofread your work yourself.

Working with Writing Styles

Obviously, not all documents are created equal. Some are stiff and formal, while others are relaxed and jaunty (and others, like portions of this book, are just downright silly). Each of these styles requires different standards of grammar. For example, in more relaxed writing, jargon and clichés are okay, whereas technical writing contains longer and more complex sentences.

For these different kettles of fish, Grammatik lets you choose from a number of different writing styles and levels of formality. And, if you're feeling spunky enough, you can even create your own custom styles. The next few sections tell you everything you need to know.

Selecting a Different Style

To select a different style, pull down the **Preferences** menu in Grammatik's main screen and select the **Writing style** command (or just press **W**). You'll see the Select Writing Style screen shown here.

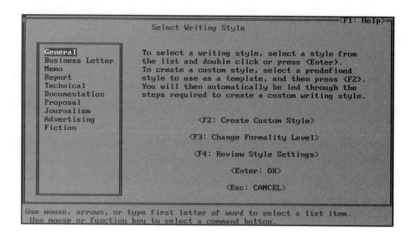

Use the Select Writing Style screen to choose a different writing style.

Before choosing a style, you might want to review its individual grammar settings. To do this, press **F4** or click on the **Review Style Settings** button. Grammatik displays the first of four screens that contain the various rule classes. To navigate the screens, use the following techniques:

- ☞ Press **Enter** or click on the **Enter: Next** button to go forward.

- ☞ Press **Backspace** or click on **Backspace: Previous** to go backward.

- ☞ Press **Esc** or click on **Esc: CANCEL** to return to the Select Writing Style screen.

The first three screens (Grammar Rules, Mechanical Rules, and Style Rules) list various check boxes with scary-sounding names. If a check box is activated (if it has an "X" in it), it means that Grammatik checks your document for that rule if you use this style. The fourth screen, Thresholds, lists this style's limits for things like sentence length and the number of sentences using passive voice.

To navigate the style list faster, press the first letter of the style you want.

To choose a different style, return to the Select Writing Style screen, use the up and down arrow keys to highlight a style, and then press **Enter**. Or you can double-click on the style with a mouse.

Changing the Formality Level

The level of *formality* is a measure of how exacting Grammatik is when it checks your documents. The Informal level is the most easygoing (it'll accept contractions, such as *it'll*, for example), while the Formal level won't let you get away with much.

To change the formality level, press **F3** or click on the **Change Formality Level** button in the Select Writing Style screen. You'll see the Select Level of Formality screen with a list of the three levels: **Informal**, **Standard**, and **Formal**. Select the one you want by highlighting it and pressing **Enter**, or by double-clicking on it.

Creating a Custom Style

Once you've used Grammatik for a while, you may notice certain types of ignorable errors keep cropping up. For example, Grammatik may complain about sentences being too long, or numbers that should be spelled out (if you've used "2" instead of "two"). Believe me, it doesn't take long before these things get awfully annoying. The remedy isn't to chuck Grammatik out the window, but to create your own styles that don't check for these errors.

Here are the steps to follow to create your own custom style:

1. In the Select Writing Style screen, highlight the style upon which you want to base your custom style.

2. Press **F2** or click on the **Create Custom Style** button. The Select Style to Customize screen appears.

3. Grammatik lets you create up to three custom styles (Custom 1, Custom 2, or Custom 3), so highlight one from the list and then press **Enter** or click on the **Enter: OK** button. Grammatik prompts you to enter a name for the style.

4. Enter a name (no more than 23 characters) and press **Enter** or click on the **Enter: OK** button. Grammatik displays the first of the rules screens.

5. Go through the rules check boxes on-screen, activating those you want to use and deactivating those you want to ignore.

6. When you're done, press **Enter** or click on the **Enter: Next** button to move to the next screen.

7. Repeat Steps 5 and 6 for each of the screens. When you exit Screen 4, Grammatik asks if you're ready to save the style.

8. Press **Enter** to save it. Grammatik returns you to the Select Writing Style screen and displays the new style at the bottom of the list.

WordPerfect's Speller checks spelling, doubled words, and unusual capitalizations anyway (see Chapter 22, "Using the Spell Checker and Thesaurus"), so you can speed up Grammatik by creating a custom style that doesn't use these checks. You'll find each of these rules on the Mechanical Rules screen.

Quitting Grammatik

When you've had enough of independent clauses and indefinite pronouns, you can quit Grammatik by returning to the main screen and selecting **Quit** from the File menu (or by pressing **Q**).

The Least You Need to Know

This chapter showed you the ins and outs of using Grammatik, WordPerfect 6's new grammar-checking program. Here's a recap:

☞ To start Grammatik, select Writing Tools from the Tools menu, and then select Grammatik from the dialog box.

☞ To start Grammatik's interactive check, select **Interactive** from the **C**hecking menu (or just press **I**).

☞ When Grammatik flags a possible error, check out the **Edit** menu for a list of your options.

☞ To quit the interactive check, select one of the commands from the **Quit** menu.

☞ Grammatik can allow for different writing styles. To work with a different style, select the **Writing style** command from the **Preferences** menu (or just press **W**) and choose the style you want from the list that appears.

☞ To use a different level of formality, press **F3** or click on the **Change Formality Level** button, and then select the level you want from the list.

Special bonus: virtual text page.
(There's virtually no text on it.)

Chapter 24

Image Is Everything: WordPerfect's Graphics Boxes

In This Chapter

- Sprucing up your documents with clip art
- Creating fancy boxes for your text
- Moving and sizing graphics boxes
- Editing graphics boxes
- More fun time-wasting tools that just about guarantee you'll never get your work done

Television commercials assure us nowadays that "image is everything." And since they couldn't put it on TV if it wasn't true (!), we need to think about what kind of image our documents present to the outside world. You've seen in earlier chapters how a few fonts and other formatting options can do wonders for drab, lifeless text. But *anybody* can do that kind of stuff. To make your documents really stand out from the crowd, you need to go graphical with clip art figures and text boxes. Happily, WordPerfect has the tools that not only get the job done, but make the whole thing a snap. This chapter gives you the graphics nitty-gritty.

TECHNO NERD TEACHES...

If you want to learn how to use WordPerfect's graphics lines, turn to Chapter 28, "A Dozen Great WordPerfect Ideas," to see them in action.

Adding Graphics Boxes to a Document

To keep your regular text and your graphics (images such as clip art figures and logos) separate, most WordPerfect graphics appear inside *graphics boxes*. These boxes are like islands floating in the sea of your document because the regular text flows around them. But unlike real islands, graphics boxes can be moved and sized, and you can apply a fistful of formatting options to them.

What can you put inside a graphics box? Well, all kinds of things, really, but the most common are clip art images and text.

Adding a Clip Art Image to a Document

If you don't have the time, inclination, or talent for creating your own graphic images, don't worry. WordPerfect comes with its own clip art collection. *Clip art* is professional-quality artwork you can incorporate into your documents free of charge. With WordPerfect, you get a few dozen images of everything from a dragon to a windmill. But the real fun begins after you've added the graphic because you can then move it around, change its size, rotate it, or add a caption—you name it.

Adding a clip art figure is as easy as opening a file. The first thing you should do is position the insertion point where you want the image to appear in the document. Then pull down the Graphics menu and select the Retrieve Image command. WordPerfect displays the Retrieve Image File dialog box, in which you can select the file you want in one of two ways:

☞ If you know the name of the file you want to use, enter it in the Filename text box and select **OK**.

☛ If you're not sure which file you want, select the **File List** button or press **F5**, and then choose **OK** in the Select List dialog box that appears. WordPerfect displays the File List dialog box, shown below. Now highlight the file you want to retrieve and choose Select. The image appears in your document.

If you'd like to take a gander at the graphic before retrieving it, select the File Manager command (or press **F5**) in the File List dialog box. When the File Manager appears, highlight the file you want to view and select the Look command.

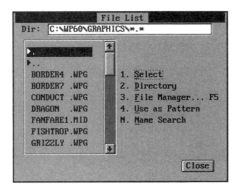

Use the File List dialog box to select the image you want to retrieve.

Once you have your image in the document, you can move it around, change its size, add a caption, and more. I'll show you how to do these things later in this section.

Adding a Text Box to a Document

Throughout this book I've placed various notes, tips, and cautions in separate sections like this:

Placing text in its own box like this is a great way to highlight important material and catch the reader's attention.

You can do the same thing in your WordPerfect documents by creating a *text box*. Here are the steps to follow:

1. Begin by positioning the insertion point where you want the box to appear.

2. Pull down the Graphics menu, select Graphics **B**oxes, and select Create in the cascade menu. WordPerfect displays the Create Graphics Box dialog box.

3. Select the Create Text command. WordPerfect displays a box in which you enter the text.

4. Type the text you want to appear in the box, add any formatting you need, and then press **F7**.

5. Select **OK**. WordPerfect returns you to the document and inserts the text box. (See below.)

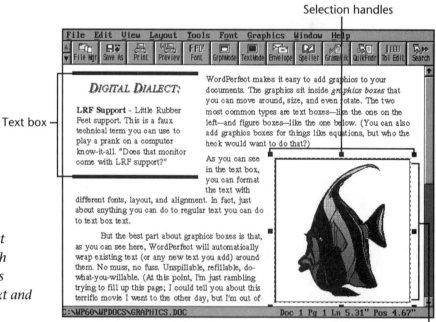

Selection handles

Text box →

A WordPerfect document with graphics boxes containing text and clip art.

Figure box

Editing a Graphics Box

If you need to make changes to a graphics box, you have to select it first. If you're going to be sizing the graphics box with your mouse (as explained a little later on), click on the box. Every graphics box has a border that defines its boundaries. When you select a box, WordPerfect displays black squares or boxes called *selection handles* around the frame of the graphics box. (Take a look at the figure box in the picture shown earlier to see an example of these selection handles.)

For other editing chores, you need to display the Edit Graphics Box dialog box (shown below) using either of the following methods:

☞ With your mouse, double-click on the graphics box.

☞ Pull down the Graphics menu, select Graphics **B**oxes, and select Edit. In the Select Box to Edit dialog box that appears, select **D**ocument Box Number and enter the number of the graphics box (WordPerfect numbers the boxes according to their position in the document). Select the Edit Box button.

While you're in the Edit Graphics Box dialog box, you can work with the document's other graphics boxes by selecting either the **Previous** button (you can also press **Home, Page Up**) or the **Next** button (**Home, Page Down**).

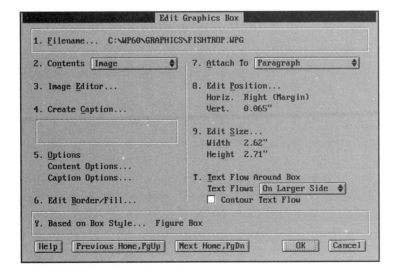

Use the Edit Graphics Box dialog box to, well, edit your graphics boxes.

Editing the Contents of a Graphics Box

If you want to change the text inside a text box or the figure inside a figure box, display the Edit Graphics Box dialog box, and then do one of the following:

- For a figure box, select the Filename command, and then go through the procedure described earlier to select the new image file.

- For a text box, select the Edit Text command. WordPerfect displays the text box text where you can make your changes. When you're done, press **F7** to return to the Edit Graphics Box dialog box.

Moving a Graphics Box

When you add a graphics box to a document, its position isn't set in stone; you can move it anywhere you like. There are two methods you can use:

- With your mouse, position the mouse pointer inside the box you want to move, hold down the left mouse button (the mouse pointer changes to a four-headed arrow), and then drag the box to its new location. As you're dragging, you'll see a dotted outline around the box that tells you where the new location will be. When the dotted line is where you want it to be, release the mouse button.

- If you don't have a mouse, you can still move a graphics box. Begin by displaying the Edit Graphics Box dialog box. Use the Attach To pop-up list to choose where you want the graphic positioned relative to (Paragraph, Page, etc.). Then select the Edit Position command. In the dialog box that appears, use the controls in the **Horizontal Position of Box** and the **Vertical Position of Box** groups to position the box. (Just to make our lives complicated, the controls that appear will vary depending on which option you selected in the Attach To pop-up list.) When you're done, select **OK**.

Sizing a Graphics Box

If a graphics box doesn't have the dimensions you want, changing the size is no problem. Again, you can use either of two methods.

As with moving graphics boxes, sizing them is infinitely easier with a mouse. Select the box you want to size, and position the mouse pointer over one of the selection handles (the pointer will change to a two-headed arrow). Hold down the left mouse button, and then drag the selection handle until the box is the size and shape you want. When you release the button, WordPerfect resizes the box. Which selection handle should you use? Well, if you want to change the size horizontally or vertically, use the appropriate handle on the middle of a side. To change the size in two directions at once, use the appropriate corner handle.

Alternatively, display the Edit Graphics Box dialog box and select the Edit **S**ize command. In the Graphics Box Size dialog box that appears, activate the Set **W**idth and Set **H**eight radio buttons and use their text boxes to enter the new dimensions. Select **OK** when you're done.

If you think you'll be changing the contents of the graphics box at some future date, you might consider activating the Automatic Width and Automatic Height radio buttons. This tells WordPerfect to adjust the dimensions of the graphics box automatically to accommodate the contents of the box.

Setting the Border and Fill Styles for a Graphics Box

As I mentioned earlier, every graphics box has a border surrounding it. The default border is a bit drab, but if you'd like something with a little more pizzazz, WordPerfect comes with over a dozen different border styles.

You can also change something called the *fill style*. The fill style is the background on which the contents of the box are displayed. The default is plain white, but there are all kinds of weird and wonderful patterns you can use. Here are some example boxes with various borders and fill styles.

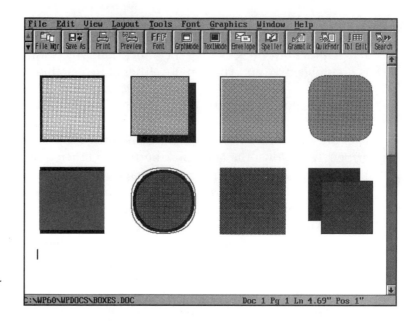

A few of WordPerfect's border and fill styles.

To change the border and fill styles, display the Edit Graphics Box dialog box and select the Edit **Border/Fill** command. WordPerfect displays the Edit Graphics Box Border/Fill dialog box. You use the following techniques to change the border and fill style:

☞ To change the border, select the **Based on Border Style** command, highlight a border style in the Border Styles dialog box, and then choose Select.

☞ To add a shadow effect, select the Shadow command, choose a Shadow Type from the Shadow dialog box, and then select **OK**.

☞ To set the fill style, select the Fill command and select Fill Style in the dialog box that appears. Highlight a fill style in the Fill Styles dialog box, and then choose Select. Select **OK** to return to the Edit Graphics Box Border/Fill dialog box.

When you're done, select the **Close** button to return to the Edit Graphics Box dialog box.

Wrapping Text Around a Graphics Box

One reason it's so easy to use graphics boxes is that WordPerfect automatically wraps the regular document text around the box. And moving or sizing the box is no problem because the text adjusts as you move or size the graphics box.

By default, WordPerfect wraps text around the box border and wraps on the side of the object that has the largest amount of white space. To change these defaults, display the Edit Graphics Box dialog box, and then use the **Text Flows** pop-up list to select a wrapping option (On Larger Side, On Left Side, etc.). If you want the text to follow the contours of the graphics box contents, activate the **Contour Text Flow** check box.

Adding a Caption to a Graphics Box

Captions provide an easy way to add explanatory text to a figure box or other graphic. For example, if you use a caption to name a figure (for example, Figure 1), you can use the name to refer to the figure from the document text (for example, "Take a look at Figure 1 to see what I mean").

To add a caption, display the Edit Graphics Box dialog box and select the Create Caption command. In the screen that appears, enter the caption and press **F7**. When you select **OK** to return to the document, WordPerfect displays the caption below the graphics box.

Working with the Image Editor

WordPerfect also includes an Image Editor for working with the images inside figure boxes. The Image Editor is a set of controls that allow you to manipulate image attributes such as rotation, scaling, colors, and more. To check out the Image Editor, display the Edit Graphics Box dialog box, and then select the Image Editor command. WordPerfect displays the Image Editor, as shown in the following figure.

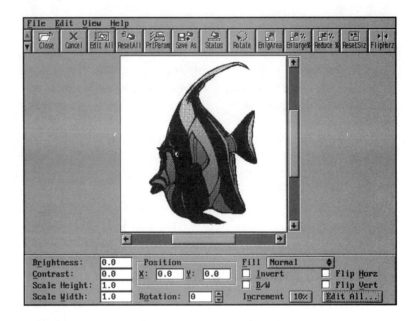

The Image Editor screen.

Here's a summary of the available controls:

Brightness   Sets the brightness (or the *saturation*) of the colors in the image. Enter a value between –1.0 (totally black) and 1.0 (totally white). You can also adjust the brightness by pressing comma (,) to darken the image, or by pressing period (.) to lighten it.

Contrast   Sets the contrast between the light and dark areas of the image. Enter a value between –1.0 (only a slight contrast) and 1.0 (major contrast). You can also decrease the contrast by pressing less than (<) or increase the contrast by pressing greater than (>).

Scale **Height** and Scale **Width**   Scales the height and width of the image. A value of 1.0 represents the current height or width. Entering, say, 0.5 reduces the height or width by one half. (Note that these values don't have anything to do with the size of the graphics box; these settings only affect the size of the image inside the graphics box.)

Position   Moves the image within the box (not to be confused with moving the entire box, which we discussed earlier). For the X text box, entering a positive number moves the image right; entering a negative number moves the image left. For the Y text box, entering a positive number moves the image up; entering a negative number moves the image down.

Rotation Rotates the image. Use the spinner to set the number of degrees of rotation (between 0 and 359). You can also rotate the image by pressing plus (+) or minus (–).

Fill Controls the colors inside the image. You can choose Normal, Transparent (i.e. no colors), or **White**.

Invert Changes the image colors to their complementary values (red changes to green, blue changes to yellow, and so on).

B/W Displays the image in black and white.

Flip Horz Flips the image along its horizontal axis.

Flip Vert Flips the image along its vertical axis.

To close the Image Editor, pull down the File menu and select Close, or press **F7**.

If you botch the editing job, you can reset the image to its original settings by pressing **Ctrl+Home**.

The Least You Need to Know

This chapter took you through some of WordPerfect's fun graphics tools. Here's what happened:

- ☞ You can insert graphics boxes anywhere in your document, and WordPerfect will automatically wrap the existing text around the box.

- ☞ To include clip art images in a document, select the Graphics menu's **Retrieve Image** command, and then specify the file you want to use.

- ☞ To add a text box, select **Graphics Boxes** from the Graphics menu, and then select **Create**. In the Create Graphics Box dialog box, select the **Create Text** command.

- ☞ To move a graphics box, drag it with your mouse. Or, display the Edit Graphics Box dialog box and select the Edit **Position** command.

continues

continued

☞ To size a graphics box, use your mouse to click on it and drag the selection handles. Or, display the Edit Graphics Box dialog box and select the Edit Size command.

☞ To change the border or fill pattern, display the Edit Graphics Box dialog box, and then select the Edit Border/Fill command.

☞ To change the attributes of a figure box image, display the Edit Graphics Box dialog box, and then select the Image Editor command.

Chapter 25

Techniques for Terrific Tables

In This Chapter

- ☛ What is a table and how is it useful?
- ☛ Creating tables from scratch or by converting existing text
- ☛ Populating a table with data
- ☛ Miscellaneous table editing techniques
- ☛ Using formulas to turn mild-mannered tables into powerful spreadsheets, able to leap tall calculations in a single bound

In this chapter, you'll learn a bit of computer carpentry as I show you how to build and work with tables. Don't worry, though, if you can't tell a hammer from a hacksaw; the kinds of tables we'll be dealing with are purely electronic because in WordPerfect, a *table* is a rectangular grid of rows and columns in a document. You can enter all kinds of info into a table, including text, numbers, and graphics. And if you're feeling really ambitious, you can even create formulas that turn the table into a reasonably powerful spreadsheet. No guff. This chapter takes you ever-so-gently through everything you need to know.

What Is a Table?

Despite their name, tables aren't really analogous to those big wooden things you eat on every night. Instead, as I've said, a WordPerfect table is a rectangular arrangement of rows and columns on your screen. The picture below shows an example table.

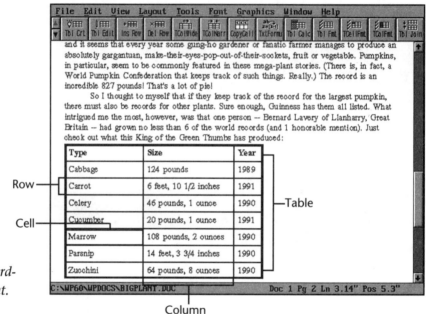

A table in a Word-Perfect document.

Row

Cell

Table

Column

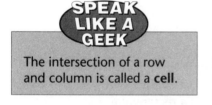

The intersection of a row and column is called a **cell**.

Way back in Chapter 14, "Making Your Lines and Paragraphs Look Good," you learned how to use tabs to make your text line up all nice and pretty. So why use a table when tabs can do a similar job? Good question. Here are just a few advantages that tables bring to the table (sorry about that):

☛ Each table cell is self-contained. You can edit and format the contents of a cell without disturbing the arrangements of the other cells.

☛ The text wraps inside each cell, making it a snap to create multiple-line entries.

☛ You can format a table as a whole, including the font, justification, and the style and color of the lines that separate each cell.

☛ You can create formulas that perform calculations on one or more table cells. You can add 'em up, multiply 'em together, or divide 'em by the square root of the price of tea in China. Whatever you need.

WordPerfect Woodworking: How to Build a Table

WordPerfect gives you two ways to create a table: you can either build it from scratch by creating the table and then entering the info, or you can convert existing text into a table. The next couple of sections show you each of the methods.

Building a Table from Scratch

If you don't have the table data already in your document, it's usually easiest to create the table first and then enter the data later. Follow these steps to create a table:

1. Position the cursor where you want the table to appear in the document.

2. Pull down the Layout menu, select Tables, and then select Create. (Alternatively, press **Alt+F7**, and then select Create in the Tables group.) WordPerfect displays the Create Table dialog box, shown below.

 You can also display the Create Table dialog box by clicking on this button in the Tables Button Bar.

Use the Create Table dialog box to specify the size of the table.

3. Use the Columns spinner to enter the number of columns for the table. (Don't sweat it if you're not sure how many columns you need; you can always add more columns—or delete extra ones—later on.)

4. Use the **R**ows spinner to enter the number of rows for the table. (Again, you can just guess at the number of rows you need and make any adjustments later.)

5. Select **OK**. WordPerfect displays the table editing window. (See "Table Refinishing: Editing a Table," to learn more about this window.)

6. Select **Close**. WordPerfect returns you to the document and inserts the table.

Miraculously Converting Existing Text into a Table

If you already have some text formatted with tabs, you can still get into the table act because WordPerfect makes it easy to convert existing text into a table. You begin by selecting the text you want to convert. Then pull down the Layout menu, select Tables, and then select Create. In the Create Table from Block dialog box that appears, make sure the Tabular Text radio button is active, and then select **OK**. When the table editing window appears, select **Close**. (Again, see "Table Refinishing: Editing a Table," later in this chapter, to get the scoop on the table editing window.)

Entering Table Values

Once you've created your table, your next task is to enter the table values (or you may need to make changes to the existing values if you converted some text into the table). As I mentioned earlier, the intersection between each row and column in a table is called a *cell*, and you enter your text into these cells.

To try this out, click on the cell you want to work with, or use the up and down arrow keys to move the cursor into the table. Then use the following keyboard techniques to get around:

To move	Press
Right one column	Tab
Left one column	Shift+Tab
Up one row	Up arrow
Down one row	Down arrow
To the first cell in the row	Ctrl+Home, Home, left arrow
To the last cell in the row	Ctrl+Home, End
To the first cell in the column	Ctrl+Home, Home, up arrow
To the last cell in the column	Ctrl+Home, Home, down arrow
To the first cell in the table	Ctrl+Home, Home, Home, up arrow
To the last cell in the table	Ctrl+Home, Home, Home, down arrow

Now just enter the value you want to appear in the cell. Here are some guidelines to keep in mind:

- ☛ If your text is longer than the width of the cell, WordPerfect wraps the text and adjusts the height of the cell to accommodate the entry.

- ☛ To start a new line in a cell, press **Enter**.

- ☛ To enter a tab, press **Home, Tab**.

TECHNO NERD TEACHES...

If you have cells with multiple lines, pressing the up arrow and down arrow keys will only move you from line to line. To hop over a cell with multiple lines, press **Alt+up arrow** or **Alt+down arrow**.

Table Refinishing: Editing a Table

Okay, now that you've built your table and filled it with data, it's time to step back a little and cast a critical eye on your creation. Do you need to format the table characters? Would you prefer it if a particular column was wider or narrower? How about trying a different border?

For some table chores, you can simply use the formatting commands you suffered through earlier in this book. For example, to change the font of a cell, just highlight the cell text and then choose your font options (as described in Chapter 13, "Making Your Characters Look Good").

Other table tasks (such as changing the border style) can only be done using the table editing window you saw earlier. To check it out, position the cursor inside the table, pull down the Layout menu, select **Tables**, and then select **Edit** (or just press **Alt+F11**). WordPerfect displays your table in the table editing window, shown below.

 You can also display the table editing window by clicking on this button in either the Tables or WPMain Button Bar.

	A	B	C
1	Type	Size	Year
2	Cabbage	124 pounds	1989
3	Carrot	6 feet, 10 1/2 inches	1991
4	Celery	46 pounds, 1 ounce	1990
5	Cucumber	20 pounds, 1 ounce	1991
6	Marrow	108 pounds, 2 ounces	1990
7	Parsnip	14 feet, 3 3/4 inches	1990
8	Zucchini	64 pounds, 8 ounces	1990

C:\WP60\WPDOCS\BIGPLANT.DOC   Cell A1 Doc 1 Pg 2 Ln 3.41" Pos 1.44"

Table_A   Table Edit
Column Width Ctrl+Arrows Ins   Del   Move/Copy   Calc   Names   Close
  1 Cell 2 Column 3 Row   4 Table 5 Formula 6 Lines/Fill 7 Join 8 Split

The table editing window.

The Table Editing Window

Before you perform any kind of editing in the table editing window, you need to let WordPerfect know whether you want to work with a single cell, multiple cells, whole rows or columns, or the entire table. Here are the guidelines to follow:

- ☞ If you want to work with a particular cell, select it by either clicking on it with your mouse or by using the arrow keys.

- ☞ To work with multiple cells, select the ones you want to work with. Use the same techniques you learned for selecting text back in Chapter 11, "Block Partying: Working with Blocks of Text."

- ☞ To work with a whole row or column, just select a single cell in the row or column. You'll then specify that you want to work with the entire row or column later in the operation (how you do this depends on which operation you're performing).

- ☞ To work with the entire table, select any cell. (Again, you'll specify you want to work with the table as a whole later, as explained below).

Here's a quick rundown of just some of the ways the table editing window lets you muck about with your tables:

Changing the width of a column   Select any cell in the column and then press either **Ctrl+left arrow** (to make the column narrower) or **Ctrl+right arrow** (to make it wider).

Inserting a new row into the table   Select any cell in the row below which you want the new row to appear, and then select the Ins button. In the Insert dialog box, activate the Rows radio button and select **OK**.

Inserting a new column into the table   Select any cell in the column to the right of which you want the new column to appear, select Ins, activate Columns, and then select **OK**.

Deleting the contents of a cell   Highlight the cell, select Del, activate the Cell Contents radio button, and then select **OK**.

Deleting a row or column   Highlight a cell in the row or column and select Del. In the Delete dialog box, select either Columns or Rows, and then select **OK**.

Formatting one or more cells   Select the cells and then select the Cell command; for columns, select Column; for rows, select **R**ow; for the entire table, select **T**able. In each case, a Format dialog box (for example, Cell Format) appears with various formatting options. Select the options you want and select **OK**.

TECHNO NERD TEACHES...

Most of the Format dialog boxes include a Number Type command. If your table includes numbers, you can use this command to format the numbers to include dollar signs, percent signs, and more.

When you've finished formatting the table, select the **Close** button in the table editing window to return to the document.

Formatting with the Tables Button Bar

To make your table formatting and editing even easier, the Tables Button Bar includes a fistful of buttons that put most of the table editing window stuff a mere mouse click away. Here's a rundown:

Button	Function
Ins Row	Inserts a row above the current row.
Del Row	Deletes the current row.
TColWide	Widens the current column.
TColNarr	Narrows the current column.
Tbl Fmt	Displays the Table Format dialog box.
TCellFmt	Displays the Cell Format dialog box.
TColFmt	Displays the Column Format dialog box.

Number Crunching: Working with Formulas

Although many tables simply display information, you can also use *formulas* to turn the table into a spreadsheet that performs calculations. A formula is an expression that calculates a result. Most formulas consist of one of more values (called *operands*) combined with one or more *operators*. In WordPerfect, an operand can be any one of the following:

☞ A number.

☞ A function (a predefined formula that comes with WordPerfect).

☞ The value of another cell in the table. To reference other cells, you use the cell's table address. The *address* of a cell is a combination of the column and row that form the cell. For example, the cell in the top left corner of a table is formed by the intersection of column A and row 1, so this cell's address is A1. To reference a cell from another table, precede the cell's address with the name of the table (the first table you created is Table A, the second is Table B, and so on) followed by a dot (for example, Table A.A1).

Operators combine the operands mathematically. The following table lists the operators you can use in your table formulas.

Operator	Example	What it does
+	A1+A2	Adds two operands together
−	A1−A2	Subtracts A2 from A1
*	A1*A2	Multiplies two operands
/	A1/A2	Divides A1 by A2
^	A1^A2	Raises A1 to the power of A2

For example, suppose your document is an invoice of items purchased. The invoice includes a table that shows the quantity ordered, the item ordered, and the price of the item. The invoice also needs to show the *extended price* for each item (the quantity ordered multiplied by the unit price of the item). Suppose the first item has the quantity ordered in cell A2 and the unit price in cell C2. To calculate the extended price, you'd use the following formula:

A2*C2

The following picture shows an example of an invoice that uses calculation in a table.

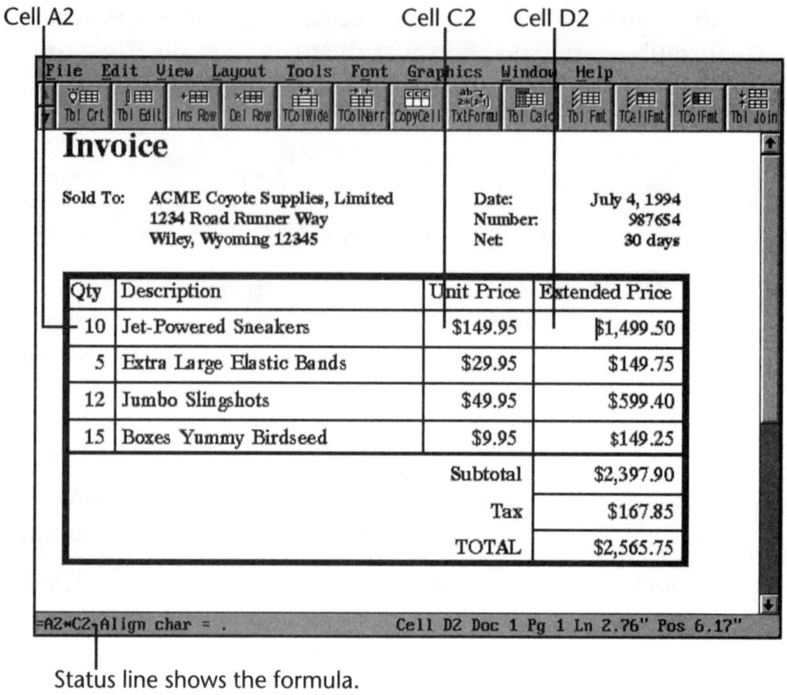

Cell A2   Cell C2   Cell D2

A table that uses formulas for calculations.

Status line shows the formula.

Creating a Formula

Without further ado, follow these steps to create a formula and display its result in a table cell:

1. Pull down the Layout menu, select Tables, and then select Edit (or press **Alt+F11**).

2. In the table editing window, select the cell where you want the result of the formula to appear.

3. Select the Formula command. WordPerfect displays the Table Formula dialog box, shown on the following page.

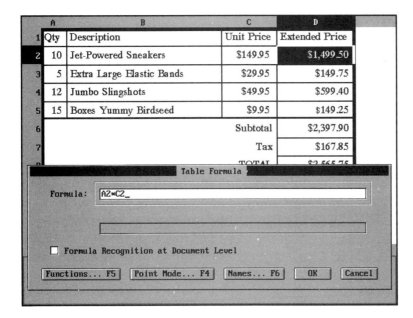

	A	B	C	D
1	Qty	Description	Unit Price	Extended Price
2	10	Jet-Powered Sneakers	$149.95	$1,499.50
3	5	Extra Large Elastic Bands	$29.95	$149.75
4	12	Jumbo Slingshots	$49.95	$599.40
5	15	Boxes Yummy Birdseed	$9.95	$149.25
6			Subtotal	$2,397.90
7			Tax	$167.85
8			TOTAL	$2,565.75

Table Formula

Formula: `A2×C2_`

☐ Formula Recognition at Document Level

[Functions... F5] [Point Mode... F4] [Names... F6] [OK] [Cancel]

Use the Table Formula dialog box to enter the formula.

4. Enter an operand in the Formula text box.

5. Enter an operator in the Formula text box.

6. Repeat Steps 4 and 5 until the formula is complete.

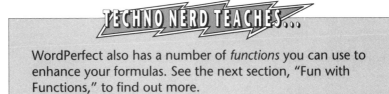

TECHNO NERD TEACHES...

WordPerfect also has a number of *functions* you can use to enhance your formulas. See the next section, "Fun with Functions," to find out more.

7. Select **OK**.

8. Select **Close**. WordPerfect returns you to the document and displays the formula result in the cell.

Fun with Functions

A *function* is a predefined formula that calculates a special result. Word-Perfect comes with dozens of functions that can calculate everything from the maximum value in a list of numbers to the monthly payment for a loan. Most functions take the following form

NAME(argument1, argument2,...)

where NAME is the name of the function and *argument1* and *argument2* are the values the function uses to calculate its result (these values are called *arguments*). These values can be numbers, text, other functions, or table cells. For example, suppose you want to calculate the average of the numbers in cells A1, A2, and A3. WordPerfect's AVE function can do the job, as follows:

AVE(A1,A2,A3)

By the way, if you're using consecutive cells, you can use the colon operator (:) to reference the cells in a short form notation. For example, instead of saying A1,A2,A3, you could say A1:A3.

Follow these steps to insert functions in your formulas:

1. Using steps 1–3 from the last section, display the Table Formula dialog box.

2. Position the cursor where you want the function to appear and select the **Functions** button (or press **F5**). WordPerfect displays the Table Functions dialog box.

3. Highlight the function you want to use.

4. Select the **Insert** button. WordPerfect returns you to the Formula text box and inserts the function. If the formula has arguments, you'll see placeholders where the arguments should go. For example, the AVE function is inserted as AVE(List).

5. Replace the function placeholders with the actual arguments you want to use in the function.

6. Select **OK** to return to the table editing window, and then select **Close** to return to the document.

The Least You Need to Know

This chapter showed you the ins and outs of WordPerfect tables. This is a rather large topic, and there's no way a single chapter can do it justice. However, we did manage to cover all the basics, which is enough to get you started. Just to help things sink in, here's a quick review:

☞ A *table* is a rectangular grid of rows and columns.

☞ To create a table, pull down the **Layout** menu, select **Tables**, and then select **Create**. If you're creating a table from scratch tell WordPerfect the number of rows and columns you need.

☞ To enter table text or numbers, select a cell and then type in the value.

☞ The table editing window lets you change column widths, insert or delete rows or columns, format cell fonts and alignment, and modify the table's border style. To display the table editing window, place the cursor inside the table, pull down the **Layout** menu, select **Tables**, and select **Edit** (or you can simply press **Alt+F11**).

☞ A *formula* is an expression that performs calculations and returns a result. It consists of one or more operands (such as numbers, text, or cell addresses) combined with one or more operators (such as +, –, and *). To display the result of an expression in a cell, display the table editing window, select the cell, select the **Formula** command, and then enter the expression in the Table Formula dialog box.

**It's OK to write on this page;
you paid for it.**

Chapter 26
A WordPerfect Miscellany

In This Chapter

- ☛ Navigating a document with bookmarks
- ☛ Arranging document text in columns
- ☛ Creating a document summary
- ☛ Using WordPerfect's Merge feature

This chapter presents four handy WordPerfect features for your fun and pleasure: bookmarks, columns, document summary, and merge. No, they're not related in any way, but I wanted to fit them in somewhere because they can be quite useful. Happy reading!

Where Was I? Working with Bookmarks

When they stop reading a book, most people insert a bookmark of some kind (a piece of paper, the phone bill, the cat's tail, whatever) so they know where they left off. You can apply the same idea to your WordPerfect documents (if you're using version 6, that is). You can mark special points in your documents with the electronic equivalent of a bookmark, which lets you leap to those points quickly.

Creating a Bookmark

Your bookmarks can refer to either a specific spot inside a document or an entire text block. To create a bookmark, follow these steps:

1. Position the cursor where you want to insert a bookmark. If you want the bookmark to mark a text block, select the block.

2. Pull down the Edit menu and select the Bookmark command, or press **Shift+F12**. The Bookmark dialog box appears.

3. Select the Create command. WordPerfect displays the Create Bookmark dialog box, shown below.

Use the Create Book-mark dialog box to identify your bookmark.

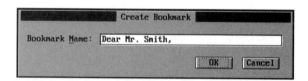

4. The Bookmark Name text box shows WordPerfect's suggested name for the bookmark (this is usually the first few words to the right of the cursor). You can accept the program's suggestion, or enter your own name.

5. Select **OK** to return to the document.

Finding a Bookmark

Once you've defined your bookmarks, you can use them to jump giddily through your document. All you have to do is select the Edit menu's Bookmark command again, highlight the bookmark you want in the Bookmark list, and then select one of the following commands:

Find   Select this command to make WordPerfect leap immediately to the marked spot.

Find and Block   If you created the bookmark for a text block, choose this command to reselect the block.

Using the QuickMark Feature

If you have a favorite spot in a document, you can label it with a special bookmark called a QuickMark. QuickMarks let you find a specific spot quickly and easily by using a simple key combination.

To set a QuickMark, position the cursor on the spot and press **Ctrl+Q**. (If your brain is unwilling to memorize yet another key combination, you can also pull down the Edit menu, select Bookmark, and then select the Set QuickMark button.)

To find the QuickMark, just press **Ctrl+F**. Now *that's* quick! (Just for the record, the non-quick method is to choose the Edit menu's Bookmark command and select the Find QuickMark button.)

TECHNO NERD TEACHES...

One of the best uses for a QuickMark is to mark your current position before you go traipsing off to another part of the document. If you set up a QuickMark before you go, you just have to press **Ctrl+F** to return to where you were.

Working with Columns

WordPerfect, of course, is good for more than just the odd letter or memo. All kinds of people are using the program to self-publish things like newsletters, booklets, pamphlets, fanzines, and more. To give these kinds of documents a more professional look, WordPerfect lets you arrange text into columns like you see in newspapers and magazines (see the following figure). The next few sections show you how to define columns and enter text into them.

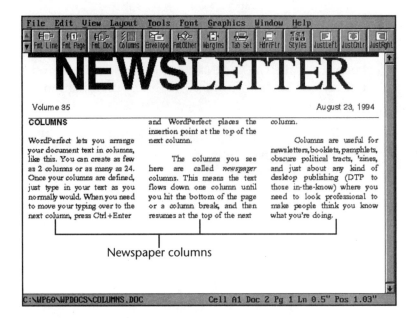

A sample of news-paper columns in WordPerfect.

Defining Columns

Columns have always been one of those features that many people avoided like the plague because, well, they just seemed too complicated and weren't worth the bother. However, WordPerfect has changed all that, and now it's easier than ever to set up and use columns. To prove it for yourself, just follow these steps to define columns for your document:

1. Position the cursor in the paragraph where you want to start the columns. (If you haven't entered the document text yet, that's okay; it's perfectly acceptable to set up your columns first and then type in the text.)

2. Pull down the Layout menu and select the Columns command. WordPerfect displays the Text Columns dialog box, shown below.

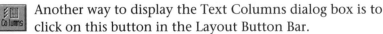 Another way to display the Text Columns dialog box is to click on this button in the Layout Button Bar.

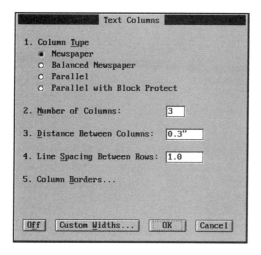

Use the Text Columns dialog box to define your columns.

3. Under Column Type, choose from the following options:

    Newspaper   The text flows down the page until it hits either the bottom of the page or a *column break* (see "Typing Text in Columns" to learn about column breaks). The text then resumes at the top of the next column.

    Balanced Newspaper   The same as Newspaper, except the columns are adjusted to be of equal length.

    Parallel   The document text is grouped in rows across the page (much like a spreadsheet). In most cases, it's easier to create a table than to use parallel columns (see Chapter 25, "Techniques for Terrific Tables," for details).

    Parallel with **B**lock Protect   The same as **P**arallel, except that WordPerfect makes sure that each row is kept together. If part of one row extends onto the next page, WordPerfect shoves the entire row onto the next page.

4. Use the **N**umber of Columns text box to enter the number of columns you want.

5. Use the **D**istance Between Columns text box to specify how much real estate appears between columns.

6. Use the Line Spacing Between Rows to set the line spacing (single-spaced, double-spaced, etc.).

7. If you'd like to place borders around or between the columns, select the Column **B**orders command to display the Create Column Border dialog box, and then select Border Style. In the Border Styles dialog box that appears, highlight either **Column Border (Between Only)** (to place a border between the columns) or **Column Border (Outside and Between)** (to place a border both between and around the columns), and then choose Select. Select **OK** to return to the Text Columns dialog box.

8. Select **OK**. WordPerfect returns you to the document and converts the existing text into columns.

Typing Text in Columns

Once you have your columns defined, your next step is to fill in the columns by typing some text (unless, of course, you converted existing text into columns). Here are some guidelines to follow when typing text columns:

- ☛ Typing text in a column isn't all that different from typing text in a normal document. Just place the cursor in the column you want to use, and start pecking away. If the columns are empty, you have to begin at the top of the first column.

- ☛ If you want to move the cursor to the next column before you reach the end of the page (this is called inserting a column break), press **Ctrl+Enter**.

- ☛ Entering text in parallel columns is slightly different than entering text in newspaper columns because you generally work across the rows instead of down the columns. In this case, position the cursor in the first column, type your text, and insert a column break (again, by pressing **Ctrl+Enter**) to move to the next column in the same row. When you insert a column break in the last column, WordPerfect starts a new row and moves the cursor back to the first column.

☞ To navigate your columns, use the keys listed in the following table:

To move to	Press
The same line in the column to the left	Alt+left arrow
The same line in the column to the right	Alt+right arrow
The first column	Ctrl+Home, Home, left arrow
The last column	Ctrl+Home, End
The top of the current column	Ctrl+Home, up arrow
The bottom of the current column	Ctrl+Home, down arrow

Working with Document Summaries

A *document summary* is just about what you'd expect: a summary of a document's vital statistics (when it was created, who wrote it, the subject matter, and so on). You can also include a descriptive name for the file and then use this name in the File Manager to supplement the cryptic 8-character name required by DOS. (See Chapter 20, "Using WordPerfect's File Manager," to learn more about File Manager.)

Creating a Document Summary

To create a summary for the current document, pull down the File menu and select the Summary command. You'll see the Document Summary dialog box as shown on the following page. This is a fairly simple affair, as dialog boxes go. It's mostly text boxes, so just fill in the blanks (use the scroll bar to display more fields). Note that WordPerfect fills in the Revision Date and Creation Date text boxes automatically. In particular, if you'd like to get out from under the yoke of those impossible-to-decipher DOS file names, be sure to fill in the **Descriptive Name** box (you can enter up to 255 characters, so there's lots of room to be *very* descriptive).

```
                    Document Summary
  Document Summary Fields
Revision Date:     6/16/94 12:41 pm
                     Display-Only
Creation Date:     3/5/94 11:54 am

Descriptive Name:

Descriptive Type:

Author:

Typist:

Subject:

Setup... Shft+F1   Select Fields... F4   Extract Shft+F10

Print   Shft+F7   Save... F10   Delete   F9   OK   Cancel
```

Use the Document Summary dialog box to enter an overview of your document.

TECHNO NERD TEACHES...

To set up File Manager to display your descriptive document names, pull down the **File** menu, select **File Manager**, and then select **OK** to display the File Manager. Select the **Setup** button or press **Shift+F1**. In the File Manager Setup dialog box, activate the Descriptive **Names** and Types radio button and select **OK**. File Manager now displays the usual 8-character mess on the left, and the descriptive name on the right.

Customizing the Document Summary Dialog Box

The fields you see in the Document Summary dialog box aren't set in stone. WordPerfect actually has dozens of fields you can include in the summary to record things like a department name, editor's name, or project name. To customize the Document Summary dialog box, follow these steps:

1. In the Document Summary dialog box, choose the **Select Fields** button or press **F4**. WordPerfect displays the Select Summary Fields dialog box, as shown on the following page.

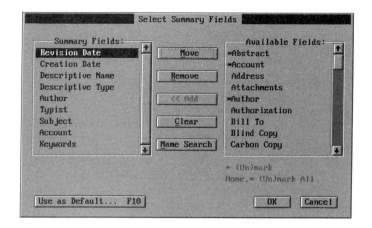

Use the Select Summary Fields dialog box to specify which fields you want to appear in the Document Summary dialog box.

2. To add a field to the summary, highlight it in the Available Fields list and select the Add button.

3. To remove a field from the summary, highlight it in the Summary Fields list and select the Remove button.

4. To move a summary field to a new position, highlight the field in the Summary Fields list and select the Move button. Now use the up and down arrow keys to position the field and press **Enter**.

5. If you want this summary configuration for all your documents, select the **Use as Default** button or press **F10**.

6. When you're done, select **OK** to return to the Document Summary dialog box.

Merging for Mass Mailings

If you've ever received one of those "standard reply" letters addressed "To Whom It May Concern" or to "Occupant," you know how impersonal and cold they are. They have about as much charm as a tax audit. But if you have to send out a mass mailing of a few dozen or even a few hundred pieces, who has time to personalize each one? The solution is to take advantage of modern technology and check out WordPerfect's Merge feature, which can automatically personalize (is that an oxymoron?) your letters, thank-you notes, or envelopes.

How does it perform such magic? It's quite simple really. Let's say you want to send out a letter to a few dozen customers, and you want each letter to begin with a friendly "Dear Frank," or "Dear Martha," or whatever. You begin by entering all the pertinent data for each person in a table in a separate file. This includes each person's first name, last name, address, and so on. Now you write the basic letter and, in the spot where each person's first name will appear, you place a special code that says, essentially, "insert each person's first name here." That's about it really. When you run the merge, WordPerfect goes through the table of data, and for each person, it extracts the first name, creates a copy of the letter, and inserts the name at the spot you specified. In other words, the two files are *merged* to produce a new document. (It's also pretty easy to extend the merge to include each person's last name, address, and so on.)

Step 1: Defining the Data File

The hardest part of a merge (or, at least, the most time-consuming), is creating the data file. Entering data for dozens or hundreds of people or companies is no one's idea of fun, but at least you know you'll only have to do it once.

There are a couple of ways to create a data file, but by far the easiest and most straightforward is to enter everything into a table. (If you're not familiar with WordPerfect tables, this might be a good time to review the material in Chapter 25, "Techniques for Terrific Tables.") The idea is that each row in the table represents a particular person (or company, or whatever), and each column represents a specific chunk of info, such as the person's first name, last name, address, and so on.

How do you know what information to include in the data file? Well, it depends entirely on what you want to use in the merge. In a basic letter, you'll need first name, last name, address, city, state, and ZIP code. If you're writing thank-you notes for charitable donations, you'll need to keep track of the amount of the donation so you can refer to it in the note.

Start a new document and then follow these steps to create your merge data file:

1. Pull down the **T**ools menu, select **M**erge, and select **D**efine. Or simply press **Shift+F9**. WordPerfect displays the Merge Codes dialog box.

    You can also display the Merge Codes dialog box by clicking on this button in the Tools Button Bar.

2. Activate the Data [Table] radio button and select **OK**. The Merge Codes (Table Data File) dialog box appears.

3. Select the Create a Table with Field Names command. The Field Names dialog box appears.

4. In the Field Name text box, enter a name for a field in your data table and press **Enter**. (Make sure the name reflects the type of data that will appear in the field, such as First Name.)

5. Repeat step 4 until you've entered all the fields you need, and then select **OK**. WordPerfect creates a table showing the field names in the first row with a blank row underneath.

6. Enter your data into the table. (Don't forget to save the file.)

The picture below shows a data file with some data entered into the table.

First Name	Last Name	Address	City	State	ZIP Code	Gift
Gary	Larceny	47 Ewe Turn Way	Fearnot	PA	12345	Solar-powered flashlight
Cheryl	Lass	444 Memory Lane	Bald Head	ME	23456	Inflatable dartboard
Whoopi	Cushion	987 Cattle Drive	Ben Hur	TX	34567	Non-slip ski wax
Larry	Budmelman	1010 Info Autobahn	Belcher	NY	45678	Parachute that opens on contact
Axl	Fell	567 Road to Wellville	Worstville	OH	56789	"Look Ma, No Hands!" alarm clock
Glint	Westwood	1 Picabo Street	Okay	OK	67890	Cork anchor

A data file with some data entered into the table.

Step 2: Defining the Form File

Your next step is to set up the form file to receive the info from the data file. This involves two things: creating the basic "skeleton" of the document you want to send out, and inserting *merge codes* that tell WordPerfect where you want it to stick the data file data. The following steps spell everything out:

1. In a new document, pull down the Tools menu, select Merge, and then select **Define**, or simply press **Shift+F9**. WordPerfect displays the Merge Codes dialog box.

2. Make sure the Form radio button is activated, and then select **OK**. WordPerfect displays the Merge Codes (Form File) dialog box. If you want to enter a code now, skip to step 5.

3. Select **OK** to return to the document, and then enter the regular document text until you reach a place where you want to insert some data file info (such as a first name).

4. Pull down the Tools menu, select Merge, and then select **Define**, or press **Shift+F9**, to return to the Merge Codes (Form File) dialog box.

5. Select the Field command. The Parameter Entry dialog box appears.

6. If you know the name of the field you want (the name that appears at the top of the column in the data file), enter it in the Field text box and select **OK**. (If you're not sure about the name, select the **List Field Names** button or press **F5**. WordPerfect displays the List Field Names dialog box. Select **Change Data File** or press **F4**, enter the name of the data file, and then select **OK**. Now highlight the field and choose **Select**.) WordPerfect inserts the merge code into the document—for example, **FIELD**(First Name).

7. Repeat steps 3–6 until the form file is complete.

The following picture shows an example form file that uses codes for the columns in the data file shown earlier.

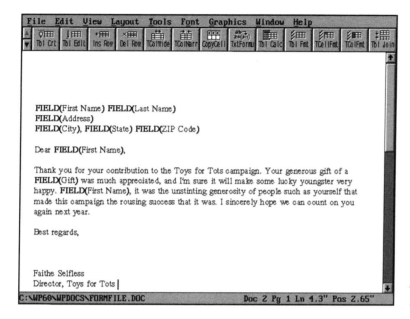

A form file with several merge codes.

Step 3: Running the Merge

Well, it's all over but for the shouting, as they say. The hard part's done, and all that remains is to perform the merge. Here's what you do:

1. Pull down the Tools menu, select Merge, and then select Run (or just press **Ctrl+F9**). WordPerfect displays the Run Merge dialog box.

    Clicking on this button in the Tools Button Bar will also start the Merge.

2. In the Form File text box, enter the name of the form file.

3. In the Data File text box, enter the name of the data file.

4. Use the Output pop-up list to select a destination for the merge results:

   Current Document   Tacks the merge results onto the end of the current document.

   Unused Document   Creates a brand new document and uses it to hold the merge results.

Printer   Sends the merge results directly to the printer.

File   Creates a separate unopened file and uses it to hold the merge results.

5. Select the **Merge** button. WordPerfect performs the merge.

The Least You Need to Know

This chapter presented a hodgepodge of four unrelated—but decidedly useful—features. Here's a retrospective look at what the heck happened:

☞ Use bookmarks to mark specific spots in your document. To create a bookmark, select Bookmark from the Edit menu (or press **Shift+F12**), and then select **Create**. To find a bookmark, select Bookmark from the Edit menu, highlight the bookmark name, and select Find.

☞ A QuickMark is a special bookmark that you can set and find quickly. To set a QuickMark, press **Ctrl+Q**. To find a QuickMark, press **Ctrl+F**.

☞ To display your text in columns, position the cursor, pull down the Layout menu, and select **Columns**.

☞ To create a document summary, pull down the **File** menu and select the **Summary** command.

☞ Merging is a three-step procedure: defining the data file, defining the form file, and running the merge.

Chapter 27
Customizing WordPerfect

In This Chapter

☞ Taking control of WordPerfect's windows

☞ Using the Zoom feature to see the forest instead of the trees (or vice-versa)

☞ Setting the Button Bar options

☞ Making your mouse behave

☞ Doing WordPerfect's colors

☞ Numerous techniques that'll help you put your best WordPerfect foot forward

WordPerfect is one of those programs you can accessorize. Oh, sure, it looks fine in its basic outfit—but add a bauble here, a trinket there, and you get a whole new look. The good news is that this new look also makes WordPerfect both easier to use and more powerful. A fairy tale? No way. Just read this chapter to find out how easy it all is.

Customizing WordPerfect's Windows

As you learned in Chapter 19, "Working with Multiple Documents," WordPerfect version 6 displays each open document in its own window.

You can have all kinds of fun with these windows by adding things like scroll bars and frames. In fact, you might have so much fun that you decide you want *every* document you open to use these features. However, selecting everything you need from the pull-down menus each time is a drag. Instead, you can define a default window setup that WordPerfect will use for each document. To do this, pull down the View menu and select the Scree**n** Setup command, or press **Ctrl+F3**. You'll see the Screen Setup dialog box, shown here.

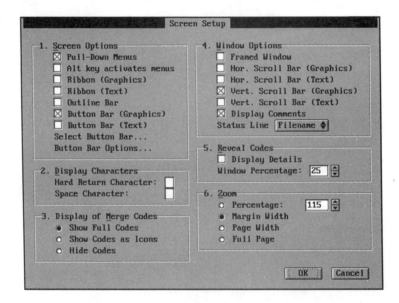

Use the Screen Setup dialog box to customize your document windows.

The **W**indow Options group contains everything you need. Here's a summary of the available options:

Framed Window   As described in Chapter 19, a window frame lets you size, move, and close windows easily. Activate this check box to put a frame around every document you open.

Hor. Scroll Bar (Graphics)   Horizontal scroll bars are great for using a mouse to navigate a document that's too wide to fit on the screen (see Chapter 8, "Day-to-Day Drudgery II: Navigating Documents"). If you use graphics mode, activate this check box to display a horizontal scroll bar in every window. (For text mode types, activate the Hor. Scroll Bar (Text) check box.)

Vert. Scroll Bar (Graphics)   You use vertical scroll bars with a mouse to navigate a document from top to bottom (again, Chapter 8 is the place you oughta be to learn about vertical scroll bars). Activate this check box to display a vertical scroll bar in graphics mode for every document. (Activate the **V**ert. Scroll Bar (Text) check box for text mode.)

Display Comments   Comments are boxed sections of text that appear on the screen, but not in printouts (see Chapter 17, "Other Ways to Look Good"). If you'd prefer *not* to see these comments in your windows, deactivate this check box.

Status Line   This option controls what WordPerfect displays on the left side of the status line that appears at the bottom of each window. Your choices are **F**ilename, **F**ont, or **N**othing.

Once you've chosen the options you want, select **OK** to put them into effect.

Who's Zooming Who: The Zoom Feature

Normally, WordPerfect displays your document pages at more or less life size. If you're in graphics mode or page mode, however, you can enlarge or reduce the size of each page with WordPerfect's Zoom feature.

To check out Zoom, pull down the View menu, select Zoom, and then select one of the following commands. (Note that these options have no effect on what your documents look like when you print them out.)

Select	To
50%	Reduce the page size to 50% of normal.
75%	Reduce the page size to 75% of normal.
100%	See the page at normal size.
125%	Increase the page size to 125% of normal.
150%	Increase the page size to 150% of normal.
200%	Increase the page size to 200% of normal.
300%	Increase the page size to 300% of normal.

continues

continued

Select	To
Margin Width	Increase the size of the page so the area between the margins takes up the full width of the screen.
Page Width	Increase the size of the page so the area between the left and right edges (including the margins) takes up the full width of the screen.
Full Page	Reduce the size of the page so you can see the entire page on-screen.

Marg ▼ Each Zoom option is also available in this Ribbon drop-down list.

You can also use WordPerfect's Screen Setup dialog box to specify a default Zoom. Select Screen Setup from the View menu, and then select either the Margin Width, Page Width, or Full Page radio button. You can also activate the Percentage option and use its spinner to specify a Zoom percent (enter a number between 40 and 800).

Customizing the Button Bars

As you've seen throughout this book, WordPerfect's Button Bars give you push-button access to many of the program's features. WordPerfect also gives you a few customization options to make the Button Bars even more convenient. Pull down the View menu, select Button Bar Setup, and then select Options. WordPerfect displays the Button Bar Options dialog box, as shown below.

Use the Button Bar Options dialog box to customize the position and style of the Button Bars.

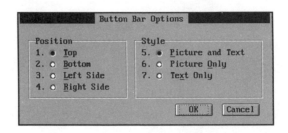

The radio buttons in the Position group control where WordPerfect displays the Button Bars on the screen. You can choose Top (the normal position), **Bottom**, **Left Side**, or **Right Side**. The Style radio buttons control the look of the buttons. The normal style is Picture and Text, but you can also select Picture Only or Text Only.

Customizing Your Mouse

One thing that's been clear throughout this book is that a mouse can be a real timesaver. But its benefits are lost if it's not set up properly, so WordPerfect lets you customize certain aspects of your mouse. Just pull down the File menu, select the Setup command, and then select **Mouse** from the cascade menu. You'll see the Mouse dialog box, shown here.

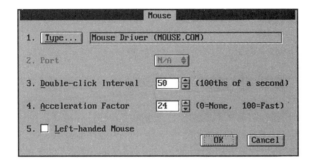

Use the Mouse dialog box to customize your rodent.

Here's a summary of the available options:

Type This option lets you select a mouse *device driver* (a program that lets WordPerfect talk to your mouse). If your mouse works fine, ignore this option. Otherwise, select it, highlight your mouse from the list that appears, and then choose Select. If you're not sure about all this, choose the Auto Select command to let WordPerfect try its hand.

Port This option is only applicable to certain kinds of mice (called *serial* mice). Again, if your mouse is working, ignore it. Otherwise, just try different values until the mouse does work.

Double-click Interval This option sets the amount of time you're allowed between two mouse clicks before WordPerfect interprets them as a double click. If you find that your double clicks aren't always recognized, use a higher setting. If two single clicks are sometimes interpreted as a double click, use a lower setting.

Acceleration Factor   This option controls how responsive the mouse pointer is to your mouse movements. If you find the pointer is hard to control because it's moving too fast, use a lower setting. If the pointer just seems to creep along, try a higher setting.

Left-handed Mouse   If you're a southpaw, activate this check box to swap the left and right mouse buttons.

When you're done, select **OK** to put the new settings into effect.

Doing WordPerfect's Colors

Let's face it, WordPerfect's basic color scheme is pretty dull (unless, of course, you *like* drab gray)—but that's okay because, after all, this is just a word processor; it's not like you have to wear it in public or anything. However, we can all use a little extra color in our lives occasionally, so WordPerfect gives you a choice of color schemes (or you can even create your own).

To see how it's done, first pull down the File menu, select Setup, and select Display. In the Display dialog box, you have the choice of working with graphics mode colors or text mode colors. Select the appropriate option. (I'll assume from here on that you're using graphics mode, in which case the Graphics Mode Screen Type/Colors dialog box appears.)

Depending on the scheme you chose, you may need to see a dialog box to notice any difference.

The Color Schemes box displays a list of the available color schemes (yes, there really is one called "Clown Town"; obviously some people just have *way* too much time on their hands). Highlight the one you want and choose the **Select** command. Choose **Close** in the Display dialog box to put the new colors into effect.

If you think you could do a better job of color selection, why not try creating your own scheme? Here are the steps to follow:

1. In the Graphics Mode Screen Type/Colors dialog box, select the Color Schemes box, and then select the Create option. WordPerfect prompts you to enter a name for the scheme.

2. Type in your own silly name for the scheme and select **OK**. You'll see the Edit Graphics Screen Colors dialog box, shown below. The Screen Elements list shows various features of the WordPerfect landscape, and the Sample Colors box shows you the color of each feature.

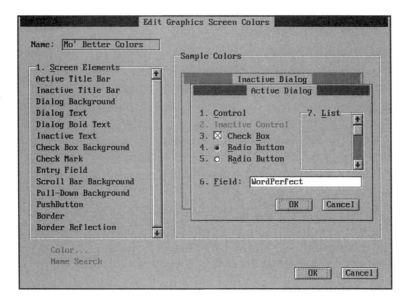

Use the Edit Graphics Screen Colors dialog box to create your own color scheme.

3. Highlight an item in the Screen Elements list, and then select the Color command. The Colors dialog box appears.

4. Use the arrow keys to highlight the color you want (or click on the color with the mouse), and then choose the Select button. WordPerfect returns you to the Edit Graphics Screen Colors dialog box and updates the Sample Colors area to show you what the new color looks like.

5. Repeat Steps 3 and 4 to set the colors for the other screen elements.

6. When you're done, select **OK**, and then close the other dialog boxes to put your new scheme into effect.

The Least You Need to Know

This chapter took you through a few neat features designed to make your WordPerfect life easier. Here's a recap:

- ☞ To customize WordPerfect's windows, pull down the View menu and select Screen Setup, or press **Ctrl+F3**.

- ☞ To get a different slant on your documents, pull down the View menu, select Zoom, and then select one of the commands in the cascade menu that appears.

- ☞ The Button Bar puts all kinds of WordPerfect commands only a mouse click away. To customize the position and style of the Button Bars, pull down the View menu, select the Button Bar Setup command, and then select Options.

- ☞ If your mouse is being temperamental, choose Setup from the File menu and select the Mouse command. The Mouse dialog box lets you set up the mouse so that it works the way you want it to.

- ☞ To do WordPerfect's colors, pull down the File menu, select Setup, and select Display.

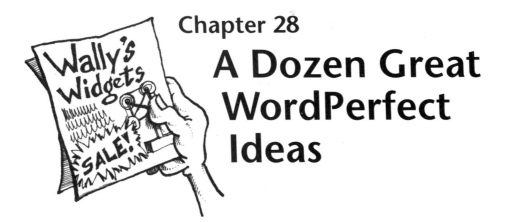

Chapter 28
A Dozen Great WordPerfect Ideas

Like most people, after forking out hard-earned cash (your own or your company's) for WordPerfect, you're probably looking to get your money's worth. Does this mean you need to fixate on each feature and memorize mundane minutiae? Not on your life! No, to get the most out of WordPerfect—or any piece of software, for that matter—you need to put it to work doing practical, useful things either around the home or at the office. To get you started, this chapter suggests a veritable bounty of handy—and sometimes even interesting—WordPerfect ideas and assorted stupid computer tricks.

1. Backing Up Your Files with File Manager

Computers are relatively reliable beasts, but one of these days your hard disk will crash, or you'll accidentally delete your last six months' work, or a virus will trash your precious files. To help you sleep better at night, you should regularly make backup copies of your documents to a floppy disk. If you have created backups and disaster strikes, at least you can restore your work.

Does all this mean you have to rush out and fork out big bucks for a dedicated backup program? Nah. WordPerfect's File Manager has a Copy command that you can press into service as a basic backup utility. The following steps show you how it's done:

1. Place a formatted floppy disk in the appropriate disk drive.

2. In File Manager, select the files you want to back up.

3. Select the Copy command. WordPerfect asks if you want to copy the marked files.

4. Select Yes. The Copy dialog box appears.

5. In the Copy Marked Files to text box, enter **a:** if the disk is in drive A, or **b:** if it's in drive B.

6. Select **OK**.

You can make backing up a little easier by changing a couple of File Manager setup options. In File Manager, select the **Setup** button or press **Shift+F1** to display the File Manager Setup dialog box. In the Sort List by group, activate the **Date/Time** radio button. Then activate both the Descending Sort and **WP Documents Only** check boxes. Select **OK** to exit; you see only WordPerfect documents in the list, *and* they are sorted by date. How does this help? Well, the documents you worked on most recently appear at the top of the list. Since these are the ones you're most likely to back up, it's easy just to mark everything you need and crank up the Copy command.

2. Using Templates to Avoid Reinventing the Wheel

In word processing lingo, a *template* is a special document that contains predefined text, graphics, formatting, and styles. The template acts as a sort of skeleton from which you can create other documents.

For example, if you use WordPerfect to create memos, most of your memos will probably have the same basic structure: a header showing your company information and maybe a logo, the word "Memo" in large type, headings such as "To," "From," and "Subject," and whatever else you need to display. To save some work, you could create a memo template that includes just those constant elements that appear in every memo. You could then fill in the variable info, such as the recipient's name, the date, the subject of the memo, and the memo text itself.

You create a template just like you would any other document. Remember, though, to include only the text, formatting, and graphics that you want to appear in every document created from the template. When you save the template, be sure to give it an extension different from the one you use for your other documents. For example, .WPT (WordPerfect Template) and .DOT (DOcument Template) are commonly used for templates (for example, MEMO.DOT).

To use a template, follow these steps:

1. Open the template document.

2. Pull down the File menu and select the Save As command, or press **F10**. WordPerfect displays the Save Document dialog box.

3. In the Filename text box, enter a name for the new document (use your normal document extension this time), and then select **OK**.

4. Fill in the missing information to complete the document.

Templates are useful for any kind of document you create regularly. The next few sections take you through some template examples.

Templates are also a great way to achieve a consistent look and feel between departments. Assuming everyone uses WordPerfect, just issue the template file to all employees and show them how to use it.

3. Template #1: The Fax Cover Sheet

When you produce documents for faxing, you probably begin by creating a cover sheet for the fax transmission. However, each of the cover sheets you create is probably identical to the others, except for things like the recipient's name and fax number. So it makes sense to create a fax cover sheet template, like the one shown on the following page. As you can see, you just need to fill in the recipient, his fax number, the date, the subject of the fax, the number of pages, and whatever extra notes are required.

```
 File   Edit  View  Layout  Tools  Font  Graphics  Window  Help
```

ACME Coyote Supplies, Limited
1234 Road Runner Way, Wiley, Wyoming 12345
Voice: (123) 555-4567   FAX: (123) 555-5678

fax transmittal

            to: _____

           fax: _____

          from: Fred Funk

          date: _____

            re: _____

         pages: (Including this page)

NOTES:

`C:\WP60\WPDOCS\FAX.DOT`   Cell B1 Doc 1 Pg 1 Ln 1.93" Pos 1.88"

A fax cover sheet template.

Here are some notes to keep in mind when creating this template:

You may be tempted to insert a date code in the Date field (as explained in Chapter 17, "Other Ways to Look Good"). This adds the current date each time you open the template (which is good), but it also *changes* the date each time you open the completed cover sheet (which is bad). Instead, insert the date as text when you're filling in the cover sheet data.

☞ The company info at the top is part of the document's header. (See Chapter 15, "Making Your Pages Look Good," to get the goods on headers.)

☞ I created the two lines that run across the page (the one below the header and the one below the "pages" section) by using WordPerfect's Graphics Line feature. To use this feature, position the insertion point where you want the line to appear, pull down the Graphics menu, select Graphics Lines, and then select Create. In the Create Graphics Line dialog box, select Line Style to choose the kind of line you want, choose Select, and then select **OK**.

☞ The section that holds the fax data and their respective headings (to:, fax:, and so on) is actually a table with two columns and six rows. I used the Lines/Fill command in the table editing window to remove all the borders except the bottom ones for the data cells.

(Check out Chapter 25, "Techniques for Terrific Tables," to learn more about tables.)

☛ The entire document is formatted with two fonts: Helve-WP Bold (for the headings) and Helve-WP. These sans serif fonts have a clean look that faxes well. The fax data headings were also right-justified.

4. Template #2: An Invoice

WordPerfect's tables are a perfect way to handle documents that require calculations (see Chapter 25, "Techniques for Terrific Tables"). In particular, they make it easy to create business forms such as invoices that require things like extended totals, subtotals, tax calculations, and a grand total. Since you presumably use such forms regularly, it makes sense to create a template. The picture below shows an invoice template.

An example invoice template.

The bulk of this document is taken up by two tables. The top table is used for invoice data such as the customer, the shipping address, the date, the invoice number, and the terms. The second table holds the individual invoice line items, and it has four columns: Qty (the quantity ordered), Description (the item ordered), Unit Price (the price per unit), and Extended Price (the quantity ordered multiplied by the unit price).

Here are some tips you can use for entering the invoice formulas:

☛ The first extended price field is in cell D2. It's supposed to show the result of multiplying the quantity (the value in cell A2) by the unit price (the value in cell C2). So for this cell you'd enter the formula **A2*C2**.

☛ Instead of repeating the Extended Price formula for each of the other cells, you can use the Copy Cell feature to save a bit of drudgery. Press **Alt+F11** to display the table editing window, and then select the Extended Price cell that already has the formula. Now select the Move/Copy button, and select Copy in the dialog box that appears. In the Copy Cell dialog box, activate the **Down** radio button, enter the number of remaining Extended Price cells (there are eight more in my example), and select **OK**. WordPerfect copies the formula into the other cells and adjusts the cell addresses accordingly (for example, the formula in cell D3 becomes **A3*C3**).

☛ To get the Subtotal, you could use the SUM( ) function to enter something like this: **SUM(D2:D10)**. However, WordPerfect gives you an easier way: just enter a plus sign (+) as the formula. This tells WordPerfect to sum every cell above the current cell.

☛ To calculate the tax, multiply the Subtotal cell (D11 in my example) by the tax rate (for example, **D11*0.07**).

☛ To derive the TOTAL, you add the Subtotal (D11) and the Tax (D12).

You can use tables to create other business forms, such as purchase orders, expense reports, balance sheets, cash flow, and income statements. Use existing paper forms as your models.

5. Template #3: Overheads

You can use WordPerfect to create documents that can be used as overheads in a presentation. The following picture shows an example of an overhead template. You replace **[Slide Title]** with the title of the slide, and then you fill in the bullet points (**[First point]**, **[Second point]**, and so on).

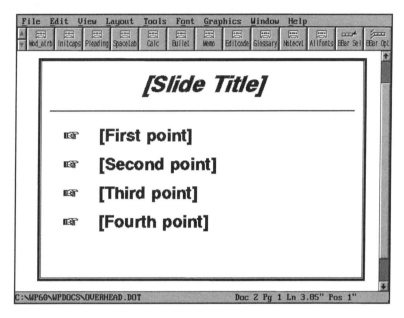

An example overhead template.

To get the bullets, you can use a special macro that comes with WordPerfect. Here are the steps to follow:

1. Position the cursor where you want the first bullet to appear.

2. Display the Macros Button Bar and click on the Bullet button. The Bullet Inserter dialog box appears.

Don't sweat it if you don't have a mouse; you can still run the Bullet macro by pulling down the **Tools** menu, selecting **Macro**, and selecting **Play** (you can also press **Alt+F10**). In the Play Macro dialog box that appears, type **bullet.wpm** in the **Macro** text box and select **OK**.

3. Select Change Bullet to display the Edit Bullet Character dialog box.

4. Select User Defined, and then press **Ctrl+W** to display the WordPerfect Characters dialog box.

5. In the **Set** pop-up list, choose **Iconic Symbols**, and then select the symbol you want to use for the bullets. The hand with the pointing finger is number 5,43.

6. Select Insert to return to the Edit Bullet Character dialog box.

7. Select **OK** to return to the Bullet Inserter dialog box.

8. Select the **Insert Bullet** command. WordPerfect inserts the bullet in the document.

9. To add subsequent bullets, position the cursor, click on the Bullet button, and then select Insert bullet.

Here are some notes you can use when creating your own template:

☛ Overhead text needs to be big so people in the back of the room can see it. For my overheads, I use a 48-point font for the title and a 36-point font for the bullet points. Helve-WP Bold is a good typeface to use because the individual letters are clean and easy to read, and they're thicker than average which makes them stand out more.

☛ Overheads usually look best with the page arranged in landscape orientation (where the text runs along the long side of the page). See Chapter 17, "Other Ways to Look Good," to learn how to set the orientation.

☛ A border around the page is often a nice touch on an overhead. To add a border, pull down the Layout menu and select **Page**. In the Page Format dialog box, select the Page Borders command, select Border Style, and then highlight the border you want from the Border Styles dialog box. Choose Select, choose **OK**, and then choose **OK** again to return to the document.

☛ To maximize the readability of the slide, set the line spacing to 1.5 (see Chapter 14, "Making Your Lines and Paragraphs Look Good").

6. Monitoring Your Finances with a WordPerfect Checkbook

In the old days of computers (way back in the '80s!), life was simple: word processing programs were only used for writing, desktop publishing programs were only used for page layout, and spreadsheets were only used for calculating. Nowadays, however, muscular programs like WordPerfect give you the electronic equivalent of one-stop shopping. So, yes, you can write with WordPerfect, but you can also do some pretty fancy page-layout stuff that used to be the domain of high-end programs. And WordPerfect's extensive table features allow you to turn the program into a veritable spreadsheet. No, it's not in the same league as Lotus 1-2-3 or Microsoft Excel, but it can handle reasonably complex calculations without a complaint.

As an example, how about turning a WordPerfect document into a digital version of your checkbook register? As you can see in the picture below, you can record all the usual stuff—check numbers, the date of each transaction, the payee or description, the payment or deposit, and whether or not the transaction has cleared the bank—and you can also convince WordPerfect to track the account balance for you automatically! No more pecking away at tiny calculator keys or fumbling with your fingers.

File Edit View Layout Tools Font Graphics Window Help

Tbl Crt | Tbl Edit | Ins Row | Del Row | TColWide | TColNarr | CopyCell | TxtFormu | Tbl Calc | Tbl Fmt | TCellFmt | TColFmt | Tbl Join

Checkbook Register
Bank: Last National Bank
Account Number: 1234567

Chk #	Date	Payee/Description	Payment	C	Deposit	Balance
	12/12/94	Opening balance			$100.00	$100.00
	12/14/94	Deposit			$500.00	$600.00
1	12/18/94	Christmas presents	$348.50			$251.50
	12/19/94	Withdrawal	$100.00			$151.50
	12/28/94	Salary			$500.00	$651.50
2	12/31/94	Bert's Beer Store	$221.37			$430.13

=G6-D7+F7 Align char = .   Cell G7 Doc 1 Pg 1 Ln 3.96" Pos 6.77"

The checkbook template.

If you've read Chapter 25, "Techniques for Terrific Tables," creating the checkbook register will pose no problems. Here are a few notes about how I've set things up:

- ☞ The cells in the Date column have been formatted as dates. (In the table editing window, select Column to display the Column Format dialog box, select Number Type, and then select **Date**. To pick out an appropriate date format, choose the Select Date Format command.)

- ☞ The cells in the Payment, Deposit, and Balance columns have been formatted as Currency and aligned on the decimal point.

- ☞ You can make WordPerfect print the column headings at the top of each new page. In the table editing window, select a cell in the header row, select Row, activate the Header Row check box, and then select **OK**.

The only moderately tricky concept is the formula you use to track the account balance. You begin the register by entering an opening balance transaction. Enter the current balance in your account in the first cell below the Balance header (cell G2 in my register). For subsequent transactions, the balance is calculated by either subtracting the value of the transaction (if it's a payment) or adding the value of the transaction (if it's a deposit). Since we don't know in advance whether a given transaction is going to be a payment or deposit, we can take both into account by using the following calculation to derive the current balance:

Previous Balance – Payment + Deposit

For example, once you enter the second transaction, the previous balance is cell G2, and the transaction value is either in the Payment column (cell D3) or the Deposit column (cell F3). So the formula that calculates the new balance in cell G3 is as follows:

G2–D3+F3

Enter this formula in cell G3 and then copy it each time you add a new transaction (as described earlier in this chapter).

7. Creating Your Own Business Cards

If you're part of the growing SOHO movement (Small Office, Home Office), you can use WordPerfect to create your own snazzy business cards. The only material you need is the appropriate paper for printing the cards (the stock should be thick enough that the cards don't appear flimsy, but not so thick that your printer chokes on it). The rest just requires a modicum of imagination and creativity.

The secret to creating business cards is WordPerfect's Subdivide feature. Subdivide breaks up a single page into two or more *logical pages*; WordPerfect treats each of these logical pages as though it were a separate page on its own, so it makes it easy to format each logical page as a separate entity.

In our business card example, each logical page contains the text and graphics for a single card. Here are the steps to follow to subdivide your pages:

1. Pull down the Layout menu and select **Page**. WordPerfect displays the Page Format dialog box.

2. Select the Subdivide **P**age command. The Subdivide Page dialog box appears.

3. Use the Number of Columns spinner to enter the number of logical pages that will appear across the physical page. Business cards are typically 3 1/2 inches wide, so enter **2** (I'm assuming you're using paper that is 8 inches wide).

4. Use the Number of **R**ows spinner to enter the number of logical pages that will appear down the physical page. Most business cards are 2 inches tall, so enter **5** (I'm assuming your paper is 11 inches tall).

5. Select **OK** to return to the Page Format dialog box, and then select **OK** to return to the document. WordPerfect displays the first subdivided page.

At this point, you just enter and format the info you want to appear on the card (including any graphics you want to include, such as a logo). When you're done, move to the bottom of the "page" and press

Ctrl+Enter to start the next logical page. In most cases, you can create each subsequent card just by copying and pasting the information from the first card. The picture below shows a subdivided page with some example business cards.

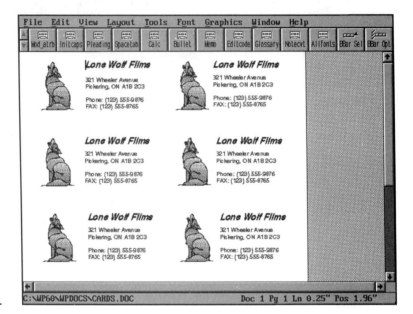

Some business cards on a subdivided page.

TECHNO NERD TEACHES...

Subdivided pages have endless uses: name tags, phone message sheets, dinner place cards, invitations—you name it. In each case, first determine the dimensions of the object you want to create, and then use these dimensions to determine how many logical pages to create.

8. Creating a Drop Cap

A *drop cap* is the first letter of a paragraph that is much larger than the regular paragraph text and extends down into the text. The following picture shows an example. Drop caps are often used in articles and newsletters to add a touch of class to the proceedings.

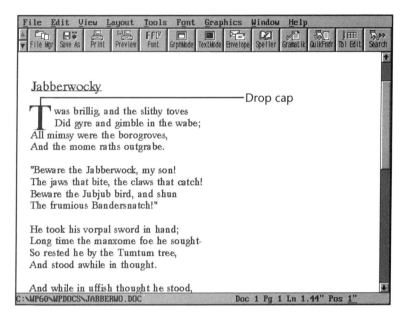

An example of a drop cap.

Here are the steps to follow to create a drop cap:

1. Position the cursor at the beginning of the paragraph and delete the first letter.

2. Pull down the Graphics menu, select Graphics **B**oxes, and then select **C**reate to display the Create Graphics Box dialog box.

3. Select the Create **T**ext command and then type the first letter of the paragraph. You also need to format the letter, as appropriate. In particular, you should set the type size to be about two and a half times the size of the regular paragraph text. For example, if you're using a 12-point font, format the letter with a 30-point font. When you're done, press **F7**.

4. Select the Edit **B**order/Fill command, select Based on Border Style, highlight **[None]** in the Border Styles dialog box, choose **S**elect, and then choose **C**lose.

5. Select Edit **P**osition, choose **L**eft in the Horizontal Position pop-up list, and then select **OK**.

6. Select the Edit **S**ize command, activate the **A**utomatic Width, Based on Box Content Width radio button, and then select **OK**.

7. Select **OK** to return to the document.

You may need to move or size the text box to get it just right. See Chapter 24, "Image Is Everything: WordPerfect's Graphics Boxes," to get the details.

9. Saving Bits of Boilerplate Text

Boilerplate is text you use over and over. It could be your company's name and address, a set of instructions, or a good joke. WordPerfect's Append feature lets you take the idea of boilerplate text to new heights. (We first looked at Append back in Chapter 11, "Block Partying: Working with Blocks of Text.")

Since Append lets you easily add text to a document, why not create a separate file to hold all your boilerplate phrases and passages? (You could call it BOILER.DOC or something.) Any time you come across some new text that you want to add to the file, just select it, pull down the Edit menu, select Append, and then select the To File command. In the Append To dialog box that appears, enter the name of the boilerplate file and select **OK**. You must open the boilerplate document when you need to use something from it. To learn how to work with multiple open documents, check out Chapter 19, "Working with Multiple Documents."

10. Searching for and Replacing Misused Words

The Replace feature that you learned about back in Chapter 12, "Search and Ye Shall Replace," is one of those features for which you'll find endless uses. But perhaps one of the best is to weed out words used improperly. For example, you might need to replace some instances of *affect* with *effect* (one of my own personal bugaboos). Here's a list of some of the most commonly confused words you might want to check for (in most cases you can reverse the *Search for* and *Replace with* terms, depending on which usage is correct):

Search for	Meaning	Replace with	Meaning
affect	To influence	effect	A result
already	Action has happened	all ready	Entirely ready
alright	None (no such word)	all right	
all together	As one	altogether	Entirely
any body	Any human form	anybody	Any person
averse	Disinclined	adverse	Opposed
breath	Inhalation	breathe	To inhale
capitol	Govt. building	capital	Seat of govt.
censure	To blame	censor	To expurgate
continual	Frequently recurring	continuous	Uninterrupted
different than	(Improper usage)	different from	
hanged	Refers to a person	hung	Refers to an object
i.e.	That is	e.g.	For example
irregardless	None (improper usage)	regardless	
momento	None (no such word)	memento	
plaintiff	A party in a lawsuit	plaintive	Mournful
regretful	(Improper usage)	regrettable	
seasonable	Timely	seasonal	Periodical

11. Keeping Track of Document Revisions

Some documents may go through a dozen amendments or more, so it becomes crucial to know which version you're dealing with. If you include the codes (not just text) for the date and time, WordPerfect updates everything each time you work on the file, so you always know when it was last modified.

The ideal place for these date and time codes is a header or footer (which I covered in Chapter 15, "Making Your Pages Look Good"). When you're in the header or footer editing screen, pull down the Tools menu, select **Date**, and then select the **Code** command.

You may also want to include the document's file name in the header or footer. To do this, pull down the Layout menu and select **Other** to display the Other Format dialog box. Then select the **Insert Filename** command. In the Insert Filename dialog box, select either **Insert Filename** (to insert the name of the file only) or **Insert Path and Filename** (to insert the file's drive and directory, as well as its name). Select **OK** to return to the Other Format dialog box, and then select **OK** to return to the document.

If you don't want to clutter a header or footer with a date code, you can also use the Document Summary feature to keep track of revisions. Return to Chapter 26, "A WordPerfect Miscellany," to find out more.

12. Using QuickLists to Avoid Sharing Conflicts

The QuickLists we looked at earlier in the book (see Chapter 21, "Finding Files Quickly with QuickLists and QuickFinder") are great if you have several people sharing a computer. If everyone uses different files, you can set up a QuickList for each person so he can easily work with his own files (and keep his grubby hands off yours).

The best way to do this is to create a separate subdirectory for each person. You can use the person's name to make it clear which directory belongs to whom. Here's how it's done:

1. In File Manager, select the **Change Default Dir** command. WordPerfect displays the Change Default Directory dialog box.

2. Use the **New Directory** text box to enter the full name of the new directory. For example, if you want to create a subdirectory

named MARGE attached to the main WP60 directory, you enter **C:\WP60\MARGE**.

3. Select **OK**. WordPerfect asks if you want to create the directory.

4. Select Yes. WordPerfect creates the directory.

When creating the QuickLists for each person, you use the name of her directory and the *.* file specification ("*.*" is the wild-card way to designate every file in a directory). For example, if one person's directory was C:\WP60\MARGE, you enter the following for her QuickList:

c:\wp60\marge*.*

A fine example of nothing to see.

Chapter 29
Installing WordPerfect

When I was a kid, I used to get nervous whenever I got Christmas presents that said "Some assembly required" on the box. I *knew* what this meant. First of all, it meant I couldn't play with the toy right away—a major bummer. Second, it meant that someone, usually my father or a slightly inebriated uncle, would have to do the assembling. Several hours and several missing parts later, the poor thing would have been relegated to a corner somewhere, half-assembled and sad-looking.

Installing computer software still fills me with the same apprehension. Most installation programs are written by people who assume that everybody will know what they mean when they say, "Change the BUFFERS setting in your CONFIG.SYS file to 30."

I'm happy to report that the WordPerfect installation program (it's called Install) is at least a little friendlier than most. If you're feeling gung-ho and would like to try your hand at this installation thing, here are the steps to follow:

1. Place the disk labeled **Install 1** into drive A or drive B (whichever one it fits into).

2. At the DOS prompt (the C:\> or C> thing), type **A:INSTALL** if the disk is in drive A, or **B:INSTALL** if the disk is in drive B. Then press **Enter**. The Install program displays its welcome screen.

3. If the three boxes near the bottom of the screen display as red, green, and blue, press **Y**; otherwise, press **N**. The WordPerfect 6.0 Installation screen appears, as shown below.

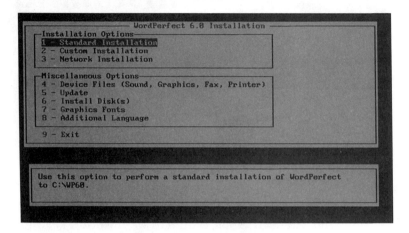

The WordPerfect 6.0 Installation screen.

4. Press **1** to choose the **Standard Installation**. Install then shows you the directories it will use during the installation.

5. Press **N** to tell Install you don't want to change these directories. Now Install tells you how much of your precious hard disk real estate WordPerfect will usurp.

6. Press **Y** to continue. Install displays the Replace Existing Files Options screen.

7. Press **2** to avoid being bothered during the installation. You're asked whether you want to "Add program directory to the path."

8. Nod your head knowingly and press **Y** to move on. Install, ever persistent with the questions, now asks about installing "additional Graphics Drivers."

9. Say "Don't be silly" and press **N**. You're then asked about installing printer drivers.

10. If you have a printer, it's a good idea to set it up here. Press **Y**, and Install displays a long list of printer types (see the picture which follows). If you don't have a printer, skip ahead to step 13.

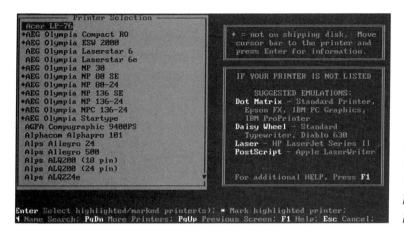

Use this screen to tell WordPerfect what kind of printer you have.

11. Use your keyboard's up and down arrow keys to highlight your printer, press the **Spacebar** to mark the printer, and then press **Enter**. Install asks if you want to select the printer you marked.

12. Press **Y**. Install sets up your printer and asks if you want to install another. If you do, press **Y** and repeat steps 11 and 12. Otherwise, press **N**. (You may also be asked if you want to install the "printer (.ALL) file." Just press **Y** to continue.) Install tells you to insert the disk labeled **Install 2** in drive A (or drive B, if that's the one you're using).

13. Remove the **Install 1** disk, insert **Install 2**, and press **Enter**. Install may ask if you want to install another printer. Press **Y** or **N**, as appropriate. When you've finished installing printers, Install copies more files from the disk and then prompts you to insert the **Install 3** disk.

13. At this point, Install spends most of its time copying files from the installation disks. When it's done with each disk, it will let you know and ask you to insert the next disk. Just follow the on-screen prompts and you'll be fine.

14. When Install is done, it will start WordPerfect and ask you to enter your registration number. If you have the number handy (it's on your registration card), type it and press **Enter**. Otherwise, just press **Enter**.

15. If you installed more than one printer, WordPerfect asks which one to use as the default. Use the up and down arrow keys to highlight the printer to use, and then press **Enter** twice. WordPerfect returns you to the DOS prompt.

Speak Like a Geek Glossary

acceleration factor   How quickly the mouse pointer moves across the screen when you move the mouse on its pad.

active window   The window you're currently slaving away in. You can tell a window is active if it has the blinking *cursor*, or if its title bar is a darker color than the other windows.

alphanumeric keypad   The keyboard area that contains the letters, numbers (the ones across the top row, not the ones on the *numeric keypad*), and other punctuation symbols.

ASCII text file   A file that uses only the American Standard Code for Information Interchange character set (which is just techno-lingo for the characters you see on your keyboard).

bit-spit   Any kind of computer-created correspondence.

block   A selection of text in a document.

boilerplate   Text that you reuse over and over. It's the word processing equivalent of the old maxim, "Don't reinvent the wheel."

boot   Computer geeks won't tell you to start your computer they'll tell you to *boot* it. This doesn't mean you should punt your monitor across the room. The term *booting* comes from the phrase "pulling oneself up by one's own bootstraps," which just means that your computer can load everything it needs to operate properly without any help from the likes of you and me.

byte   Computerese for a single character of information. So, for example, the phrase "This phrase is 28 bytes long" is, yes, 28 bytes long (you count the spaces too—but not the quotation marks).

cascade   A cool way of arranging windows so that they overlap each other while still letting you see the top of each window.

cascade menu   A menu that appears when you select certain *pull-down menu* commands.

cell   In a *table*, the intersection of a row and column. Each cell has its own address within the table, which is created by combining the letter and number of the column and row, respectively, that form the cell.

character formatting   Changing the attributes of individual characters by adding things such as bold or italics, or by using different fonts.

character set   A collection of related characters.

check box   A square-shaped switch that toggles a *dialog box* option on or off. The option is turned on when an "X" appears in the box.

churn   To endlessly rewrite and revise a section of text.

click   To quickly press and release the left mouse button.

clipboard   An area that holds data temporarily during cut-and-paste operations.

command button   A rectangular doohickey (usually found in *dialog boxes*) that, when chosen, runs whatever command is spelled out on its label.

commands   The options you see in a *pull-down menu*. You use commands to tell WordPerfect what you want it to do next.

cursor The vertical bar (it's horizontal in *text mode*) that you see inside WordPerfect's typing area; it tells you where the next character you type will appear.

cursor control keys The keys (which you'll find on a separate keypad or mixed in with the *numeric keypad*) that you use to navigate a document.

delay The amount of time it takes for a second character to appear when you press and hold down a key.

dialog boxes Ubiquitous windows that pop up on the screen to ask you for information or to seek confirmation of an action you requested (or sometimes just to say "Hi").

directory A storage location on your hard disk for keeping related files together. If your hard disk is like a house, a directory is like a room inside the house. See also *subdirectory*.

disk See *floppy disk*.

double-click To quickly press and release the left mouse button *twice* in succession.

double-click interval The maximum amount of time between mouse clicks that WordPerfect will allow for a double-click to be registered.

drag To press and *hold down* the left mouse button and then move the mouse.

drop-down list A *dialog box* control that normally shows only a single item but, when selected, displays a list of options.

endnote A section of text placed at the end of a document that usually contains asides or comments that embellish something in the regular document text. See also *footnote*.

extension The three-character ending to a DOS file name. The extension is separated from the main name by a period.

file   An organized unit of information inside your computer. If you think of your hard disk as a house, files can be either servants (your programs) or things (data used by you or by a program).

file name   The name of a file (duh). File names usually consist of a primary name (that can be a maximum of 8 characters), followed by a period (.), followed by an extension (that can be a maximum of 3 characters). Primary names and extensions can't contain spaces or any of the following characters:

$$+ = \backslash \, | \, [\,] \, ; : , . < > ? /$$

file specification   A combination of drive letter, directory name, legal *file name* characters (such as letters and numbers), and *wild-card characters* (* and ?) that specifies the files you want to work with (for example, c:\wp60\wpdocs*.doc).

floppy disk   A portable storage medium that consists of a flexible disk protected by a plastic case. Floppy disks are available in a variety of sizes and capacities.

font   A distinctive graphic design of letters, numbers, and other symbols.

footer   A section of text that appears at the bottom margin of each page in a document. See also *header*.

footnote   A section of text placed at the bottom of a page. It usually contains asides or comments that embellish something in the regular document text. See also *endnote*.

formatting   The process of setting up a disk so it can read and write information. Not to be confused with *character formatting*.

frame   A border that surrounds a *window* and lets you *maximize*, *minimize*, move, and size the window.

fritterware   Any software that causes you to fritter away time fiddling with its various bells and whistles.

function keys   The keys located either to the left of the *numeric keypad* or across the top of the keyboard. There are usually 10 function keys (although some keyboards have 12), and they're labeled F1, F2, and so on. In WordPerfect, you use these keys either by themselves or as part of key combinations.

graphics mode   A new mode introduced in version 6 that gives WordPerfect true *WYSIWYG* capabilities. The disadvantage is that it is slightly slower than *text mode*.

hard page break   A *page break* that you insert yourself. Text always breaks at this point, regardless of the margin sizes.

header   A section of text that appears at the top margin of each page in a document. See also *footer*.

hyphenation   The process where WordPerfect splits larger words in two at the end of a line and inserts a hyphen. This can help improve the spacing in your paragraphs.

kilobyte   1,024 *bytes*. Usually abbreviated as just *K*.

landscape orientation   When the lines on a page run across the long side of the page. See also *portrait orientation*.

margins   The empty spaces that surround your text on the page. WordPerfect's standard margins are one inch high on the top and bottom edges of the page, and one inch wide on the left and right edges.

maximize   To increase the size of a window to its largest extent. See also *minimize*.

megabyte   1,024 *kilobytes* or 1,048,576 *bytes*. The cognoscenti write this as *M* or *MB* and pronounce it *meg*.

menu bar   The horizontal bar on the top line of the WordPerfect screen. The menu bar contains the *pull-down menus*.

minimize   To reduce the size of a window to its smallest extent. See also *maximize*.

mouse potato   The computer equivalent of a couch potato. Someone who spend lots of time in front of the screen.

numeric keypad   A separate keypad for entering numbers on most keyboards. It actually serves two functions: when the Num Lock key is on, you can use it to enter numbers; if Num Lock is off, the keypad cursor keys are enabled, and you can use them to navigate a document. Some keyboards (called extended keyboards) have a separate cursor keypad so you can keep Num Lock on all the time.

ohnosecond   The brief fraction of time in which you realize you've just made a HUGE blunder.

orphan   A first line in a paragraph that appears by itself at the end of a page. See also *widow*.

page break   A line that appears across the screen, telling you where one page ends and the next one begins.

page mode   A mode that shows you page elements—such as page numbers, *headers*, and *footers*—that you normally only see once you print a document.

point   To move the mouse pointer so it rests on a specific screen location.

port   The connection into which you plug the cable from a device such as a mouse or printer.

portrait orientation   When the lines run across the short side of a page. This is the standard way most pages are oriented. See also *landscape orientation*.

pull-down menus   Hidden menus that you open from WordPerfect's *menu bar* to access the program's commands and features.

quadruple-click   To quickly press and release the left mouse button four times in succession. Quadruple-clicking a paragraph selects the entire paragraph.

radio buttons   *Dialog box* options that appear as small circles in groups of two or more. Only one option from a group can be chosen.

RAM   Stands for Random Access Memory. The memory in your computer that DOS uses to run your programs.

repeat rate After the initial *delay*, the rate at which characters appear when you press and hold down a key.

right ragged Left-justified text. The right side of each line doesn't line up, so it looks "ragged."

scroll bar A bar that appears at the bottom or on the right of a window whenever the window is too small to display all of its contents.

scrolling To move up or down through a document.

soft page break A *page break* inserted automatically by WordPerfect. The position of the break depends on the margin sizes.

spamming To write (or speak) ramblingly and aimlessly on a hodge-podge of subjects. ("I got his memo, but you could tell he was just spammin' me; the guy doesn't know what the heck he's talking about.")

style A predefined collection of formatting and layout options that you can apply to text all at once.

subdirectory A *directory* within a directory.

table A rectangular grid of rows and columns that can hold text, numbers, graphics, and the results of formulas.

text box A screen area you use to type in text information such as a description or a file name.

text mode WordPerfect's normal operating mode. It runs faster, but you don't get *WYSIWYG* (or the cool 3-D effects you get with *graphics mode* or *page mode*).

triple-click To quickly press and release the left mouse button three times in succession. In WordPerfect, triple-clicking a sentence selects the entire sentence.

type size A measure of the height of a font. Type size is measured in *points*; there are 72 points in an inch.

typeover mode   A WordPerfect mode in which the characters you type replace existing characters (instead of being inserted between them). Use the Insert key to toggle between this mode and insert mode.

watermark   A translucent image or section of text that prints "underneath" existing text on a page.

widow   The last line in a paragraph that appears by itself at the top of a page. See also *orphan*.

wild-card characters   Characters used to designate multiple *files* in a *file specification*. The question mark (?) substitutes for a single character, and the asterisk (*) substitutes for multiple characters.

window   A screen area where WordPerfect displays your documents.

word processing   Using a computer to write, edit, format, and print documents. A high-end word processor such as WordPerfect also lets you add complicated features such as *footnotes* and indexes, and even has desktop publishing options that let you do true page layout.

word wrap   A WordPerfect feature that starts a new line automatically as your typing reaches the end of the current line.

WYSIWYG   What-You-See-Is-What-You-Get. The feature that enables you to see on your computer screen what you end up getting from your printer. It's pronounced *wizzy wig*.

Index

Who cares what you think? WE DO!

We take our customers' opinions very personally. After all, you're the reason we publish these books. If you're not happy, we're doing something wrong.

We'd appreciate it if you would take the time to drop us a note or fax us a fax. A real person—not a computer—reads every letter we get, and makes sure that your comments get relayed to the appropriate people.

Not sure what to say? Here are some details we'd like to know:

- ☞ Who you are (age, occupation, hobbies, etc.)
- ☞ Where you bought the book
- ☞ Why you picked this book instead of a different one
- ☞ What you liked best about the book
- ☞ What could have been done better
- ☞ Your overall opinion of the book
- ☞ What other topics you would purchase a book on

Mail, e-mail, or fax it to:

Faithe Wempen
Product Development Manager
Alpha Books
201 West 103rd Street
Indianapolis, IN 46290

FAX: (317) 581-4669
CIS: 75430,174

Special Offer!

Alpha Books needs people like you to give opinions about new and existing books. Product testers receive free books in exchange for providing their opinions about them. If you would like to be a product tester, please mention it in your letter, and make sure you include your full name, address, and daytime phone.